The Chowhound's™ Guide to
the New York Tristate Area

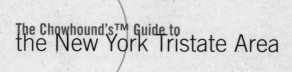

The Chowhound's™ Guide to
the New York Tristate Area

Chowhound.com

Introduction by Jim Leff

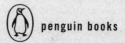
penguin books

PENGUIN BOOKS
Published by the Penguin Group
Penguin Group (USA) Inc., 375 Hudson Street, New York, New York 10014, U.S.A.
Penguin Group (Canada), 10 Alcorn Avenue, Toronto, Ontario, Canada M4V 3B2
   (a division of Pearson Penguin Canada Inc.)
Penguin Books Ltd, 80 Strand, London WC2R 0RL, England
Penguin Ireland, 25 St Stephen's Green, Dublin 2, Ireland
   (a division of Penguin Books Ltd)
Penguin Group (Australia), 250 Camberwell Road, Camberwell, Victoria 3124, Australia
   (a division of Pearson Australia Group Pty Ltd)
Penguin Books India Pvt Ltd, 11 Community Centre, Panchsheel Park, New Delhi—110
   017, India
Penguin Group (NZ), cnr Airborne and Rosedale Roads, Albany, Auckland 1310,
   New Zealand (a division of Pearson New Zealand Ltd)
Penguin Books (South Africa) (Pty) Ltd, 24 Sturdee Avenue, Rosebank, Johannesburg
   2196, South Africa

Penguin Books Ltd, Registered Offices:
80 Strand, London WC2R 0RL, England

First published in Penguin Books 2005

10 9 8 7 6 5 4 3 2 1

Copyright © Chowhound, Inc., 2005
All rights reserved

Some of the contents of this book first appeared in *ChowNews,* an e-mail newsletter.

CIP data available
ISBN 0 14 30.3440 5

Printed in the United States of America
Set in New Century Schoolbook with Trade Gothic
Designed by Sabrina Bowers

Contents

A Dining Guide Like No Other

You'll notice that many popular and excellent places such as Tomoe Sushi, Magnolia Bakery, Babbo, Union Square Cafe, and Grimaldi's Pizza aren't mentioned in these pages. It's not that we don't like them. We do! But our pizza coverage doesn't grab every worthy slice, and our dumpling roster is short a *shu mai* or two. *The Chowhound's Guide* doesn't aim for comprehensiveness (though it does offer exhaustive surveys of lesser-known Italian restaurants and sushi bars, really interesting brunches and high-quality street cart vendors, nearly every taqueria on Roosevelt Avenue, and all the best Cuban and Vietnamese sandwiches, as well as many other highly essential topics). Over the years, Chowhound.com has covered nearly the entire universe of edibility, but this guide focuses on recent "chowconnaissance," to ensure the freshest possible info and to fit it into a portable size.

The goal is not to catalog every obvious choice. We've concentrated on places that are white hot among those who eat to a different drummer: the front-line food lovers determinedly smoking out the sensations of tomorrow. *The Chowhound's Guide* is an eye-opening plunge into the world of adventure dining, spotlighting places that have recently excited the expert and iconoclastic diners known as chowhounds. Most eateries described herein will be completely unknown to you—virgin finds never before mentioned in guidebooks or newspaper food sections. Here, for your chowing pleasure, are more than a thousand cutting-edge dens of deliciousness—intriguing alternatives to the oft-hyped usual suspects. It's the ultimate hip map to edible treasure, by and for those who live to seek it out.

Everyone knows about the cheesecake at Junior's; that's old news. Our cheesecake roundup skips this obvious choice, instead offering enticing tips like a little Mexican bakery/cafe in Queens that's been determined (via the scientific industriousness of one of our passionate kooks) to bake "benchmark" cheesecake. We've found knockout great guacamole as a menu non sequitur at a tony Upper East Side French wine bar, and a homespun Thai restaurant operating as a sideline within a midtown Blimpie's sub shop.

Any food guide will tell you about L'Ecole, the French cooking school. Only *The Chowhound's Guide* will hip you to L'Ecole's early bird service—the shift where the teachers cook, instead of the students. Most foodies know about Di Fara Pizzeria (first touted by chowhounds, by the way), but we'll tell you which of the owner's kids, who rotate kitchen duty, inherited the cooking gene and which just go through the motions. You've heard of Noho Star, and you may know that it serves both Chinese and American dishes and makes its own (great) ginger ale. But did you know about its life-changing chocolate pudding? No?!? Then dive into this book and don't expect to come out for a good long while. And expect to get very very hungry!

○○○ Tips for Using *The Chowhound's Guide*

The central presumption of this guide is that as a chowhound, you're willing to go out of your way for greatness. If you must have the most extremely delicious pizza or soufflé, you want to hear about the standouts, and will gladly trek across town for them. If you can approach this guide with a free-ranging, ready-to-chow mind-set, let us make you so cuckoo-for-Cocoa-Puffs ravenous that you jump out the door in a delirious frenzy. If you're stubbornly determined to settle for options close by, our neighborhood index will direct you to convenient killer chow and tempt you into ranging just a bit wider.

There are two vastly different ways to use this guide. We expect that you'll flip between the two.

1. Right Brain: If you don't know what or where you feel like eating, boy, is this the guide for you. These pages contain pure, distilled gastronomic foreplay, designed to get you "in the mood." Just browse; we'll soon have you on your way to satisfying cravings you didn't realize you had.

2. Left Brain: If you hanker for a given cuisine, search the cuisine index. If you want to stay local, check the nabe index. If you'd like to see our thoughts on a specific place, rifle through the alphabetical index.

Our respondents take pride in their opinions because their names are attached to them. It pays to note whose taste matches your own and weigh tips accordingly, but don't feel obliged to pay close attention to the players (whose Chowhound.com nicknames appear within asterisks). Our editors have selected only the most promising tips from reliable reporters, always watching for corroboration. If we note that a restaurant is recommended by *Jack Sprat*, that doesn't mean we haven't weighed in other opinions as well.

Alternative eating doesn't necessarily mean "cheap eats." Different pleasures come at different prices, so both snobs and reverse snobs miss out on too much enjoyment. Chowhounds embrace the full spectrum. Their mantra is "deliciousness is deliciousness"; a wonderful brownie baked with ample love, skill, and pride is as worthy of respect as the richest Persicus caviar. You'll get the best possible use from this guide if you, too, embrace deliciousness in all its many manifestations.

Finally, there's no thrill like making your own finds. Put this guide to ample use, but don't be a slave to it. Sever the cord sometimes and adventurously chow where no hound has ever chowed before. Report back by joining the conversation on Chowhound.com, and maybe we'll include you and your tip in our next edition!

○○○ How Do You Build a "Chowhound's Guide"?

Easy! First, build a Web site and attract five hundred thousand people per month. Prevent its savvy intensity from becoming diluted as the community grows huge. Work to keep conversation focused, rather than lapsing into brawls, ads, and chatty digressions—as large online discussions do. Train teams to watch vigilantly for sham testimonials, deflect the nutty .01 percent who aim to derail things, and keep it all rolling on a shoestring budget with a skeleton staff and lots of pure chowhound fervor. The result: a deliriously informative unorganized mayhem of thousands of daily reports from across the continent, penetrable only by the most ardent chowhounds. Like at a good used book store, everyone leaves with an armful of bounty, but few ever find exactly what they were looking for.

So . . . recruit fleets of chow-savvy editors to read through each posting, scouring for primo tips. Organize the information, weigh opinions, gauge consensus, and look up addresses and phone numbers, producing an e-mailed summary called *ChowNews* (in editions for New York Tristate, San Francisco Bay Area, and Greater Los Angeles) sent to subscribers each week (information at www.chowhound.com/chownews/ny.html). Now readers can enjoy the chow tips without having to outswim the tidal wave.

But if you tried to make a book by printing out every issue of *ChowNews*, you'd get disorganized, nonupdated, unindexed clots of papers, useless for zeroing in on great bites. So instead cull the best recent *ChowNews* info, reedit, reconsolidate, index, and cross-reference, and have throngs of chowhounds vet all for currency and quality—working quickly so the tips don't go stale.

If this guidebook seems unlike any other, now you understand why. Only obsessed raving zealots could produce a food guide this good. Swarms of them at every stage, contributing, supervising, and editing with ferocious intensity. It's a rare occurrence, and we invite you to savor the unique results.

○○○ Don't Trust This Book

All prices and hours mentioned in this guide are iffy. For that matter, so are the tips themselves. Why? Because things change fast in the food world. So call ahead to make sure that dynamite lasagna deal is still on, and that the place hasn't turned into a tanning parlor. And don't shoot the messenger if a new chef has come aboard and is blithely melting Velveeta all over everything.

If the world of edibility is so flaky and changeable, why bother with this guide? Simple: even though chow information, like a croissant, starts to stale from the moment it's produced, you will still eat a quadrillion times better if you crib from *The Chowhound's Guide* than if you don't. The goal—of this guide, of dining out, of life itself—is to increase your odds of eating deliciously, and we are your best possible ally, because we are battalions of obsessive-compulsive true believers who are at least as picky as you are. And this is literally as fresh as a book can possibly be. Since the users of Chowhound sign their names to their opinions, pride compels them to offer timely tips. And this guide's editors have selected recently confirmed information. Plus, the folks at Penguin, themselves chowhounds, have expedited production.

But still, caveat eater. Call ahead to confirm prices and other details, and always remember that last week's superb artichoke pizza might be next week's inedible nightmare.

◦◯◦ Chowhound Profiles

Profiles of some randomly selected Chowhound.com regulars are scattered throughout the guide. We've asked them a number of questions, and predictably, everyone offered different perspectives on everything—with one unexpected exception. When asked about their favorite guilty pleasures, fully half our respondents (in both New York and San Francisco) cited Popeye's fried chicken. We swear we weren't paid for the mass market product placement.

◦◯◦ The Real Purpose

Finally, let me confess something. In the end, it doesn't matter if you're out there reading this . . . *any* of you. I've recruited the most obsessive and fussy eaters to build the largest food community in the world, tended to its growth, appointed staff to encapsulate its output into *ChowNews,* and convinced Penguin to release this volume all from one motivation: for many years I have lusted to hold exactly this book in my hands. Yes, this has all been a grotesquely elaborate vanity project for me, me, me. I've tricked hundreds of thousands of experts into coughing up their best tips, created machinery to process and cull those tips, and duped a major publisher into spitting out the savviest, deepest, chowiest guide to New York Tristate dining ever produced. It all stems from my dream of harnessing the know-how of chowhounds everywhere to ensure that I'll make out sublimely wherever I go or whatever I crave. You can all go do as you like. I've got my book and I'm ready to go eat.

Ciao,
    —Jim Leff, Alpha Hound

About Chowhounds

Chowhounds existed long before a Web site gathered them into an international network. Chowhounding predates even prostitution. Among Neanderthals were those who roamed a valley or two out of their way to where the mastodons ran particularly tasty—and who always insisted on the tender cheek meat.

Chowhounds ignore conventional wisdom and hype. They refuse to eat where they're told, preferring to scout for hidden gems. This culinary treasure hunting is fueled by the conviction that the landscape is rife with unheralded greatness awaiting joyful discovery. And so chowhounds plumb outlying neighborhoods; they screech their cars to a halt upon spotting promising-looking Peruvian chicken parlors; they horde take-out menus with a covetousness that would alarm even fervent butterfly collectors. All this to avoid the unthinkable horror of ingesting a bite lacking the potential to change their lives. A chowhound cannot bear the thought that something shatteringly wonderful might have been discovered if they'd only trekked two blocks farther.

Chowhounds are open to the full spectrum of deliciousness. They sit up straight in four-star palaces and swirl their merlot with eyebrow-cocked insouciance, yet they also know to ask curbside tamale vendors for atole, the traditional accompanying beverage. They appreciate subtle cooking where poetic statements are made with ethereal gestures as much as lusty cooking requiring hearty digging in. They adjust; they acclimatize; they're culinary chameleons gleaning the essential experience from each milieu.

If one knows one's options, one can always score. Being a chowhound is all about acquiring the ability to sate every craving not just adequately but extraordinarily. Since even billionaires find themselves in formal dining settings for less than 10 percent of their ingesting lives, all chowhounds build portfolios of superior breakfast muffins, falafel sandwiches, and ice-cream sundaes as well as options for swanky business lunches and Saturday night dates. You may grab a quick sandwich at work. A chowhound goes twenty blocks out of the way for a better one. You may pick up a bag of cookies from a convenience store. A chowhound orders cookies from a certain bakery in Wisconsin.

Chowhounds eat on the cutting (and spooning and forking) edge: they're aware of a new immigrant group's influx before city agencies catch on, they navigate the roads of obscure corners of the city with more aplomb than cabbies, and most of all, they know all the best places to eat. They won't settle for anything less than cooking that makes them shut their eyes and moan with pleasure. Chowhounds are always on the lookout for greatness, and their discoveries will be tomorrow's vaunted places. They are the buzzers rather than the buzzees.

One joy of this peculiar hobby is that the objects of a chowhound's affections are more viscerally satisfying than those of, say, antiques collectors. After all, you can't literally consume your new Hepplewhite mahogany Pembroke table. You can only look at it, point at it, show it off—locked always in the cold dualism of finder and found. Compare and contrast, if you will, with a slice of fresh, eggy golden brown coconut custard pie. Food is not just acquired, it's encompassed at the cellular level. And while Mr. Hepplewhite is as dead as his era, the cultural aspects of cuisine are vividly alive, immersive, *ingestible*. There is much to be experienced on the chowhounding trail: adventures to undertake and otherness to embrace and internalize.

In the end, it's more than just about food. In an age when humongous engines of marketing ensnare multitudes to blandly familiar brands, chowhounds are the conscientious objectors. Having resisted the hypnotic trance of directed consumption, they use their free will to make smart choices. By refusing to settle for easy mediocrity, they ensure that a great many of their occasions are special ones—and support the artisans, holdouts, and geniuses who aim for more than the extraction of maximal profit from minimal effort. The more people awakened to the heady pleasures of treasure hunting, the more treasures there'll be for us all to enjoy.

Acknowledgments

The Chowhound's Guide to the New York Tristate Area was edited by Deven Black, Jake Klisivitch, Jim Leff, Frank Leone, Limster, Fred Manny, Caitlin McGrath, and Chris Van Der Rhodes.

The material in this guide was adapted and edited from *ChowNews,* a weekly e-mail publication chock-full of primo chow tips culled from the Chowhound.com message boards. (Read a sample issue at www.chowhound.com/chownewshny.html.) The editorial staff of *New York Tristate ChowNews* is:

Editors: Frank Leone, Deven Black, and Mark Hokoda
Assistant Editors: Tom Steele and an Impondymous
Executive Editor: Jim Leff
Managing Editor: Pat Hammond
Copy Editor: Caitlin McGrath
Linker: Karen Ostler and a Mannonymous

The wait staff for the Chowhound.com Web site is:

Alpha Hound: Jim Leff
Web Tamer: Bob Okumura
Pack Management: Pat Hammond
Technical Attaché: Pierre Jelenc
Bone Counter: Leslie Huang
Legal Beagles: Andrew "Wonki" Kim and Molly McEnery
   (Wilson Sonsini Goodrich & Rosati)
LSD (not the drug): Jeremy Osner and Pierre Jelenc
Logo Artist: Cecil Lehar
Korean Military Adviser: Michael Yu

Brad Heintz is the evil genius behind CHEW (the Chowhound Editing Wizard). Limster created Nabe Converter, our program for indexing, and Pierre Jelenc and Paul Trapani provided technical help. Office space was provided by Lawsuites.net. This guide would have left several dead and countless wounded without BBEdit, Bare Bones Software's legendary text editing software.

The editors would like to thank our agent, Daniel Greenberg of Levine Greenberg Literary Agency (and Melissa Rowland and Elizabeth Wooldridge of LGLA as well), and, at Penguin, our editors Jennifer Ehmann and David Cashion; managing editor Matt Giarratano; copy editor Amy Mintzer; production editors Jennifer Tait and Noirin Lucas; and designer Sabrina Bowers.

Deep debt of gratitude to: Bob Okumura (Chowhound cofounder); Pat Hammond, Andy Penn, and Wayne Frost; Dave Feldman, Seth Godin, Jay and Michelle Itkowitz; Brian Platton and George Sape of Epstein Becker & Green; David Shenk, the aggrieved spouses, and varyingly significant others; the Sainted Arepa Lady; and, most of all, the awesome hounds of Chowhound.com.

213 GRAND: Exemplary Noodles and Pork

213 Grand Street Gourmet (Chinatown)
213 Grand St.
Manhattan, NY
212-226-4231
Chinese (Hong Kong)/Chinese (Dim Sum)

Check out all the impeccably fresh prepared items in the windows at **213 Grand Street Gourmet**. Then duck inside for superb lo mein with ginger, scallions, and beef. The noodles are perfectly al-dente, cooked to order, and all ingredients are top-notch (tender and flavorful beef, well-balanced sauce). Baby pig—with very tender meat and thin, crispy skin—is no less than superb, reports *Ahab*. *Deena* recommends their dim sum, roast pork (they'll trim it as lean as you'd like), and chow fun (best dry, not soupy).

The Outer Boroughs on **THREE DOLLARS** a Meal

Cafe Mexicano (Brooklyn)
671 Union St.
Park Slope, Brooklyn, NY
718-623-6754
Mexican

Di Fara Pizzeria (Brooklyn)
1424 Avenue J
Midwood, Brooklyn, NY
718-258-1367
Pizza/Italian

El Guatón Pizzeria (Queens)
68-14 Roosevelt Ave.
Woodside, Queens, NY
718-478-1199
Chilean Pizza

Homefood (Queens)
38-05 Main St.
Flushing, Queens, NY
718-463-6868
Chinese

La Taqueria (Brooklyn)
72 7th Ave.
Park Slope, Brooklyn, NY
718-398-4300
Mexican

Matamoros Puebla Grocery
(Brooklyn)
193 Bedford Ave.
Greenpoint, Brooklyn, NY
718-782-5044
Mexican

Nio's Trinidad Roti Shack
(Brooklyn)
2702 Church Ave.
Flatbush, Brooklyn, NY
718-287-9848
Trinidadian

Northern Dumplings (Queens)
22A 40th Rd.
Flushing, Queens, NY
Chinese (Beijing)

Tacos Nuevo Mexicano I
(Brooklyn)
491 5th Ave
Park Slope, Brooklyn, NY
718-832-0050
Mexican

Yi Mei Bakery (Queens)
8126 Broadway
Elmhurst, Queens, NY
718-898-8005
Chinese Bakery

In Brooklyn $3 gets you:

- a slice of cheese pizza at **Di Fara's** (but bring extra cash because you can't eat just one);
- two doubles (smashed curried chickpeas between fried roti) at **Nio's Roti Shack**;
- two tacos of your choice at **Tacos Nuevo Mexicana**;
- a tamale, with change to spare, at **Cafe Mexicana**;
- a fresh-tasting open-faced veggie taco at **La Taqueria** (splurge another buck for a nice cantaloupe agua fresca);
- two $1.50 *sopes* at **Matamoros Puebla Grocery**.

In Queens $3 gets you:

- sixteen incredible freshly made dumplings from **Northern Dumpling**;
- a HUGE baked beef or chicken empanada or Chilean hot

dog *completo* (beef frank, sauerkraut, tomatoes, avocados, and mayo) on a large homemade roll at **El Guatón Pizzeria**;

- up to three pastries at **Yi Mei Bakery**, where *Jessica Klonsky* recommends pineapple crusted bun stuffed with dried pork or with cheese danish filling (really a dried milk powder/butter/sugar mixture called "nai3 su1"), best fresh out of the oven;
- at least one order of amazing scallion pancakes at **Homefood**.

○ **Cafe Mexicano:** *see also* p. 299.
○ **Di Fara Pizzeria:** *see also* p. 107.
○ **Matamoros Puebla Grocery:** *see also* p. 297.

A Rave for **360**

360 (Brooklyn)
360 Van Brundt
Red Hook, Brooklyn, NY
718-246-0360
Eclectic New American

Adam Neaman on **360**: "Once in a blue moon, you find a magic restaurant, where the food is insanely good, the service brilliant, and the prices too low relative to the food quality to keep you from going three days in a row (I did last weekend). 360 in Red Hook is my new magic restaurant." Another poster sniffs that 360 is more suited to the Upper West Side than Red Hook (which is fast gentrifying).

A $20 three-course prix fixe meal included heirloom tomato soup with fresh mozzarella and basil oil, delicate and crispy dorade (sea bream) with olive paste and haricots verts, and pork loin with sliced green apples. Lots of very good wines under $30, and a knowledgeable sommelier to help you select.

Other choices highly praised by the hounds: appetizers of beef *borek*, sardines or cheese in puff pastry, entrées of pollack or pork chop, both with vegetables.

An à la carte menu is also available. The owner is a wine guy, so its short but interesting list is all French wines from lesser-known regions at reasonable markups. Cash only, and not open every day (call for hours).

50 CARMINE: Great Homestyle Cooking with Pizzazz

50 Carmine (Greenwich Village)
50 Carmine St.
Manhattan, NY
212-206-9134
Italian

Sarah Jenkins' 50 Carmine excels at great homestyle cooking prepared with market-driven ingredients and served at reasonable prices. Spicy razor clams in chili pepper broth, fonduelike pasta with a multitude of cheeses, *papardelle* in wild boar sauce, and just-short-of-muttony lamb with chanterelles are all winners, says *Abbylovi*. Other recommendations: outrageously good short ribs over polenta, duck, mussels, and sautéed skate wings with greens over smashed potatoes (simple, really fresh, well-prepared, and way satisfying). All pastas are first-rate except the red wine clam sauce one, which is a definite Avoid. Better desserts can be found in the neighborhood, but among the restaurant's offerings, olive oil cake's the standout, says *Nyufoodie*.

A: Sophisticated Minimalism

A Cafe (Upper West Side)
947 Columbus Ave.
Manhattan, NY
212-531-1643
New American/French/Caribbean

Who needs a fancy kitchen to make good food? The chef at **A** uses three toaster ovens and a slow cooker to create everything served. This guy is a miracle worker. The "kitchen" is roughly the size of an elevator, yet A turns out solid stuff like duck confit and jerk pork chops, reports *Gregg*. The menu changes frequently and it's BYO and very inexpensive. The dining room's been expanded but is still almost as small as the kitchen. In spite of the seeming austerities (even the name is minimalist!), the place feels incredibly sophisticated and romantic.

ADIRONDACK Chowhounding

Friends Lake Inn (Warren County)
963 Friends Lake Rd.
Chestertown, NY
518-494-4751
American

L-Ken's (Albany County)
1565 Central Ave.
Albany, NY
518-869-6279
Diner or Coffeeshop

Mr. B's Best (Albany County)
91 Broadway
Albany, NY
518-432-4165
Sandwich Shop

Oscar's Smokehouse
 (Warren County)
22 Raymond Ln.
Warrensburg, NY
518-623-3431
Barbecue/Store

Owl at Twilight (Essex County)
Olmstedville Rd. (Rte. 29)
Olmstedville, NY
518-251-4696
Spanish/Latin American/French

Sisters Cafe & Take Out
 (Essex County)
Main St. (Rte. 29)
Olmstedville, NY
518-251-5629
Diner or Coffeeshop

The Spanish-South American-French fusion menu at **Owl at Twilight** offers everything from rack of lamb to Nicaraguan beef preparations to a quote from Hegel. The wine list is long and select, and ingredients are top-notch, reports *Aidan*.

Sisters is an absolutely wonderful place for breakfast or a burger, and the owners are super nice and accommodating.

Chowhound Nametag: Iron Frank

○○○

Location: Manhattan, New York City.

Occupation: Personal trainer/*ChowNews* editor.

Cholesterol Level: Normal, last time I checked.

Number of Visits to McDonald's in Past Decade: Maybe a dozen . . . but only to use the bathroom.

Farthest Out of the Way Traveled Just for Chow: Vancouver, for my yearly dim sum roundup.

Nabe Most Full of Explorable Unknown Chow: Roosevelt Avenue in Queens.

Top Chinatown Pick: New Green Bo is still the most consistent. Every other place is a one-dish wonder (like Yummy Noodles for their rice casseroles).

Underrated by Chowhounds: Ba Xuyen, Sushi Yasu, Pho Bang, Village Yokocho, Cafe Zaiya, Oms/B.

Weight Management Tip: Keep moving—walk to and from wherever you're going to eat if possible. And if it doesn't taste great, don't eat it. (Have it wrapped, give it to someone else who will appreciate it, and move on to the next spot.)

Favorite Comfort Chow: Village Yokocho for yaki onigiri, fried squid legs, yakiniku don.

Guilty Pleasure: Bubble Tea from Ten Ren Tea Company.

Favorite Gelato Flavor: Pistachio.

Chowhounding Rules of Thumb:
1. Look in the window to see what people are eating.
2. Pay no attention to Zagat ratings.
3. Don't eat at pizzerias with more toppings than customers.
4. If a restaurant gives you the takeout menu, especially in Chinatown, ask if they have any other menu with different items.
5. Learn about a few dishes the restaurant's country of origin is famous for, and order them to instill confidence in the staff that you want the real deal.

Favorite restaurant that never disappoints me and where I'm most likely to run into other Chowhounds: Sripraphai.

L-Ken's is an old-fashioned drive-in with signage and decor that looks authentic because it is original. There are locally made hot dogs and great fries, says *elvislives*, but she raves most about the clam roll—about a six-inch high pile of fried clam strips on top of a hot-dog roll, served with choice of tartar or cocktail sauce on the side. The clam strips are golden, crispy, tasty, and just the right chewy/tender texture.

Mr. B's Best roasts beef and turkey in-house, then thinly slices them in a huge pile served on a fresh homemade kaiser roll with a big chunk of lettuce, thick slices of local tomato, raw onion, and your choice of sauce (special sauce, horseradish, BBQ). Kinda like Arby's, except really, really good.

The sign on top of **Oscar's Smokehouse** says "Hams–Bacon," but that's just the tip of the meatburg at this butcher shop cum gourmet grocery. There's pork in a variety of forms, as well as chicken, turkey, and cheeses sold individually or combined into both smoked and unsmoked sausages. Jams, jellies, mustards, bacons, and more round out the selection,

Friends Lake Inn, a beautiful old restored inn, offers guests a meal plan including full dinner and breakfast. Great cheese selection, and the on-site wine shop ensures a great wine list at very reasonable prices. Breakfast is a buffet with homemade granola, fresh fruit, bagels and full lox spread, homemade blueberry muffins, yogurt, etc., but that's just the warm-up for hot, made-to-order omelets, frittatas, and homemade corned beef hash.

See also Miscellaneous *Upstate* Tips and Upstate *Barbecue*. And see nabe index for upstate counties.

○ **Oscar's Smokehouse:** *see also* **p. 29.**

ALIAS: Trendy with Good Reason

Alias (Lower East Side)
76 Clinton St.
Manhattan, NY
212-505-5011
New American

Nothing but raves for trendy **Alias**, whose menu, which focuses on fresh and seasonal ingredients, is tweaked daily and changed substantially every week. So don't expect to actually find any of the following dishes, but you can get an idea of what to expect via a meal report from *elvislives*, who says that every dish draws on deep flavors. For example, there's a delicious red and yellow beet salad with DiPalo ricotta and garlic croutons, and another with chunks of bosc pear mixed with balsamic roasted onions, topped with a slice of grilled blue cheese bruschetta. Nova Scotia salmon one night was served atop a bed of tasty grilled chard and veggies, and superlative braised shortribs were served with little blue corn dumplings. Those ribs were phenomenal, rich, and super tender, with hints of garlic, citrus, and other intriguing flavors. For dessert: a heavenly butter tart.

ALISEO for Central Italian Roasted Meaty Fare

Aliseo Osteria del Borgo (Brooklyn)
665 Vanderbilt Ave.
Prospect Heights, Brooklyn, NY
718-783-3400
Italian

The focus at Aliseo, a little restaurant reminiscent of a classical central-Italian *rosticceria*, is on meat, usually roasted or cured. *Faren* reports that the chef/owner is very welcoming and clearly a fanatic for quality. Red-wine-marinated figs come with a variety of cheeses and melt-in-your-mouth prosciutto. *Porchetta* (herbed roast pork) comes room temperature and has a nice crunchy skin. Wines come by the bottle, carafe, or glass. They won't serve tap water, but the bottled water is free(!). The standard coffee is espresso, but they'll make a *macchiato* if asked.

Good brunch, too. *Lambretta76* says very rich parmigiana bread and asparagus parmigiana frittatas are smallish but have nice earthy egg flavor. *Tricolore* salad is large enough to share, and the balsamic vinegar with it is exceptional. A couple of soups (red beet with apricot and pureed string bean) and a couple of sandwiches are also available. Cash only.

Heavenly ANGEL FOOD CAKE

Buttercup Bake Shop
  (Midtown East)
973 2nd Ave.
Manhattan, NY
212-350-4144
Bakery

Unnamed bakery/coffee shop
  (Chinatown)
East side of Bowery, just south
  of Canal St.
Manhattan, NY
Chinese Bakery

A tiny bakery/coffee shop in Chinatown makes delicious individual-sized angel food cakes shaped like overgrown cupcakes. You'll know you're at the right bakery when you see the cakes cooling in the window. Whatever you do, don't order anything else here, though—no matter how inviting it might appear.

Farther uptown, **Buttercup Bake Shop** makes good angel food cake.

○ **Buttercup Bake Shop**: *see also* p. 224.

APPLE Picking

Breezy Hill Orchard
  (Dutchess County)
828 Centre Rd.
Staatsburg, NY
845-266-3979
Farm or Farm Stand

Greig Farm (Dutchess County)
227 Pitcher Ln.
Red Hook, NY
845-758-1234
Farm or Farm Stand

Mead's Orchards
   (Dutchess County)
15 Scism Rd.
Red Hook, NY
845-756-5641
Farm or Farm Stand

Montgomery Place Orchards
   (Dutchess County)
Rte. 9G and 199, 12 miles west
   of Taconic Pkwy.
Red Hook, NY
845-758-6338
Farm or Farm Stand

Outhouse Orchards
   (Westchester County)
130 Hardscrable Rd.
Croton Falls, NY
914-277-3188
Farm or Farm Stand

Prospect Hill Orchards
   (Ulster County)
40 Clarkes Ln.
Milton, NY
845-795-2383
Farm or Farm Stand

Salinger's Orchard and Farm
   Market (Westchester County)
230 Guinea Rd.
Brewster, NY
845-277-3521
Farm or Farm Stand

Hounds name their favorite spots for apple picking (a couple even accessible via mass transit):

- Elizabeth Ryan's **Breezy Hill Orchards** (near Rhinebeck): over fifty apple varieties, mostly heirlooms, and pears as well. They also make Hudson Valley cider and Maeve's cider (both hard). Good bakery.
- **Greig Farm**: apples are just one of the pick-your-own fruits here. Big farm stand and animals make this a fun day trip for families.
- **Prospect Hill Orchards**: low trees for easy apple picking, but pears are high. Charge by the pound instead of the bushel. Limited selection of varieties.
- **Mead's Orchards**: peaches, Italian plums, and apples for picking, and a huge selection of pumpkins, squashes, and gourds.
- Carless city dwellers craving a taste of country life can go apple picking via public transit. *Alex R* advises taking Metro North to the Croton Falls Station, where

both **Outhouse Orchards** and **Salinger's** are less than five minutes away by cab.

- **Montgomery Place** Stand is a farm stand connected to a real farm, but there's no pick-your-own. We're just sneaking it in because they have such excellent corn (so juicy the stalks drip), great tomatoes (Cherokee purple, German stripe, Brandywine, etc.), nectarines, peaches, and raspberries. Really good bread and local jam and honey, reports *lucia*.

○ Montgomery Place Orchards: *see also* p. 295.

The Sainted **AREPA LADY**

The Sainted Arepa Lady (Queens)
northwest corner of Roosevelt Ave. and 79th St.
Jackson Heights, Queens, NY
Colombian

The Sainted Arepa Lady has long been *Jim Leff*'s single top pick (if pressed to choose one) for NY area deliciousness. The following was his early report:

When people ask me to name my favorite food in New York, I inevitably answer—without hesitation—"arepas from the Arepa Lady." This saintly woman grills Colombian corn cakes on her street cart weekends after 10:30 p.m., and they are magical.

I don't know her name; such knowledge would detract from my appreciation of her as an archetype. While I speak pretty decent Spanish, I've never been able to fully follow her conversation, but it doesn't matter. I go when I'm feeling blue, stand under her umbrella, and feel a healing calm wash over me as she brushes the sizzling corn cakes with butter. Zen-masterlike in her complete absorption in the task, she grills the things with infinite patience and loving care.

Everyone adores the Arepa Lady. The people on the

street treat her with reverence and respect; there's always a small entourage of hangers-on standing around her cart or sitting on folding chairs. Fast cars and smoke-billowing trucks zoom down the street, the 7 train crashes by overhead, partying Latinos cavort up and down the block, but the Arepa Lady's peacefulness absorbs it all, transforms it, and gives back . . . corn cakes.

The arepas themselves are snacks from heaven. Coursely ground corn, fried in pancakes about six inches in diameter and an inch thick, slathered with butter and topped with shredded white cheese, they're brown and crunchy, chewy and a little bit sweet, the butter and cheese imbuing the whole with salty, dairy meltiness.

Nearby, others grill arepas on street carts, but they are not the Arepa Lady (look for the tiny, ageless woman with the beatific smile). They all use the same ingredients and similar grills, but only her arepas have that certain cosmic expansiveness. You try one, and your first reaction is "Mmm, this is delicious." But before that thought can fully form, waves of progressively deeper feelings begin crashing, and you are finally left silently nodding your head. You understand things. You have been loved.

I've brought Malaysian designers, Russian cookbook authors, Catalan drummers, and German set painters to the Arepa Lady on the way home from shamefully gluttonous food outings, way too full to object very forcefully, clutching their sides in pain. I drag them there for the proverbial "one more bite." Her sanctified vibe somehow coaxes them to try a nibble, and suddenly eyes brighten and appetites rekindle. My guests invariably swoon over the things, even when sampled after binges so overindulgent that they had sworn never to eat again. The magic of the Arepa Lady gives them the strength to eat on.

She sets up on the northwest corner of Roosevelt Avenue and Seventy-ninth Street, and both she—and several taco trucks—are within walking distance of the E, F train Roosevelt Avenue stop (at Seventy-fourth Street), the third stop into Queens. For a shorter walk but a longer ride, take the 7 train to Eighty-second Street.

Flavorful and Tender
ARGENTINIAN Meat

Hacienda de Argentina (Upper East Side)
339 E. 75th St.
Manhattan, NY
212-472-5300
Argentinian

Hacienda de Argentina is a mecca for South American meat. *Parillada mixta*, an Argentine mixed grill, includes short ribs, sweetbreads, steak and chicken, but they'll replace the chicken with more traditional blood sausage (*morcilla*) upon request. *Faren* says all meats are very flavorful and tender and recommends gnocchi in a light tomato sauce (fabulous—light, tasty, and totally pleasing) for a meat alternative. Get the empanada sampler and meaty, delicious short ribs. Good homemade bread, too. Everything is à la carte; entrées arrive without sides. Service gets raves.

ASIAN FUSION

Asiate (Midtown West)
80 Columbus Circle, in Mandarin
    Oriental Hotel
Manhattan, NY
212-805-8881
French/Japanese

Chubo (Lower East Side)
6 Clinton St.
Manhattan, NY
212-674-6300
Eclectic

Kuma Inn (Lower East Side)
113 Ludlow St., 2nd Fl.
Manhattan, NY
212-353-8866
Japanese

Ma-Ya Thai Fusion Cafe
    (East Village)
234 E. 4th St.
Manhattan, NY
646-313-1987
Eclectic Thai

Sumile (Greenwich Village)   Vong (Midtown East)
154 W. 13th St.   200 E. 54th St.
Manhattan, NY   Manhattan, NY
212-989-7699   212-486-9592
Eclectic French   French/Thai

Vong was one of the original fusion restaurants and it still pleases. *TK Baltimore* describes foie gras flavored with ginger and warm sliced mango as "melty-licious," and the grilled beef main course served in a ginger broth with noodles is wonderful, too—as is mango tart with basil ice cream.

Kuma Inn's friendly owner/chef, King Phojanakong, is of Thai and Filipino parentage, and he brings both cultures to the food he cooks right behind the counter where you order. Small plates ($7–10) of salmon, tuna, or scallops are marinated with Asian fruits, chayote, ginger, or mirin and sake. Little slices of London broil, delicate vegetable spring rolls, long beans, and more, are treated with Filipino/Thai twists that make the food here distinctive, reports *djk*, who says everything's delicious, though you might have to order a lot of plates to get a full meal.

Chubo's Asian-influenced menus are all prix fixe: $24 for appetizer, entrée, and dessert. Skip dessert and the bill drops to $20. Recommended dishes include thyme-roasted hake, oat-crusted smoked salmon cakes, and flavorful grilled salmon. Relaxed vibe and good service. Good date place.

The menu at **Sumile** (in the old Domicile space) is loosely based on Japanese cuisine, but ingredients come from across Asia and preparation is French. Menu items are presented as Asian tapas—about $14 each. *Craig* praises veal head and foie gras terrine with crispy duck tongue and mizuna salad, impeccable poached halibut, and a highly refined dish of duck breast with sake and foie gras mousse, among other items. The wine list features reasonable prices on small production wines. Food and wine are solid and well chosen, report *Fred and Wilma*, who praise the service but find the room itself a disaster.

The fusion concept at **Ma-Ya** extends from their long cocktail list (lychee cosmopolitans, sake mojitos, etc.) through dessert. Calamari is very tasty and green curry chicken is perfectly cooked, but fried pork on toast is oily, reports *JH Jill*. Good mango sticky rice with coconut sauce and fried roti filled with evaporated milk for dessert. There's a music space downstairs.

Asiate is a Japanese-influenced French restaurant in the

Mandarin Oriental Hotel on Columbus Circle, graced with beautiful views of the city, thanks to its thirty-fifth-floor location. Chef Norie Sugie, who has cooked with Charlie Trotter, is cooking cuisine that can only just barely be called fusion; Japanese influences are seen in minor touches like sprinkles of nori atop mini baguettes and *amuses* of gruyère gougères. Some of the decadent dishes enjoyed by *banh cuon* include appetizers of prawns with truffle shavings and handmade pasta noodles (steamed en papillote with house spicy xo sauce covered with large black truffle shavings), clam étouffé (geoduck, razor, and ark clams in a buttery coconut broth), and caesar salad soup (warm pureed lettuce dotted with bits of grain and parmesan foam). Suckling pig is a total knockout: two pressed rectangles of roasted pig with crispy skin, a spherical croquette of minced pig trotter parts encrusted in panko breadcrumbs, a portion of braised pig cheeks resting on lightly sautéed cabbage and apple puree spiced with fennel and sumac. Don't miss the rosé champagne by Vranken, plus a nice selection of sakes by the glass. Dinner is prix fixe at $65 for a leisurely three-course meal and $85 for a seven-course tasting.

ASTORIA Beyond Greek

Al Dayaa (Queens)
22-75 31st St.
Astoria, Queens, NY
Lebanese

Balkh Shish Kabab (Queens)
23-10 31st St.
Astoria, Queens, NY
718-721-5020
Afghan

Cina Romanian Restaurant
    (Queens)
45-17 28th Ave.
Astoria, Queens, NY
718-956-0372
Romanian

Dhaka Cafe Jhill (Queens)
35-55 33rd St.
Astoria, Queens, NY
718-937-4200
Bangladeshi

El Farolito (Queens)
25-39 Steinway St.
Astoria, Queens, NY
718-204-7711
Argentinian

El Mariachi (Queens)
33-11 Broadway
Astoria, Queens, NY
718-545-4039
Mexican

Girassol Churrascaria (Queens)
33-18 28th Ave.
Astoria, Queens, NY
718-545-8250
Brazilian

Joseph Livoti Pork Store (Queens)
37-21 Ditmars Blvd.
Astoria, Queens, NY
718-721-1579
Italian Deli

Kabab Cafe (Queens)
25-12 Steinway St.
Astoria, Queens, NY
718-728-9858
Egyptian

La Casa Del Pan (Queens)
33-20 30th Ave.
Astoria, Queens, NY
718-721-7991
Colombian Bakery

La Casa Del Pan (Queens)
38-02 Broadway
Astoria, Queens, NY
718-726-7946
Colombian Bakery

Laziza of New York Pastry
 (Queens)
23-78 Steinway St.
Astoria, Queens, NY
718-777-7676
Jordanian/Palestinian

Malagueta (Queens)
25-35 36th Ave.
Long Island City, Queens, NY
718-937-4821
Brazilian

Pollos y Mas (Queens)
30th Ave. and 36th St.
Astoria, Queens, NY
718-204-9484
Peruvian

VOLO Gastronomia (Queens)
28-09 Ditmars Blvd.
Astoria, Queens, NY
718-278-8878
Italian/Istrian

Astoria was known, until recently, as a heavily Greek nabe. But no more. Diversity rules!

VOLO Gastronomia is a cafe/panin/takeout place—with some seating—that serves a few things from the legendary Piccolo Venezia. It's quite a find, even if only for the chance to try excerpts from the menu of NYC's best Istrian/Italian kitchen for less than astronomical prices. "What a gem! My panino with speck, taleggio and radicchio was nicely pressed on their homemade focaccia bread and the combination of flavors was fantastic. I had a little room left to try some gelato and boy was I glad I did—the hazelnut was the best I ever had, better than in Italy!

Coffee was outrageous," raves *mets31*. The display cases in the back are filled with great-looking prepared foods like crab cakes and cannelloni. There are also deli meats (like bresaola, prosciutto, and cappacola) and cheeses for sale by the pound.

Baba ghanoush at **Al Dayaa** is creamy, garlicky, and smoky and served with delicious olive oil on top. The meat combo comes with chicken kabob, shish kebab and kofta kebab on top of amazing rice pilaf (with almonds, pine nuts, and ground beef), reports *AndyK*. There are a couple of tables in the back if you want to eat in.

At **El Mariachi**, both food and service earn high marks, though it might be best to stick to relatively simple dishes. Tacos, huevos rancheros, *chilaquiles*, and salsa draw praise.

The two **La Casa del Pan** locations specialize in coffee and Colombian breakfast treats. Chowhound *dpw206* recommends *pan de bono*, especially if you can get a fresh warm one (they also reheat well at home).

Cina serves tasty stuffed cabbage and other homey Romanian specialties with flair in elegant surroundings with excellent service, all at very reasonable prices . . . which makes one wonder why the place is so empty. Flavors are intense, says *john knoessel*, who recommends *mici* (koftalike ground beef and pork sausages served with spicy mustard) and eggplant spreads. Other hounds suggest pork tenderloin with bacon and garlic and tripe soup in a buttery broth with chopped garlic and sour cream. Lunch specials are especially good.

Malagueta and **Girassol** for Brazilian. The latter makes fantastic tilefish in red sauce and spit-cooked sirloin.

Kabab Cafe is a perennial Chowhound favorite. Get whatever chef/owner Ali suggests. Veggie appetizers usually shine, as do specials.

Stop off at **Laziza** Bakery for Middle Eastern baked goods to take home or eat at its one lonely table. Coffee and tea, too. Don't miss the sensational Palestinian *kunefe* (koo-NEFF-uh), a very rare specialty.

Peruvian **Pollos y Mas**, as the name implies, specializes in chicken. Arroz con pollo and *plato tipica* are good, but even better with green sauce.

Argentinian **El Farolito** sometimes has trouble coordinating dishes for groups, but the owner treats customers like gold, and the food's great.

Balkh Shish Kabob for Afghan *aushak* (dumplings) and tea.

Dhaka Jhill is a very inexpensive Bangaladeshi—whole fish about $6. Naan is fresh.

Joe's Pork Store makes their own sausages (including great cheese sausage with hunks of provolone, fennel-laced sweet sausage, and spicy hot red sausage). Also good sopressata and a hot version of dry pancetta. The cold case includes pork ribs, shoulders, and loins, and also smoked and fresh mozzarella and fresh ricotta. "This store is a treasure and I always like to support handmade food by people who love what they do," says *alithang*.

See also The State of Astoria *Greek* and Great *Mexican* in Long Island City.

Plus see nabe index for places in Astoria and nearby Long Island City.

○ **Kabab Cafe:** *see also* **p. 191.**
○ **Malagueta:** *see also* **p. 208.**

ATLANTIC AVENUE Arabic

Damascus Bread & Pastry Shop
  (Brooklyn)
195 Atlantic Ave.
Cobble Hill, Brooklyn, NY
718-625-7070
Lebanese/Syrian Bakery

Lunchette (Brookyln)
145 Court St.
Cobble Hill, Brooklyn, NY
718-624-9325
Yemeni

Sahadi Importing Co. (Brooklyn)
187 Atlantic Ave.
Brooklyn Heights, Brooklyn, NY
718-624-4550
Middle Eastern

Tabouleh Restaurant (Brooklyn)
136 Smith St.
Cobble Hill, Brooklyn, NY
718-797-3313
Jordanian/Palestinian

Waterfalls Cafe (Brooklyn)
144 Atlantic Ave.
Cobble Hill, Brooklyn, NY
718-488-8886
Lebanese

Yemen Cafe (Brooklyn)
176 Atlantic Ave.
Cobble Hill, Brooklyn, NY
718-834-9533
Yemeni

The area around Atlantic Avenue in Brooklyn is one of the nation's oldest Arab communities and home to immigrants from almost all the Arab countries, which means many great shops and restaurants serving the Arab community.

The only thing western-hemispheric about **Lunchette** is its name, a holdover from an earlier establishment in the location. There's an Arabic menu in the window but no English equivalent. The food is Yemeni, and the staff and customers are very friendly. Just ask them to cook you some lunch and enjoy the feast.

Waterfalls' excellent authentic Lebanese falafel, hummus, shwarma, salads, soups, and smoky baba ghanoush are all lovingly prepared by a friendly family. They've started baking their own soft and fresh bread in a new bread oven, but it's hard to keep up with demand (they run out, and tend not to serve it with takeout orders), so check before ordering. Vegetarian items shine. A favorite strategy is to order a vegetarian combo plate and add meat. Servings are large.

Tabouleh doesn't look like much from the outside, but the interior is immaculate and the food is incredible, reports *Dipsy*, who says the line of car service drivers going in and out testifies to its quality. The Jordanian owner takes pride in his cooking and prepares about four daily items, one a rice, one chicken (often in a spicy red sauce), one lamb, etc. You order from the counter, where everything looks fresh and is beautifully presented.

Yemen Cafe, located above the Yemeni barbershop, serves food just a little different from other places, perhaps more like what Yemenis eat at home. Yemeni *fatta* (buttery bread strips served with a large bowl of honey and more butter or as an entrée with meat) is a favorite of *driggs*. *Jim Leff* agrees, and theorizes that it's called that 'cuz the more you eat, the fatta you get.

No matter where you end up, almost everyone recommends stopping at **Sahadi** for take-home hummus, baba ghanoush (the latter prepackaged only; don't get it from the big bowl), pitted kalamata olives, and dark chocolate-covered almonds. Also pick up some soft, triangle-shaped pocketless pitas from **Damascus Bakery**, two doors down.

○ **Sahadi Importing Co:** *see also* p. 54.

AVENUE U CHINATOWN

Century Cafe (Brooklyn)
1924 Avenue U
Gravesend, Brooklyn, NY
718-648-8898
Chinese (Dim Sum)/Chinese
  (Cantonese)

Ocean Palace Pavilion (Brooklyn)
1418 Avenue U
Gravesend, Brooklyn, NY
718-376-3838
Chinese (Hong Kong)/Chinese
  (Dim Sum)

Saigon Palace (Brooklyn)
1915 Avenue U
Gravesend, Brooklyn, NY
718-646-0008
Vietnamese

Unnamed seafood restaurant
  (Brooklyn)
Across the street from 1924
  Avenue U
Gravesend, Brooklyn, NY
Chinese (Cantonese)

Win Sing Seafood (Brooklyn)
1217 Avenue U
Gravesend, Brooklyn, NY.
718-998-0360
Chinese (Dim Sum)/Chinese
  (Cantonese)

There's a growing Chinese community in the Gravesend section of Brooklyn that's not yet registered in the minds of most New York diners. Hounds have been staking out the best options, however.

Century Cafe has a few tables but no table service. Excellent dim sum is found near the back (good sticky rice wrapped in lotus leaf).

Across the street from Century Cafe is an **unnamed** inexpensive seafood restaurant. Make sure someone explains the wall posters and/or the Chinese menu because the real gems are not listed on the English menu. They'll often have sautéed twin lobsters; fresh oysters and/or scallops on the half shell steamed with black beans, scallions, and ginger; pea shoots sautéed with garlic; crispy-skinned roasted chicken served with toasted salt; sautéed clams and/or razor clams in a spicy black bean sauce; and fresh fish straight out of the tank.

Saigon Palace has excellent *pho* with outstanding broth.

Ocean Palace is slightly fancier than the other restaurants, and their menu is more accessible if less ambitious. Stick with Peking duck, fish ball dim sum, and crispy fried chicken lest ye run into one of many dud choices.

Win Sing is a sit-down dim sum house.

What to Get at Manhattan
BAKERIES

A L Bazzini Co. (Tribeca)
339 Greenwich St.
Manhattan, NY
212-334-1280
Store

Amy's Bread (Chelsea)
75 9th Ave. in the Chelsea
   Market
Manhattan, NY
212-462-4338
Bakery

Amy's Bread (Upper East Side)
972 Lexington Ave.
Manhattan, NY
212-537-0270
Bakery

Amy's Bread (Clinton)
672 9th Ave.
Manhattan, NY
212-977-2670
Bakery

Columbus Bakery (Midtown East)
957 1st Ave.
Manhattan, NY
212-421-0334
Bakery

Columbus Bakery
   (Upper West Side)
474 Columbus Ave.
Manhattan, NY
212-724-6880
Bakery

Eleni's NYC (Chelsea)
75 9th Ave., in the Chelsea
   Market
Manhattan, NY
212-255-7990
Bakery

Fat Witch Brownies (Chelsea)
75 9th Ave., in the Chelsea
   Market
Manhattan, NY
212-807-1335
Bakery

Kossar's Bialys (Lower East Side)
367 Grand St.
Manhattan, NY
212-473-4810
Kosher Eastern European
   Jewish

Mary's Off Jane
  (Greenwich Village)
34 Eighth Ave.
Manhattan, NY
212-243-5972
Bakery

Once Upon a Tart (Soho)
135 Sullivan St.
Manhattan, NY
212-387-8869
Bakery

Out of the Kitchen
  (Greenwich Village)
456 Hudson St.
Manhattan, NY
212-242-0399
American

Pasticceria Bruno
  (Greenwich Village)
245 Bleecker St.
Manhattan, NY
212-242-4959
French/Italian Café

Pasticceria Bruno
  (Greenwich Village)
506 LaGuardia Pl.
Manhattan, NY
212-982-5854
French/Italian Café

Polka Dot Cake Studio
  (Greenwich Village)
312 Bleecker St.
Manhattan, NY
212-645-0500
Bakery

Rocco Pastry Shop
  (Greenwich Village)
243 Bleecker St.
Manhattan, NY
212-242-6031
Italian Bakery/Cheese
  Shop/Pizzeria

Sarabeth's Bakery (Chelsea)
75 9th Ave., in the Chelsea
  Market
Manhattan, NY
212-989-2424
Bakery

Sarabeth's East (Upper East Side)
1295 Madison Ave., in the
  Whitney Museum
Manhattan, NY
212-410-7335
American

Sarabeth's West
  (Upper West Side)
423 Amsterdam Ave.
Manhattan, NY
212-496-6280
American

Sullivan Street Bakery (Clinton)
533 W. 47th St.
Manhattan, NY
212-586-1626
Italian Bakery

Sullivan Street Bakery (Soho)
73 Sullivan St.
Manhattan, NY
212-334-9435
Italian Bakery

Few bakeries do everything well. Some specialize in breads, others in cakes. Some have just one exceptional item. Hounds reveal where to go for what.

Perhaps the greatest concentration of quality bakers is in Chelsea Market, where you'll find at least four hound-sanctioned bakers at work: Amy's Bread, Sarabeth's, Eleni's, and Fat Witch Brownies.

Amy's Bread bakes a variety of goodies but items with chocolate stand out, especially old-fashioned chocolate cake, chocolate-cherry rolls, and sourdough twists with chocolate bits or olives. But cakes aren't available at the Chelsea Market branch, so head to the Clinton or UES locations for layered goodness. "I've never shared some people's infatuation with Amy's Bread," grouses *Jim Leff*; "their stuff always seems slightly cold-hearted to me. But I just tried their cranberry scones and Got Religion."

Sarabeth's is known for pancake brunches and scones. The Chelsea Market branch isn't a sit-down restaurant, but sells lots of baked goods and breakfast you can enjoy at the market's common tables. Their plain minimuffins are worth swooning over in their own charming way. *Jim Leff* cautions that they're a subtle pleasure; there's amazing texture and flavor, but you really have to concentrate to appreciate them. The pumpkin/sunflower varieties are merely competent, but the ones that appear plain taste anything but.

Pricey cookies are the thing at **Eleni's**, from simple ginger and butter cookies to elaborately iced sugar cookie sets.

Fat Witch Brownies: The name says it all.

Out of the Kitchen's black and white cookies are amazing, says *sweettooth*.

Black and white cookies also stand out at **Rocco Pastry Shop**. And check out their old-school cannolis, filled to order. Every once in a while they make big fat chocolate chip cookies (in classic chocolate chip, half-chocolate-covered chocolate chip, and the chocolate trifecta of half-chocolate-dipped chocolate chocolate chip). *Aki* says these are pretty big, and very thick; they look like big scones. They're more dry/flaky (in a good way) than soft/chewy; their texture is similar to shortbread—very light consistency.

Pasticceria Bruno, right next door to Rocco Pastry Shop, also has old-fashioned Italian pastries, but they're better known for French pastries and fruit tarts.

A little farther along on the same block is **Polka Dot Cake Studio,** renowned for chocolate blackout cake—a better choice than their "Brad Pitt Brownies," which *Caitlin Wheeler* says are pretty good (in spite of the dopey name) as long as you get them fresh.

Bazzini's is primarily a nut wholesaler, but has expanded to sell tasty scones and other goodies.

Cheddar dill scones, muffins, and biscotti are recommended at **Once Upon a Tart**.

Entering **Kossar's Bialys** is like stepping back in time. It's basically a bialy bakery (ovens and racks all over) with a small counter, and they still make the bialys on big old wooden racks. Also try their bialy bread. Closed Saturday.

Congo bars (crumb crust, a mixture of condensed milk with coconut, topped with chocolate and more coconut) may or may not have been invented at **Mary's Off Jane**, but they sure make a great rendition. Also check out lemon bars, Romeo and Juliets, mojito cookies, chocolate chubbies, lime-ginger scones, and banana muffins (but ONLY if they're fresh). *Amy Mintzer* says it's a rare source of Boston cream pie. Slow turnover can be a problem, so ask when the item was baked.

Get wonderful browned sugar cakes at **Columbus Bakery**.

Sullivan Street Bakery is a longtime favorite for a large and consistently well-made selection of breads, bread pizzas, Danish, and many other treats.

See also Where the Good *Desserts* Live and all listings under Bakeries and Dessert Cafes in the cuisine index.

- **Amy's Bread:** *see* pp. 85, 238.
- **Sarabeth's:** *see* p. 123.
- **Sullivan Street Bakery:** *see also* pp. 36, 67, 244.

BAMIYAN for Very Good Afghan

Bamiyan (Gramercy)
157 E. 26th St.
Manhattan, NY
212-481-3232
Afghan

Chowhound Nametag: Dave Feldman

○○○

Location: Upper West Side, Manhattan, New York City.

Occupation: Author

Number of Visits to McDonald's in Past Decade: twenty-five. Two until about three months ago, when I started eating the California Cobb salad with grilled chicken and low-fat balsamic vinaigrette.

Farthest Out of the Way Traveled Just for Chow: Going several hundred miles out of my way to eat at Arthur Bryant's in the late '60s, inspired by Calvin Trillin's *American Fried*. But I'm proudest of going two hours out of my way to get a superb plain doughnut in Rutland, Vermont.

Favorite Comfort Chow: Kabab Cafe. The baba ghanoush and humitas are comforting.

Guilty Pleasure: Not really guilty, but I love nacho cheese and all spicy versions of Doritos.

Favorite Gelato Flavor: Coffee.

Favorite Mail-order Chow: Virginia Diner for peanuts (www.vadiner.com) and Enstrom's for toffee (www.enstrom.com).

Chowhounding Rules of Thumb:
1. Passion can be gleaned in cyberspace, and Chowhound.com allows me to do "virtual Chowhounding." When I see someone whose posts I trust writing about a restaurant I haven't been to before, and that poster has the verbal equivalent of a glow in his or her eyes, I'm going.
2. If a restaurant, except in small towns, has a display ad in the Yellow Pages . . . don't go.

Longtime fave Bamiyan continues to earn praise for nicely prepared and very tasty Afghan dishes. Kabobs and other meat dishes are excellent, as are deep-fried fritters filled with spiced pumpkin. Try *aushak*, herb-stuffed ravioli topped with yogurt and crumbled ground beef.

Comprehensive **BANH MI** Roundup

An Dong (Brooklyn)
5424 8th Ave.
Sunset Park, Brooklyn, NY
718-972-2269
Vietnamese

Ba Le Deli (Chinatown)
145 Canal St.
Manhattan, NY
212-343-2657
Vietnamese

Ba Xuyen (Brooklyn)
6011 7th Ave.
Sunset Park, Brooklyn, NY
718-765-0037
Vietnamese

Ba Xuyen (Brooklyn)
4222 8th Ave.
Sunset Park, Brooklyn, NY
718-633-6601
Vietnamese

Banh M Sau Voi Cafe (Tribeca)
101 Lafayette St.
Manhattan, NY
212-226-8184
Vietnamese

Banh Mi Hiep Hoa (Brooklyn)
5701 7th Ave.
Sunset Park, Brooklyn, NY
718-567-7628
Vietnamese

Phi Lan (Midtown East)
249 East 45th St.
Manhattan, NY
212-922-9411
Vietnamese Sandwich Shop

Pho Tu Do (Chinatown)
119 Bowery
Manhattan, NY
212-966-2666
Vietnamese

Saigon Bakery (Chinatown)
59 Division St.
Manhattan, NY
212-941-1541
Vietnamese

Tan Tu Quynh (Lower East Side)
128 Hester St.
Manhattan, NY
212-966-6878
Vietnamese Sandwich Shop

Vietnam Banh Mi So 1 (Lower East Side)
369 Broome St.
Manhattan, NY
212-219-8341
Vietnamese

For the uninitiated, *banh mi* are Vietnamese sandwiches served on baguettes made from half rice and half wheat flour (very crispy outside and fluffy inside). Standard fillings include pâté, long cucumber slices, a pickled combo of carrot and daikon, mayonnaise, and hot sauce. Alternative fillings include choices of warm/hot BBQ pork, Vietnamese pork-and-seafood sausage, or Vietnamese "headcheese" of pork/beef tendon and other cuts in a firm gelatin. Most places also offer vegetarian, meatball, or chicken banh mi.

Here is a pretty comprehensive list of noteworthy Manhattan and Brooklyn banh mi, put together by *the rogue*:

Saigon Banh Mi makes only one style, the *dac biet* (aka the special), which includes everything but the kitchen sink. Lots of pork and veggies.

There are about a half-dozen styles of banh mi at **Vietnam Banh Mi So 1**, including a very good vegetarian sandwich with mushrooms, sweet radish, and rice noodles.

Pho Tu Do serves just two variations. The $2.75 "Saigon" is filled with lots of sweet crumbly pork, while for a buck more there's one filled with warm grilled pork slices. Make sure they don't overtoast the bread.

There's a good selection of meat and veggies in the sole banh mi at **Tan Tu Quynh** but the sandwiches are not packed as generously as at some other places. Same complaint at **Ba Le Deli** (with a half-dozen styles including dac biet, meatball, and chicken) and at **Phi Lan** in midtown (pricier at $6 for a pretty big—though skimpily filled—sandwich).

Banh Mi Sau Voi Cafe makes a variety of styles, but at least one hound says quality is not as high as elsewhere.

In Brooklyn, **Ba Xuyen** claims all pâté and meats are imported (frozen) from France. They're topped with five different sauces, including homemade BBQ sauce, which provide great flavor contrasts. Their newer Eighth Avenue branch is much larger than the original and features a backlit menu with large pictures of the different banh mi styles. There's also a hot case containing their signature yucca cake (shrink-wrapped, but that doesn't hurt quality), various leaf-wrapped things and other curiosity-inducing items, including a tantalizing-sounding treat: "I picked up something I thought was a spring roll that turned out to be the best bun I've ever had, at a ridiculously low $3. It was made with spaghetti-style rice noodles, pork skin, spring rolls, more vegetables than you usually see in a NY bun, and one of the better bun sauces I've ever had. It has a great spicy bite to it that I'm not used to from this dish," raves *Peter Cuce*. Sickly sweet bubble teas are made from mix. Instead, get an amazingly good *sinh to bo* (avocado shake).

Also in Brooklyn, **An Dong** uses all local meats in its over-stuffed banh mi, but *the rogue* says while the dac biet variety is very meaty tasting, it doesn't have the complex flavors other banh mi offer.

Banh Mi Hiep Hoa is another Brooklyn banh mi contender (try the #1 dac biet), making unrepentantly spicy banh mi tailored to Vietnamese tastes.

BARBECUE Deep in the Heart of Jersey

Hot Rod's Real Pit BBQ (Morris County)
100 Randolph Ave. at Joann's
Mine Hill, NJ
973-361-5050
Barbecue

This is a funky, comfortable spot off the beaten track with good barbecue. "The cornbread was hot, with accompanying maple butter—there wasn't a crumb left in very short order, which meant the hushpuppies didn't get the attention they deserved. The baked beans are to die for (they're homemade), the slaw is crisp and light and a perfect foil for the ribs in their crust of dry rub. I had the good fortune to sample a bit of their pulled pork—the genuine article. There's a sandwich of this with my name on it for my next visit," reports *Maureen*. Only open 5–10 p.m., Tuesday through Saturday. Very busy weekends, more accessible during the week.

Upstate **BARBECUE**

Brooks House of Bar-B-Q
  (Otsego County)
5560 Hwy. 7
Oneonta, NY
607-432-1782
Barbecue

Chumley's BBQ Hut
  (Orange County)
1 Durland Rd.
Florida, NY
845-651-7429
Barbecue

Jenny's Bar-B-Q
  (Dutchess County)
1639 Rte. 199
Stanfordville, NY
845-876-1151
Barbecue

Oscar's Smokehouse
  (Warren County)
22 Raymond Ln.
Warrensburg, NY
518-623-3431
Barbecue/Store

Brooks BBQ, a large barbecue restaurant with a pit out back, is located just a short drive from Cooperstown. *ScottK* finds their BBQ pork and beef tasty but obscured in sauce. Ribs the day he tried them were a bit tough. But the outstanding (dare we say "hall of fame?") item is the BBQ chicken. Cooked in a charcoal pit and mopped with a spiced, vinegar-based sauce while cooking, it's juicy and full of great, penetrating, smoky charcoal flavor. Sauce is neither required nor applied.

Meats at **Chumley's BBQ Hut** (pulled pork, brisket, chicken and tender, flavorful ribs) gets lots of praise from *Andrea*, but the sides really thrill her. Macaroni salad is fab, and shoestring fries are amazing, as are the extra rich baked beans. But accompanying corn muffins are dry, and fresh fried chips with salsa are greasy.

Jenny's is a time machine, a real throwback to the 1950s. It's attached to a motel, complete with kitschy atmosphere and an owner who doubles as waitress. *Scott Gordon* says ribs and brisket go well with great homemade fries. Open Thursday through Sunday only.

Great smoked meats at **Oscar's Smokehouse**.

○ **Oscar's Smokehouse:** *see also* **p. 5.**

Fresh **BEAN CURD**

Taste Good Soya Food (Brooklyn)
5103 8th Ave.
Sunset Park, Brooklyn, NY
718-686-6088
Chinese

Taste Good Soya Food is a bean-curd factory selling freshly made squares of pillowy bean curd, fried and frozen bean curd, soy milk, good quality bean sprouts and noodles, including rolled flat rice noodles layered with dried shrimp and scallions. Open to the public at rock-bottom prices.
　　See also *Chinatown Vendors.*

Brooklyn **BEEF SANDWICHES**

Brennan & Car Restaurant
　　(Brooklyn)
3432 Nostrand Ave.
Sheepshead Bay, Brooklyn, NY
718-646-9559
American

De Fonte's of Red Hook
　　(Brooklyn)
379 Columbia St.
Red Hook, Brooklyn, NY
718-855-6982
Italian Sandwich Shop

John's Deli (Brooklyn)
2438 Stillwell Ave.
Bensonhurst, Brooklyn, NY
718-714-4377
Sandwich Shop

Roll-N-Roaster (Brooklyn)
2901 Emmons Ave.
Sheepshead Bay, Brooklyn, NY
718-769-6000
American

The Brooklyn roast beef sandwich is almost an institution, though there's little agreement about how to define it and how it differs from roast beef sandwiches elsewhere. Each of the following is a distinct style of eatery serving a distinctive sandwich:

Brennan and Carr has waitress service and probably the best beef of the three.

John's is a simple nothing-fancy deli. *Jeff* says they've got great bread and really tasty gravy. *Brookly* says their roast beef is best on Thursdays.

Fast food **Roll-N-Roaster**'s been around more than twenty-five years. Hounds recommend their turkey sandwiches, corn nuggets, chicken tenders, and orange- and lemonades. *Ian* really likes their beef with cheese and onions on a fresh seeded roll with a side of round fries.

De Fonte's makes the perfect roast beef sandwich on gravy-soaked, sesame-seeded Italian bread, as well as terrific egg and pepper and/or potato, and anything combining fried eggplant, roasted peppers, and mozzarella.

○ **De Fonte's of Red Hook:** *see also* pp. 56, 115.

In the **BERKSHIRES**

Verdura (Berkshire County)
44 Railroad St.
Great Barrington, MA
413-528-8969
Italian

Verdura fills with New Yorkers on weekends, yet still maintains a friendly atmosphere. Try not to fill up on excellent, moist and chewy Tuscan-style bread before your meal arrives. Foie gras makes a decadent appetizer. Fish, in fritto misto or grilled trout over white beans and salsa verde, is absolutely fresh, says *bookistan*, who also enjoyed gnocchi with vegetables.

BLACK DUCK: Delicious Eponymity

Black Duck (Murray Hill)
122 E. 28th St., next to the Park South Hotel
Manhattan, NY
212-448-0888
New American

Located in a restored eighteenth-century brownstone (with nice wood floors and a fireplace) next to the Park South Hotel, **Black Duck's** eponymous dish is black pepper-crusted duck breast in cherry glace sauce. *DaveG* finds it very flavorful and juicy, and not overly peppery. Juicy rack of lamb comes properly done in a port wine sauce. The rest of the menu is seafood oriented. Portions tend toward the small side even if prices don't. Often a jazz combo plays through dinner.

BLINTZES

Artisanal (Murray Hill)
2 Park Ave.; enter on 32nd St.
Manhattan, NY
212-725-8585
French

B&H Dairy (East Village)
127 2nd Ave.
Manhattan, NY
212-505-8065
Eastern European Jewish

Cafe Edison (Clinton)
240 W. 47th St.
Manhattan, NY
212-840-5000
Diner or Coffee Shop

Diamond Dairy Kosher
  Luncheonette
  (Midtown West)
4 W. 47th St., 2nd Fl.
Manhattan, NY
212-719-2694
Kosher Eastern European Jewish

Veselka Restaurant
  (East Village)
144 2nd Ave.
Manhattan, NY
212-228-9682
Ukranian/Central/Eastern
  European

New York used to play host to a blintzkreig, and there are still venues here and there—one of which is even trendy!

Artisanal makes cheese blintzes for brunch with pomegranate seeds and quince puree. Blintzes at **Veselka** are the traditional Russian plain cheese variety. **Cafe Edison** has Polish-style blintzes and good hearty soups. From the mezzanine of **Diamond Dairy Kosher Luncheonette**, you can eat blintzes while looking down at folks haggling over jewelry. **B&H Dairy** serves blintzes at its old-style lunch counter.

- Artisanal: *see also* pp. 66, 132, 207, 266.
- Veselka Restaurant: *see also* p. 280.

More BOSNIAN BURGERS!

Bosna-Express (Queens)
791 Fairview Ave.
Ridgewood, Queens, NY
718-497-7577
Bosnian or Serbian

Istria Sport Club (Queens)
28-09 Astoria Blvd.
Astoria, Queens, NY
718-728-3181
Istrian

Cevabdzinica Sarajevo (Queens)
37-18 34th Ave
Astoria, Queens, NY
718-752-9528
Bosnian or Serbian

Rudar Soccer Club (Queens)
34-01 45th St.
Long Island City, Queens, NY
718-786-5833
Istrian

Pljeskavica—**better known as** the Bosnian burger—is famously made at **Bosna-Express** in Ridgewood. Not really a hamburger, this $6 mixture of ground beef and lamb more closely resembles a sausage patty on steroids. "The gargantuan disk of meat slathered with sweetish home-made yogurt and topped with chopped onions, and a salad of tomatoes, red and green peppers and a sprinkling of crushed red pepper (*ajvar*) sandwiched between a toasted round of traditional pita bread proved to be almost too much for me," writes *Canchito*. A similar dish, called *cevapi*, is served at **Istria** Club, **Rudar** Club and **Cevabdzinica Sarajevo**. Many butchers on Broadway in Astoria have them prepared, ready to be cooked on your grill, and also sell accompanying Adriatic brand ajvar (red pepper paste) in hot and mild versions.

BRASSERIE JULIEN

Brasserie Julien (Upper East Side)
1422 3rd Ave.
Manhattan, NY
212-744-6327
French Brasserie

We don't understand why **Brasserie Julien** doesn't get more attention. Every comment we've had on it has been positive. The latest, a lunch report from *Tasty Llama*, raved over great corn chowder, a nut-filled goat cheese and vegetable appetizer (which can be expanded into an entrée), and a charcuterie platter (especially soft and very flavorful salami).

BRAZILIAN for Breakfast and Dinner

Casa Restaurant (Greenwich Village)
72 Bedford St.
Manhattan, NY
212-366-9410
Brazilian

Having heard that the esteemed Brazilian restaurant **Casa** makes first-rate hot chocolate and French toast, *Unagi* stopped in for dinner and found it just as terrific. Entrées were perfect tilapia with onions, potatoes, and olives; grilled steak (flavored with taro flower and bacon); and a vegetarian plate of rice, beans, a fried plantain, and choice of two vegetables (including chayote and collards). An interesting wine list and selection of exotic fruit juices round out the menu.

A Loaf of **BREAD**, Yadda Yadda

Balthazar (Soho)
80 Spring St.
Manhattan, NY
212-965-1414
French Bistro

Balthazar Bakery Wholesale
   Division (Bergen County)
214 S. Dean St.
Englewood, NJ
201-503-9717
French Bakery

Corrado's Bakery
   (Grand Central)
109 E. 42nd St.
Manhattan, NY
212-599-4321
Bakery

Corrado's Bakery
   (Upper East Side)
960 Lexington Ave.
Manhattan, NY
212-774-1904
Bakery

Eli's Vinegar Factory
   (Upper East Side)
431 E. 91st St.
Manhattan, NY
212-987-0885
Store

Il Forno (Essex County)
18 S. Fullerton Ave.
Montclair, NJ
973-233-0800
Italian Bakery

Il Forno (Essex County)
199 Bellevue Ave.
Montclair, NJ
973-744-2665
Italian Bakery

Le Pain Quotidien (Citywide)
www.painquotidien.com
French/Belgian

Levain Bakery
   (Upper West Side)
167 W. 74th St.
Manhattan, NY
212-874-6080
Bakery

Mazzola Bakery (Brooklyn)
192 Union St.
Carroll Gardens, Brooklyn, NY
718-643-1719
Italian Bakery

Mazzola Bakery (Brooklyn)
195 Court St.
Carroll Gardens, Brooklyn, NY
718-797-2385
Italian Bakery

Orwasher's Bakery
(Upper East Side)
308 E. 78th St.
Manhattan, NY
212-288-6569
Eastern European Jewish Bakery

Paneantico Bakery Cafe
(Brooklyn)
9124 3rd Ave.
Bay Ridge, Brooklyn, NY
718-680-2347
Italian Bakery

Rockhill Bakehouse, at Union
Square Greenmarket
(Union Square)
130 E. 16th St., #5
Manhattan, NY
888-BREAD-11
Bakery

Royal Crown Pastry Shop
(Brooklyn)
6512 14th Ave.
Borough Park, Brooklyn, NY
718-234-1002
Bakery

Silver Bell Bakery (Corona)
4304 Junction Blvd.
Corona, Queens, NY
718-779-5156
Central/Eastern European Bakery

Sullivan Street Bakery (Clinton)
533 W. 47th St.
Manhattan, NY
212-586-1626
Italian Bakery

Sullivan Street Bakery (Soho)
73 Sullivan St.
Manhattan, NY
212-334-9435
Italian Bakery

Uprising Bread Bakery (Brooklyn)
328 7th Ave.
Park Slope, Brooklyn, NY
718-499-8665
Bakery

Uprising Bread Bakery (Brooklyn)
138 7th Ave.
Park Slope, Brooklyn, NY
718-499-5242
Bakery

While many bakeries produce good bread, you often need to hit different ones for different things. Here are tips complete with most-recommended specialties:

Sullivan Street Bakery is wildly popular with hounds as an all-around bread baker but draws particular praise for *pugliese* (the kind you can imagine Giacomo cooking in the back alleys of Naples—black, crumbly crust with a soft, dense interior, says *Flour*), ciabatta, and fresh pizza bianco. A lot of people don't know about their *schiacciata all'uva*—moist, chewy thin foccacia topped with anise seeds, tiny champagne grapes, and a little dusting of sugar (marvelous, not-too-sweet, really amazing combo of textures/flavors, says *dixieday*), and great with soft sheep or goat cheese.

Levain on the Upper West Side is also reported to make a very good ciabatta.

Balthazar's breads are delicious, but a completely different style than Sullivan Street's. Their walnut loaves deserve particular mention.

Dense old-fashioned Eastern European-style breads (black, pumpernickel, babka, seeded ryes, challah, etc.) are the specialty at **Orwasher's**, a family-run bakery on the Upper East Side. Outstanding corn rye and any breads with raisins—including surprisingly good Irish soda bread.

Eli's raisin bread is considered the best around by some hounds.

On Saturdays you can find **Rockhill Bakehouse** at the Union Square Greenmarket. *Penny* recommends their San Francisco sourdough and cheddar corn jalapeno bread. Deliciousness does not come cheaply, but their loaves stay good for up to a week.

"One of my favorite things to do is eat a whole lot of **Le Pain Quotidien's** rye bread, which is mystically soft yet dense, and get really tired and go to sleep. Take that, you atkinsheads!" roars *babar ganesh*.

The motto of **Uprising Bakery** is "Prepare to Meet Your Baker," and *Dipsy* thinks that'd be reason enough to love them even if their ciabatta weren't so damned good.

Silver Bell Bakery sells a variety of things, but *Nanaimo Bar* says its Lithuanian peasant bread made with rye flour is off the charts (and even better toasted).

Royal Crown and **Paneantico** are related, and both are very much loved by chowhounds. Chocolate (chocolate in regular dough, not chocolate dough) and fig-walnut breads are praised, and chestnut bread (available only during the holidays) is sublime, says *Timowitz*.

Mazzola Bakery gets raves for delicious, peppery lard bread with bits of baked-in salami and veins of melted-in cheese. Olive bread also gets mostly good comments, but other items draw mixed reactions, as does detached service.

Lots of whole dried figs are mixed into the dough for **Corrado Bakery's** fig-walnut bread, which is fabulous plain, says *quixote*, and among the best loaves of bread he's tried in years.

Il Forno's ciabatta is not your normal bread, reports *Melanie Wong*, a self-confessed tough-to-please bread snob from San

Francisco who actually prefers it to the vaunted ciabatta at Sullivan Street Bakery. Its crust has a tender crispness that gives way to a firmer chewiness, and the crumb is irregular in texture and airy yet suitably moist. The bread itself has more yeasty flavor and a touch more salt. And Il Forno's cookies may outshine the bread. The small turnovers are a bit tough in the pastry, but their fillings (great fresh apricot and raspberry preserve) are so excellent you won't care. Best of all: chewy/crisp almond macaroons studded with pignoli, with the perfect balance of almond flavor and sweetness.

○ **Balthazar:** see also pp. 41, 96, 104, 238.
○ **Corrado's Bakery:** see also p. 239.
○ **Levain Bakery:** see also p. 86.
○ **Royal Crown Pastry Shop:** see also pp. 239, 252.
○ **Sullivan Street Bakery:** see also pp. 22, 67, 244.

Un-American **BREAKFAST** in Queens

Buenos Aires Bakery
(Queens)
90-09 Roosevelt Ave.
Corona, Queens, NY
718-672-4046
Argentinian Bakery

Castillo del Rey (Queens)
78-23 37th Ave.
Jackson Heights, Queens, NY
Dominican

Gusty Chicken (Queens)
40-10 82nd St.
Jackson Heights, Queens, NY
718-779-2910
Colombian

La Flor Bakery & Cafe (Queens)
53-02 Roosevelt Ave.
Woodside, Queens, NY
718-426-8023
Mexican/American

La Nueva Bakery (Queens)
86-10 37th Ave.
Jackson Heights, Queens, NY
718-507-2339
Latin American Café

La Pequeña Colombia Restaurant
(Queens)
83-27 Roosevelt Ave.
Jackson Heights, Queens, NY
718-478-6528
Colombian

Plaza Garibaldi (Queens)
89-12 Roosevelt Ave.
Jackson Heights, Queens, NY
718-651-9722
Mexican

Stop Inn Cafe (Queens)
60-22 Roosevelt Ave.
Woodside, Queens, NY
718-779-0290
Irish

Shane's Bakery of Woodside
    (Queens)
39-61 61st St.
Woodside, Queens NY
718-424-9039
Irish Bakery

Taqueria Coatzingo (Queens)
76-05 Roosevelt Ave.
Jackson Heights, Queens, NY
718-424-1977
Mexican

Of course, it's all "American" (lucky for us!) . . . but don't hit the following places looking for eggs benedict!

Taqueria Coatzingo and **Plaza Garibaldi** are just two of many Mexican restaurants on Roosevelt Avenue serving *chilaquiles* for breakfast. At Coatzingo, *stuartlafonda* advises to order them with *al pastor*, ask for less hot sauce, and have them put a fried egg on top.

Gusty Chicken and **La Pequeña Colombia** make good *café con leche* with different combinations of *arepas con queso, huevos pericos* (eggs scrambled with tomato and green onions). Ask for the green hot sauce, and also *buñuelos* (like spherical doughnuts).

Buenos Aires Bakery makes nice pastries for a sweet breakfast.

Dominican **Castillo del Rey** serves *mofongo* for breakfast.

La Nueva Bakery has a good selection of Colombian and Argentine/Uruguayan pastries and cappuccino.

La Flor makes a very nice Mexican-inspired breakfast.

Stop Inn Cafe is an Irish/Greek diner whose potatoes, says *jmui*, are not to be missed.

Shane's Bakery, across the street, serves a huge Irish breakfast special with black and white pudding (also pick up a loaf of their soda bread).

○ **Buenos Aires Bakery:** *see also* **p. 87.**
○ **La Flor Bakery & Cafe:** *see also* **p. 68.**
○ **La Nueva Bakery:** *see also* **p. 175.**
○ **La Pequeña Colombia Restaurant:** *see also* **p. 281.**
○ **Taqueria Coatzingo:** *see also* **p. 214.**

Chowhound Nametag: TrishUntrapped

○○○

Location:
New Fairfield, Connecticut.

Occupation:
Paralegal and newspaper reporter, former chief elected official.

Farthest Out of the Way Traveled Just for Chow: On a business trip to Nashville, drove fifty miles south to the Loveless Cafe for a breakfast of fluffy biscuits and country ham . . . Yummmm . . .

Nabe Most Full of Explorable Unknown Chow:
Pick any neighborhood in New York City.

Underrated by Chowhounds: Carminuccio's Pizza in Newtown, Connecticut; China Grill in Manhattan.

Weight Management Tip:
There are no calories in brownie batter until it's cooked.

Favorite Comfort Chow:
Chicken valdostana at Portofino's, New Fairfield, Connecticut.

Guilty Pleasure: The "Big D" BLT at Duchess (a Connecticut fast food chain) is one darn good sandwich; make sure you get the Big D one though—not their puny little one.

Favorite Gelato Flavor:
Coconut.

Branford, CT, **BREAKFAST** Spots

Indian Neck Market
  (New Haven County)
2 Sybil Ave.
Branford, CT
203-483-8220
American

Scotty's Breakfast Connections
  (New Haven County)
1188 Main St.
Branford, CT
203-483-4597
Diner or Coffee Shop

Lenny's Indian Head Inn
  (New Haven County)
205 S. Montowese St.
Branford, CT
203-488-1500
Seafood

Waiting Station
  (New Haven County)
1048 Main St.
Branford, CT
203-488-5176
American

New Haven's famous for its brick-oven pizza. But if you're wanting breakfast thereabouts (or are passing through on 95), head seven miles to Branford's **Waiting Station**, which serves daily breakfast specials and interesting omelets with brie, sun-dried tomato, and spinach. It's very neighborhood-ish, and very crowded after church on Sundays. Eggs at **Scotty's** tend to be dry (maybe that's why you can find a table here!), but home fries are top-notch. If it's a nice day, you might want to sit outside at **Indian Neck Market**. Really fresh food, nice people, and newspapers. If you oversleep breakfast, try **Lenny's Indian Head Inn** for their massively popular fried seafood.

○ **Lenny's Indian Head Inn:** *see also* **p. 88.**

Better **BRUNCH**

Bacchus (Brooklyn)
409 Atlantic Ave.
Boerum Hill, Brooklyn, NY
718-852-1572
French Bistro

Balthazar (Soho)
80 Spring St.
Manhattan, NY
212-965-1414
French Bistro

Beso Restaurant (Brooklyn)
210 5th Ave.
Park Slope, Brooklyn, NY
718-783-4902
American/Latin American

Blue Ribbon Bakery
  (Greenwich Village)
33 Downing St.
Manhattan, NY
212-337-0404
American

Cafe Bar (Queens)
3290 36th St.
Long Island City, Queens, NY
718-204-5273
New American

Chez Laurence (Murray Hill)
245 Madison Ave.
Manhattan, NY
212-683-0284
French

Elephant & Castle
  (Greenwich Village)
68 Greenwich Ave.
Manhattan, NY
212-243-1400
American

Florent (Greenwich Village)
69 Gansevoort St.
Manhattan, NY
212-989-5779
French Brasserie

Good Enough to Eat
  (Upper West Side)
483 Amsterdam Ave.
Manhattan, NY
212-496-0163
American

good Restaurant
  (Greenwich Village)
89 Greenwich Ave.
Manhattan, NY
212-691-8080
New American/Latin American

Home Restaurant
  (Greenwich Village)
20 Cornelia St.
Manhattan, NY
212-243-9579
American

Jane Restaurant
  (Greenwich Village)
100 W. Houston St.
Manhattan, NY
212-254-7000
New American

Kitchenette (Tribeca)
80 W. Broadway
Manhattan, NY
212-267-6740
American/Diner or Coffee Shop

Kitchenette Uptown (Harlem)
1272 Amsterdam Ave.
Manhattan, NY
212-531-7600
American/Diner or Coffee Shop

Noho Star (Greenwich Village)
330 Lafayette St.
Manhattan, NY
212-925-0070
New American/Chinese

107 (Upper West Side)
2787 Broadway
Manhattan, NY
212-864-1555
Cajun/Creole

Ouest (Upper West Side)
2315 Broadway
Manhattan, NY
212-580-8700
New American

Pastis (Greenwich Village)
9 9th Ave.
Manhattan, NY
212-929-4844
French Bistro

Rose Water Restaurant (Brooklyn)
787 Union St.
Park Slope, Brooklyn, NY
718-783-3800
New American

Snacky (Brooklyn)
187 Grand St.
Williamsburg, Brooklyn, NY
718-486-4848
Japanese

Tea & Sympathy
   (Greenwich Village)
108 Greenwich Ave.
Manhattan, NY
212-807-8329
British

Toast (Harlem)
3157 Broadway
Manhattan, NY
212-662-1144
American

Most brunches are terribly boring. The following transcend that fate by being (1) uncommonly delicious or (2) interesting (that is, not just offering the usual fare) and delicious. Either way, the following are brunches fit for chowhounds (some of the most innovative are in Brooklyn, so we'll start there first):

Traditional brunch items get a Hispanic twist at **Beso** out in Park Slope, where hash browns are made with yuca instead of potatoes, marinated smoked salmon comes on a cheese *arepa* with tomato-avocado salad, and you can also get the traditional Spanish breakfast of churros served with thick hot chocolate for dipping. Service can be a little spacey.

There's nothing boring about the Sunday brunch menu at **Rose Water**, also in Park Slope, where emphasis is on the creative use of fresh, local ingredients. Start off with a meze plate of yogurt with pomegranate molasses, hummus and a dish involving lots of carrot. Follow with a poached goose egg, artichoke and pepper frittata, or duck confit sandwich. Everything is spiced and seasoned with panache. (Dinner there draws more variable reviews.)

Snacky is a Williamsburg izakaya (Japanese pub/lounge) whose small menu includes about six well-executed items, including ginger-braised pork chop, toasted sesame bread with eggs and Chinese sausage, Korean beef BBQ, dumplings, and scallion pancake, among other things. It's a pay-one-price brunch for $7 and comes with tea or coffee. Side dishes (included) are as good as mains—yaki soba, mixed sautéed vegetables, and a potato pancake.

Bacchus, in Boerum Hill, is a nicely laid out French bistro with an outside patio and good spinach and goat cheese crêpes (with mesclun salad), says *billyblancoNYC*. Crème brulée with fresh strawberries is excellent. Kitchen's not particularly creative (the New York French Greatest Hits, not that there's anything wrong with that, says *bosshogg*), but most people aren't looking for creativity at brunch, anyway. (To digress, here are dinner tips: maigret de canard, boudin with apples and mashed potatoes, monkfish with lentils, mushroom ravioli, grilled sardines, and tarte tatin.)

Chowhound *adam* recommends a gastronomic orgy at **Ouest**, starting with their top-notch baked goods basket (including a small muffin studded with a chunk of warm banana) and moving on to well-composed salads, granola with sweet cream, and monsters like fried poached eggs over duck confit.

Weekend brunch starts at 9:00 a.m. on Saturdays at **Chez Laurence**, where you can indulge in one of the city's very best croissants (plain, almond, chocolate, and ham and cheese) or rich brioche served with homemade fruit confitures. The house specialty is "egg-spresso," scrambled eggs steamed to order with your choice of ham, cheese, tomato, and/or scallions. Traditional omelets, too.

Great baked goods, endless (and promptly refilled) coffee, and an interesting menu of brunch favorites with a twist (for example, multigrain waffles with homemade applesauce and yogurt) are just some of the charms of **good Restaurant**.

At **Jane Restaurant**, hounds recommend benedict Jane (with crab and crawfish cakes) and benedict Johnny (with chicken sausage and corn pancakes). Both come with home fries. Fantastic Bloody Marys, house-made sausage, and desserts.

Noho Star serves an irresistible combo of soft-scrambled eggs with salmon caviar and wasabi sour cream.

If you desire poached eggs (with spinach in red wine sauce with lardons) or French toast as much as *adam* does, follow his lead and hit **Blue Ribbon Bakery**.

Home has a cozy heated garden and the perfect brunch condiment: house-made ketchup.

Balthazar has unbeatable eggs Benedict.

Good Enough to Eat consistently tastes great across its menu.

For a selection of brunch items on a weekday, try **Pastis** or its older sibling Balthazar.

A flexible brunch surrogate: **Elephant and Castle** and **Florent** serve breakfast every day.

Tea & Sympathy opens early enough for brunch (from 11:00 a.m. on) but officially serves breakfast only on weekends.

Brunch entrée quality is erratic at **107**, but the free muffins are awesome (in a town where it's hard to find a good muffin). *Tim H.* says blueberry's best.

Kitchenette is a perennial brunch favorite for southern-style dishes.

At **Toast**, $10 gets you a substantially sized entrée and a small juice. Coffee's extra.

The vibe is funky at **Cafe Bar**, in Astoria, Queens. Couches mix with worn industrial-looking tables, chairs, and floors; and clubby music plays even at brunch. But it's not all vibe; brunch items are prepared with serious care, and while they may seem expensive, *Dan Sonenberg* says the high quality's worth the price. He says scrambled eggs with feta are light and delicious, and come with outstanding "country fries"—sautéed potatoes, peppers, and asparagus. Fresh blood orange juice to start.

○ **Balthazar:** see also pp. 35, 96, 104, 238.
○ **Blue Ribbon Bakery:** see also pp. 104, 266, 272.
○ **Chez Laurence:** see also p. 141.
○ **Good Enough to Eat:** see also p. 85.
○ **good Restaurant:** see also p. 123.
○ **Home Restaurant:** see also p. 104.
○ **Kitchenette:** see also pp. 104, 151, 205, 240, 280.
○ **Noho Star:** see also pp. 105, 233.
○ **Pastis:** see also p. 133.
○ **Tea & Sympathy:** see also p. 207.

Chowhound Nametag: Eric Eto

○◯○

Location: Woodside, Queens.

Occupation: Graphic designer.

Cholesterol Level: On the high end of normal.

Nabe Most Full of Explorable Unknown Chow: Most of Queens where the subway doesn't run, and most of Los Angeles County.

Top Chinatown Pick:
  Manhattan: Dragon's Gate.
  Flushing: either the Xi'an stand in the Flushing Food Court or Spicy and Tasty for Sichuan.

Underrated by Chowhounds: Rajdani for Indian food in Woodside, Queens.

Favorite Comfort Chow: Friday special at Yagura (Japanese lunch counter) of *soboro-don*, which is ground beef cooked in a sweetened soy sauce paired with sweetened scrambled egg on top of rice. Also, any Japanese place where I can get grilled *sanma* (pike mackerel) with grated daikon, lemon and soy sauce, and a few bowls of rice.

Guilty Pleasure: Doritos, Entenmann's doughnuts, Pringles, McDonald's fries.

Favorite Gelato Flavor: Normally crema, but when I think about gelato, I keep thinking about a flavor I had in Florence at Vivoli. It was a chestnut gelato (during chestnut season), grainy like pureed chestnuts would be, and bursting with chestnut flavor. I remember that I paired it with some rich chocolate and it didn't match at all—the chocolate really interfered with the subtle chestnut flavor. I went back to try the chestnut gelato again, but they didn't make it that day, and I've been dreaming about it ever since.

Chowhounding Rule of Thumb: *Take a look at what's on special.* Is it just high-priced ingredients or is there reason to believe the person cooking wants to express something else? If you can glean anything about the personality of the chef from the specials, then check back with the regular menu to find items that may merit special attention. More than one item of a specific regional specialization is a really good clue. I seem to use this strategy in finer establishments as well as in many of the Mexican joints in Queens.

Favorite Unknown Cuisine: After a couple trips to Japan, I'm completely intrigued by what is called *yoshoku-ryori* (which translates as Western cuisine, basically Japanese variations on Western food). There's evidence of yoshoku in many Japanese menus, with items such as curry rice, or omelette rice, and croquettes, to name a couple of items, but this subset of Japanese cuisine is so off the radar outside of the homeland, and it has a very complex history and has legitimacy as a cuisine on its own. Culinary students study yoshoku cuisine as they would traditional Japanese, or French, or Italian cookery to go on to become chefs. Yoshoku-ryori seems to have origins in French/British/Japanese fusion from the early twentieth century. I don't know enough about its history to provide anything definitive, but there's evidence for these national origins (and more recently, we can throw Italian in the mix). The most dedicated yoshoku restaurants spend an exorbitant amount of time on prep work, especially in making sauces. For instance, demi-glace is an essential part of this cuisine, and is the base for dishes like curry, hayashi rice (beef hash rice), and tongue stew, among many others. Some places even make their own ketchup for their omelet rice. I tried to visit several yoshoku restaurants during my recent trip to Japan, to get a broader sense of the cuisine, but I realized that further visits are necessary to get a firmer grasp.

Grab Something to Eat in
BRYANT PARK

Ata-Ru (Grand Central)
151 E. 43rd Street.
Manhattan, NY
212-681-6484
Japanese

Bread and Olives
(Midtown West)
24 W. 45 St.
Manhattan, NY
212-764-1588
Lebanese

Cipriani Le Specialita
(Grand Central)
110 E. 42nd St., #5
Manhattan, NY
212-499-0599
Italian

Cucina Express
(Grand Central)
200 Park Ave.
Manhattan, NY
212-682-2211
Italian

Grand Central Dining Concourse
(Grand Central)
East 42nd St. and Lexington Ave.
Grand Central Station,
Downstairs
Manhattan, NY
www.grandcentralterminal.com/
restaurants.htm
Store

Lunchbox (Grand Central)
420 Lexington Ave. (underneath
the Graybar Building)
Manhattan, NY
212-682-3812
Sandwich Shop

Pret a Manger (Grand Central)
11 W. 42 St.
Manhattan, NY
212-997-5520
Sandwich Shop

Yagura Market (Grand Central)
24 E. 41st St.
Manhattan, NY
212-679-3777
Japanese

Yum Thai (Midtown West)
123 W. 44th St.
Manhattan, NY
212-819-0554
Thai

- On nice days Bryant Park is a lovely lunch spot. Here are some great nearby choices to pick up some quality takeout chow.
- **Yagura Market** is a Japanese takeout and grocery store with made-to-order tempura, teriyaki, and noodle dishes. Also sushi and other prepared dishes sold by weight.
- Rice bowls at **Ata Ru** are portable and only $6.75.
- **Lunchbox** fronts as a chocolatier, but if you walk to the back there's a great deli with cheap gourmet sandwiches, wraps, and panini . . . and amazing fries, says *Sara*.
- **Pret A Manger,** the British chain, serves a big variety of premade sandwiches for lunch. *Fresh Basil* recommends chicken mango almond sandwiches on five-grain bread, or salmon with cream cheese on dill rye, and great blackberry or peach fruit and yogurt drinks.
- **Cipriani Le Specialita** specializes in cakes and pastries, but also sells well-made panini and daily pasta specials.
- The food court under **Grand Central** Terminal has a variety of takeout options from various vendors. Past recommendations include pizza from Two Boots, Zocalo's enchiladas, pies from the Little Pie Company, and Cafe Spice's Indian dishes.
- **Yum Thai** is a little hole-in-the-wall counter with its menu on the wall. It's not in the immediate area, but *Evan* says #14 (pad kee mao) is worth the walk.
- **Bread and Olives** serves fresh, subtly flavored Lebanese food.
- There are two Cucina and Co. stores in the Met Life Building. If you're willing to have a late lunch, **Cucina Express** goes half price every day at 2:00 p.m. Wait a half hour for the bargain hunting throngs to abate, and by 2:30 or so you can calmly score salmon filet over Caesar salad for $3.

○ **Yagura Market:** *see also* **p. 141.**

BURGER: Queens

Austin Steak & Ale House
(Queens)
82-72 Austin St.
Kew Gardens, Queens, NY
718-849-3939
Steak House

BK Sweeney's (Queens)
42-25 235th St.
Douglaston, Queens, NY
718-225-1866
Pub

Donovan's Of Bayside (Queens)
214-16 41st Ave.
Bayside, Queens, NY
718-423-5178
Irish Pub

Donovan's Pub (Queens)
57-24 Roosevelt Ave.
Woodside, Queens, NY
718-429-9339
Irish Pub

New York Style Eats (Queens)
45-02 Queens Blvd.
Sunnyside, Queens, NY
718-937-4121
Italian/American

P J Horgan's (Queens)
42-17 Queens Blvd.
Woodside, Queens, NY
718-361-9584
Irish Pub

Donovan's is a chowhound legend, worth a trip for great cheeseburgers (must order with sautéed onions) and Guinness stout. Great price, too: just $5.95 with fries. You can sit by the fireplace, order a Guinness with your burger, and finish the night with an Irish coffee.

P J Horgan's makes really good burgers, described by *Astoriaboy* as "bar-burgers" in the Corner Bistro style. The **Austin Ale House** does a very creditable burger, including a gilded lily of a Buffalo burger (covered with Buffalo wing sauce and blue cheese), plus good fries. And there are excellent burgers at **New York Style Eats** in Sunnyside and at **BK Sweeney's** in Douglaston (skip the wings, though).

Fancy **BURGERS**

Brasserie 360 (Upper East Side)
200 E. 60th St.
Manhattan, NY
212-688-8688
French Brasserie/Japanese

Peter Luger (Brooklyn)
178 Broadway
Williamsburg, Brooklyn, NY
718-387-7400
Steak House

Craftbar (Gramercy)
43 E. 19th St.
Manhattan, NY
212-780-0880
New American

Sugiyama (Midtown West)
251 W. 55th St.
Manhattan, NY
212-956-0670
Japanese

DB Bistro Moderne
   (Midtown West)
55 W. 44th St.
Manhattan, NY
212-391-2400
French

The Sunburnt Cow (East Village)
137 Ave. C
Manhattan, NY
212-529-0005
Australian

Our first report on DB Bistro's notorious $29 burger, with short-rib meat and foie gras, said it didn't really come together. But *shortstop* reports a different take—it's so good she thinks about it constantly. Her only regret is that she ordered it medium rare instead of rare. Even medium rare, it's exceptionally juicy and doesn't even need ketchup—the roasted tomato, slivered red onion, and wisp of lettuce already on it when it's served dress it perfectly. And that bun—crispy outside, soft, but not too, inside, and crunching in contrast to the lusciousness of the burger almost to the end. Other menu standouts include tuna tartare and lobster salad with artichokes and endive.

A hamburger might not be the best medium for appreciating the finer points of Kobe beef, but if you've been curious to try, **Brasserie 360** offers a $14.95 burger made of Kobe-style beef of Western U.S. origin. That's a good $25 cheaper than the competition, and equally flavorful. The burger meat is only lightly ground, and the whole affair comes with or without cheese (cheddar or Swiss) for the same price, on a soft brioche-type bun.

Some superior venues for contemplating the virtues of Kobe are **Sugiyama**, which serves a small portion cooked at the table as part of their highest priced omakase; and **Craftbar**, where it's served as a skirt steak along with foie gras and an asparagus-based sauce.

Not exactly fancy, but certainly not your ordinary burger, **The Sunburnt Cow**, an Australian restaurant, serves the Aussie Burger; ordered "with the lot," it includes egg, bacon, cheese, pineapple, beet root, lettuce, tomato, and sautéed onion on a toasted bun. It's tasty and complex. Also on the menu: roo bangers (kangaroo sausage) and smashed potatoes.

How about nonfancy really great burgers in a fancy place? **Peter Luger's**—yes, Peter Luger's—serves burgers, but only till 3:00 p.m., and only on weekdays. At $5.95, they come with the same thick-sliced tomato and onion served as the signature appetizer. It's easily worth three times the price, as the quality of the meat is unsurpassed, of course. You can add hearty steak fries for an extra dollar! There is no serious competition here, says *RZ*, who concludes that Luger's is the Chateau d'Yquem of burgers.

○ **Brasserie 360**: *see also* p. 294.
○ **Craftbar**: *see also* pp. 264, 266.
○ **DB Bistro Moderne**: *see also* p. 266.
○ **Peter Luger**: *see also* pp. 69, 239.

BURRATA: Cheesy Creamy Wonderfulness

Agata & Valentina
(Upper East Side)
1505 1st Ave.
Manhattan, NY
212-639-1645
Store

Agata & Valentina
(Upper East Side)
350 E. 79th St.
Manhattan, NY
212-452-0690
Store

Citarella (Greenwich Village)
424 6th Ave.
Manhattan, NY
212-874-0383
Store

Citarella (Upper East Side)
1313 3rd Ave.
Manhattan, NY
212-874-0383
Store

Citarella (Upper West Side)
2135 Broadway
Manhattan, NY
212-874-0383
Store

Coluccio & Sons (Brooklyn)
1214 60th St.
Borough Park, Brooklyn, NY
718-436-6700
Italian

Di Palo Fine Foods
   (Lower East Side)
206 Grand St.
Manhattan, NY
212-226-1033
Italian Deli

Fairway Market (Harlem)
2350 12th Ave.
Manhattan, NY
212-234-3883
Store

Fairway Market (Upper West Side)
2127 Broadway
Manhattan, NY
212-595-1888
Store

Murray's Cheese Shop
   (Grand Central)
73 Grand Central Terminal,
   halfway in the market on the
   north side
Manhattan, NY
212-922-1540
Cheese Shop

Murray's Cheese Shop
   (Greenwich Village)
257 Bleecker St.
Manhattan, NY
212-243-3289
Cheese Shop

Hounds rave about burrata, fresh mozzarella—traditionally made from buffalo milk but now usually made from cows'—stuffed with a yogurtlike combination of cream and chopped-up mozzarella pieces. Watch for a trend.

Burrata is available at the locations listed above (call ahead to confirm).

- ○ **Di Palo Fine Foods:** *see also* **pp. 108, 290.**
- ○ **Fairway Market:** *see also* **p. 123.**

Better **BUTTERS** in Brooklyn

Bierkraft (Brooklyn)
191 5th Ave.
Park Slope, Brooklyn, NY
718-230-7600
Store

Blue Apron Foods (Brooklyn)
814 Union St.
Park Slope, Brooklyn, NY
718-230-3180
Store

Eagle Provisions (Brooklyn)
628 5th Ave.
Park Slope, Brooklyn, NY
718-499-0026
Polish

Grand Army Plaza Farmers'
   Market (Brooklyn)
Grand Army Plaza
Park Slope, Brooklyn, NY
Farmers' Market

Polam International (Brooklyn)
952 Manhattan Ave.
Greenpoint, Brooklyn, NY
718-383-2763
Polish Store

Sahadi Importing Co. (Brooklyn)
187 Atlantic Ave.
Brooklyn Heights, Brooklyn, NY
718-624-4550
Middle Eastern

Been imbibing barely bearable butter? Buy better—by buying beguiling butters in Brooklyn! Find super fresh and flavorful brands at these markets:

- **Sahadi** carries several brands of European butter that are higher in milk fat than their American counterparts.
- **Polam Food** carries a nice selection of ultrafresh, ultraclean tasting, paper-wrapped butters, both domestic and imported.
- **Eagle Provisions** stocks several European butters, including some from Normandy.
- **Bierkraft** stocks imported butters like the French Beurre d'Isigny, as well as superior domestics like a great brand from Vermont.
- There's a good butter selection at **Blue Apron**.
- You can find Ronnybrook Farms' high-quality butters at the **Grand Army Plaza** farmers' market on Saturdays.

○ **Blue Apron Foods:** *see also* p. 186.
○ **Sahadi Importing Co:** *see also* p. 18.

Old School **CANTONESE-**American

Golden Gate Chinese Restaurant (Riverdale)
3550 Johnson Ave.
Bronx, NY
718-549-6206
Chinese

Any item that sounds old-school Chinese-American is a good choice at **Golden Gate**. Lobster with burnt pork has been praised highly by Eric Asimov in *The New York Times*, as well as by chowhounds. Golden Gate also makes another irresistible dish: butterflied shrimp wrapped in bacon, served with onions, and garnished with peanuts. You can taste the nostalgia dripping from selections like shrimp with lobster sauce, egg foo yung, sweet-and-sour pork, and wor shu opp (served with brown gravy on a bed of lettuce).

CARNITAS Craving Fulfilled

Flor de Luna (Queens)
33–09 36th Ave.
Astoria, Queens, NY
718-392-9349
Mexican

Carnitas, Mexican roast pork, is made by a long process that involves simmering in fat, rendering much of the fat from the pork, and then finishing with a blast of heat that fries the remaining fat. *Eric Etc* describes the ideal texture as both moist and dry, slightly stringy, crunchy, bacony. It's similar to pulled pork, or pernil, but concentrated.

The holy grail choice is from the El Fogoncitico #2 truck, which uses premade carnitas meat packed into gallon drink containers. They finish off the meat on the grill and serve it in an irresistible taco. The truck parks in the Jackson Heights/Woodside area along Roosevelt Avenue. Good luck finding it (no idea, by the way, if there's an El Fogoncitico #1).

Flor de Luna makes the best carnitas *babar ganesh* has ever had in Queens. Their chipotle sauce is tops as well.

Extreme Western **CARROLL GARDENS**

Alma (Brooklyn)
187 Columbia St.
Carroll Gardens, Brooklyn, NY
718-643-5400
Mexican

De Fonte's Of Red Hook
    (Brooklyn)
379 Columbia St.
Red Hook, Brooklyn NY
718-855-6982
Italian Sandwich Shop

Ferdinando's Focacceria
    (Brooklyn)
151 Union St.
Carroll Gardens, Brooklyn, NY
718-855-1545
Italian

Margaret Palca Bakes (Brooklyn)
191 Columbia St.
Red Hook, Brooklyn, NY
718-643-3507
Bakery

Schnack (Brooklyn)
122 Union St.
Carroll Gardens, Brooklyn, NY
718-855-2879
American

The extreme western edge of Carroll Gardens (and Red Hook, which adjoins), right near the East River, is an up-and-coming food hotbed that also includes some venerable landmarks.

Alma is an upscale Mexican restaurant that's more nouvelle than authentic. . . . but is delicious, which is all that really counts.

Schnack is a funky little joint with a hip, young clientele that serves great hot dogs (rivaling Gray's Papaya), kielbasa (handmade by Jubilat, a great Brooklyn-Polish producer) and tiny burgers. Even the breakfasts are good. Check out their pickles, their special sauce, good fries, and cheap beer.

Ferdinando's Focacceria is a Sicilian joint with great panelle (chickpea fritters), rice balls, and octopus salad. Go at lunchtime for maximum freshness. And while it's nowhere near Red Hook, Joe's of Avenue U is preferred by some for similar Sicilian fare.

Also don't forget (covered in detail elsewhere): **De Fonte's** for great heroes and **Margaret Palca Bakes** for great rugelach and other baked goods.

○ **De Fonte's Of Red Hook:** *see also* **pp. 30, 115.**
○ **Margaret Palca Bakes:** *see also* **pp. 69, 105.**

CARTS, Trucks, and Sidewalk Vendors

Food Truck (Lower Manhattan)
1 State Street Plaza, corner
    of Water and Whitehall,
    near Staten Island Ferry
Manhattan, NY
American Street Cart/Truck

Gabriel's Food Cart
    (Midtown West)
50th St. and 6th Ave.
Manhattan, NY
American Street Cart/Truck

Jerk Guy (Harlem)
W. 144th St. between Frederick
    Douglass Blvd. and Adam
    Clayton Powell Blvd.
Manhattan, NY
Jamaican Street Cart/Truck

Korean Hot Dog Cart
    (Lower East Side)
Corner of Ludlow and Stanton
Manhattan, NY
Korean/American Street
    Cart/Truck

La Poblanita Taco Cart
    (Upper East Side)
on the northwest corner of
    97th St. and 2nd Ave.
Manhattan, NY
Mexican

Sorbet by Danue (Midtown East)
123 W. 56th St. in the
    Parker Meridien Hotel
Manhattan, NY
Ice Cream or Gelato

Sweet Petunia's Pushcart
   (Hudson County)
Barrow and York Streets
Jersey City, NJ
Eclectic

Trini-Pak Boyz (Midtown West)
43rd St. and 6th Ave.
Manhattan, NY
Pakistani/Trinidadian

Restaurants are flaky enough. When it comes to street vendors, it's downright impossible to be sure when these freewheeling folks will be around—or even if they'll be in operation by the time you read this. For up-to-the-minute information, query the hounds at www.chowhound.com.

Several hounds insist that chicken curry over rice at the **Trini-Pak Boyz** cart is the best in the city. Not just the best from a cart, but the best . . . period! Two portion sizes each come with lightly seasoned sautéed chickpeas and cabbage. Ask for it with everything, and you'll get hot/sweet tamarind sauce and a spicy yogurt/coriander dressing on top. It's great, raves *Mark DiBlasi*. Real good curry lamb over rice, too. The Boyz are a big chowhound fave.

Monday through Friday, from about 11:00 a.m. until 4:00 p.m. or so, a woman sells, at 97th and 2nd, what *Nina* calls absolutely delicious gorditas and tacos.

Look for **"La Poblanita,"** a really good truck at the corner of Water and Whitehall, which serves hot foods at lunchtime. Fried sole is fresh from Fulton Street Market. *Abrocadabro* describes two breaded pieces, fairly thick, with crispy not-too-thick breading, and nicely moist, fresh-tasting fish. Burgers are handmade, 100 percent sirloin, and come with lettuce, tomato, and average quality fries. Lots of other options, too.

"Gabriel's food cart has the most unbelievable Philly cheesesteaks. Mind you, I am not normally a fan of meaty, greasy fast food, so believe me when I tell you these are incredible. Spicy and full of vegetables and tasty meat (when Gabriel is cooking. Sometimes he has a substitute)," reports *cate corcoran*. The vegetables are, of course, a revisionist touch.

Be on the lookout for the **Jerk Guy** uptown making serious Jamaican jerk on the sidewalk in the traditional way: barbecued over live coals in oil drums. He moves around, but word on the street is this is the real thing. He's not mythical—we've seen the drums, at West 144th Street between Frederick Douglass Boulevard and Adam Clayton Powell.

The **Korean Hot Dog Cart** seems to be out only late Friday and Saturday nights. In addition to hot dogs with kimchi toppings, the cart sells skinless, meaty, chicken wings (really tasty, says *Brown man*), bulgogi, and grilled chicken sandwiches. Homemade juices and teas, too.

The **Sorbet by Danue** cart has a new location, but the same great sorbet, says *aleppo*. Two bucks for two scoops. All fresh fruit flavors like coconut, mango, raspberry, peach, plum, and cantaloupe. Cherry is outstanding.

In Jersey City, you'll find **Sweet Petunia's Pushcart** run by ex-WFMU DJ Leila Haddad mornings from 7:30 to at least 9:30. Everything except the bagels is homemade and, since Leila likes to experiment, you can never be sure what she'll have on hand. Choices might include stuff like cream scones with cherries, Portuguese coconut "pudding," Brazilian cheese puffs, zucchini/apricot bread, homemade empanadas, amazing homemade mushroom quiche, apple/pear galettes, Greek wedding cookies, and more, reports *robin edgerton*, who says everything is delicious.

For Chinatown carts, see *Chinatown Vendors*.

For tamale ladies, see The Search for Perfect *Tamales* (Plus digressions).

○ **Trini-Pak Boyz:** *see also* p. 141.

CENTRAL ASIAN Kosher Exotica

Beautiful Bukhara (Queens)
64-47 108th St.
Rego Park, Queens, NY
718-275-2220
Kosher Central Asian

Cheburechnaya (Queens)
92-09 63rd Dr.
Rego Park, Queens, NY
718-897-9080
Kosher Central Asian

Chio Pio (Brooklyn)
3087 Brighton 4th St.
Brighton Beach, Brooklyn, NY
718-615-9221
Kosher Middle Eastern/North
      African/Kosher Central
      Asian/Russian

Salut (Queens)
6342 108th St.
Kew Gardens, Queens, NY
718-275-6860
Kosher Central Asian

Uzbekistan Cultural Center and Tandoori Bread (Queens)
120-35 83rd Ave
Kew Gardens, Queens, NY
718-850-3426
Kosher Central Asian

Emigrants from the various Central Asian Republics have poured into Queens and Brooklyn, opening restaurants serving this exotic cuisine. Many are observant Jews, and all the following places are kosher.

The menu at **Cheburechnaya**, an Uzbek restaurant, has typical dishes like *mantee* (lamb dumplings), chebureki (pierogilike fried dumplings with potato, mushroom, or beef), and shish kebab, plus good stuff like rams' testicles. The chebureki are good, the hummus fine, the bread is excellent, but according to *el jefe* the real reason to go is the kebabs. All are outstanding, including the ram testicles. Be sure to try the Uzbek sodas (citrus, bubblegum, or anise flavored). Service, by a Korean woman, is helpful and knowledgeable (you gotta love New York!). Closed Friday night, and doesn't open Saturday night until sundown. Busy at lunch and Saturday nights.

Uzbekistan Cultural Center and Tandoori Bread makes good *lagman*, a brothy soup with chunks of lamb and noodles flavored with dill; breads; various kebabs (especially lamb and bone-in chicken), and a sweet bread called *katlama*. They've even got an Uzbek karaoke floor show!

Chio Pio is a little place serving perfect chicken kebabs. The cuisine served at **Salut** has Persian, Afghan, and Russian influences . . . and lots of dill. **Beautiful Bukhara** is another small place (about twenty-five seats) with excellent kebabs (also lagman and mantee—dumplings).

Keep in mind that kosher restaurants close Friday afternoons till after sundown on Saturday.

○ **Salut:** *see also* **p. 281.**

CENTRAL ASIAN

Raves for 'CESCA

'Cesca (Upper West Side)
164 W. 75th St.
Manhattan, NY
212-787-6300
Italian

Hounds are raving about 'Cesca, the Tom Valenti restaurant. Polenta with mushrooms and cheese is amazing, says *JBW*, whose only complaint is that excellent main dishes of pasta al forno and lamb chops are a tad heavy. *S. Willig* praises sides like caponata and cabbage, and notes that you can hear the person next to you even when the restaurant is going full blast. Gnocchi with braised duck is rich and savory, the gnocchi perfectly tender and light, the duck unctuous and toothsome, reports *winnie*, who also raves about shrimp raviolini ("such brilliance of flavor and combination of textures—wow. I can still taste it even now.") The wine list has lots of choices in the $20 to $30 range, in addition to much pricier options.

○ 'Cesca: *see also* p. 139.

Queens CEVICHE

Braulio's Y Familia Restaurant
   (Queens)
39-08 63rd St.
Woodside, Queens, NY
718-899-3267
Ecuadorian

Chabuca Limena (Queens)
85-14 Roosevelt Ave.
Jackson Heights, Queens, NY
718-779-7378
Peruvian

La Pollada de Laura (Queens)
102-03 Northern Blvd.
Corona, Queens, NY
718-426-7818
Peruvian

Eight ceviches are served at **La Pollada de Laura**. Unlike other places whose ceviches cure overnight in a lime juice mixture, these are made fresh to order and are less soupy, more like a salad. "The ceviche blew me away. It was deliciously sour and flavorful. The calamari was excellent as well, piping hot and incredibly crisp. Dipped in the juices from the ceviche, it was heavenly. I highly recommend this combination dish," reports *Wendy*. This place doesn't make its ceviche very spicy, but you can add homemade hot sauce to taste. La Pollada de Laura also offers a full Peruvian menu (*tostones* fried to perfection, but rotisserie chicken can be dry), and a friendly, helpful staff (though knowing some Spanish helps). BYOB.

Pescado mixto, pulpo (octopus), and *concha negra* ceviche at **Chabuca Limena** draw raves. *Jack Barber* said it's by far the best ceviche he's had in the city, including fusiony renditions from Patria and Chicama.

Braulios y Familia serves Ecuadorian ceviche, a little soupier than Peruvian ceviches. *Canchito* says their pulpo's good.

Long Island **CHAWCOLATE**

Got Chocolates (Suffolk County)
572 Main St.
Islip, NY
631-224-8450
Chocolate/Candy Shop

Got Chocolates sells some imported chocolate and homemade fudge, but *Paul Trapani* says high-quality homemade chocolate treats are the way to go here. Nonpareils are hearty drops rather than thin wafers. And those garishly pink white-chocolate strawberries in the display case are made with freeze-dried fruit and have excellent flavor. This same treat in block form, along with blueberry and banana versions, is available via the internet at www.gotchocolates.com.

Chowhound Nametag: Pat Hammond

oOo

Location: Westchester County, New York, via Central Maine, via St. Louis, Missouri (three moves in four years).

Occupation: I retired in 2000, but work as a crossing guard at a local elementary school (where parents and I swap chow tips). I'm an overly involved grandma too!

Cholesterol Level: I forget the total, but my "good" cholesterol is astoundingly high. Bring on the bacon!

Number of Visits to McDonald's in Past Decade:
Two or three, maybe. I prefer Popeye's chicken for fast food.

Farthest Out of the Way Traveled Just for Chow: The focus of my trip to Portugal was to find *perceves*, giant barnacles. I found them, and they were wonderful!

Nabe Most Full of Explorable Unknown Chow: New Rochelle, New York! I've just begun to plumb the wealth of Mexican restaurants there.

Favorite Comfort Chow:
Any place that serves good congee.

Guilty Pleasure:
Vanilla ice cream with Trader Joe's candied ginger puree mixed in.

Favorite Gelato Flavor:
Lemon.

CHEAP Downtown

AKA Cafe (Lower East Side)
49 Clinton St.
Manhattan, NY
212-979-6096
New American

Apolo Restaurant
   (Lower East Side)
168½ Delancey St.
Manhattan, NY
212-477-4918
Caribbean

Bereket Turkish Kebab House
   (Lower East Side)
187 E. Houston St.
Manhattan, NY
212-475-7700
Turkish

Blue 9 Burger (East Village)
92 3rd Ave.
Manhattan, NY
212-979-0053
American

Casa Adela (East Village)
66 Avenue C
Manhattan, NY
212-473-1882
Puerto Rican

Cibao Restaurant
   (Lower East Side)
72 Clinton St.
Manhattan, NY
212-228-0703
Cuban

Clinton Restaurant
   (Lower East Side)
293 E. Houston St.
Manhattan, NY
212-982-3222
Dominican

El Castillo de Jagua
   (Lower East Side)
113 Rivington St.
Manhattan, NY
212-982-6412
Dominican

Fried Dumpling (Chinatown)
99 Allen St.
Manhattan, NY
212-941-9975
Chinese

Haveli (East Village)
100 2nd Ave.
Manhattan, NY
212-982-0533
South Asian

Juicy Lucy (East Village)
85 Avenue A
Manhattan, NY
212-777-5829
Vegetarian

Mama's Food Shop (East Village)
200 E. 3rd St.
Manhattan, NY
212-777-4425
Southern

Punjabi Grocery & Deli
(East Village)
114 E. 1st St.
Manhattan, NY
212-533-9048
North Indian

Spanish American Food
(East Village)
351 E. 13th St.
Manhattan, NY
212-475-4508
Cuban

Tiny's Giant Sandwiches
(Lower East Side)
127 Rivington St.
Manhattan, NY
212-982-1690
Sandwich Shop

Win 49 (Lower East Side)
205 Allen St.
Manhattan, NY
212-353-9494
Japanese

Yonah Schimmel Knishery
(Lower East Side)
137 E. Houston St.
Manhattan, NY
212-477-2858
Eastern European Jewish

Tasty low-cost ($7 or under) options abound downtown:

- **Win 49:** bento boxes—eel, chicken, or beef—over rice, choice of two sides (including, sometimes, toothsome fried oysters), *edamame, hijiki*, a couple of Japanese pickles, and a miso soup for seven bucks plus tax. Very limited seating.
- **Bereket Turkish Kebab House:** Almost everything is good (if not super great) at this twenty-four-hour fast-food place. Get Turkish pizza (aka lahmacun, $2.50) and load it with hot sauce.
- **Punjabi Deli:** 75 cents for kulfi (Indian ice cream) or a samosa. Everything else is between $2 and $4. Taxi drivers' hangout.
- Knishes at **Yonah Schimmel's** are extremely cost effective.
- Cuban sandwiches are good bargains at **Spanish American Food** and **Clinton Restaurant**
- **Juicy Lucy:** $1.75 tamales.
- Roast chicken with rice and beans for around $5 at both **Cibao Restaurant** and **Casa Adela**.

- Fried chicken with fried rice and plantains is $5.50 at **Apolo Restaurant**.
- Roast pork with rice and beans is $4.50 at **El Castillo de Jagua** . . . and almost everything else is under $7.
- A double order of chicken livers at **Haveli** comes in under $7.
- At **Tiny's Giant Sandwiches**, try a mac daddy.
- **Blue 9** has tasty burger deals under $7.
- **Mama's** place: four pieces of chicken and one side for $8. Get an extra side and serve two for $9.
- Many little delicious meals at **AKA cafe** for about $7.
- $7 buys 35 dumplings from Fried **Dumpling**.

Party at the **CHEESE CAVE**

Artisanal Restaurant (Murray Hill)
2 Park Ave. enter on 32nd St.
Manhattan, NY
212-725-8585
French

Artisanal Cheese Center (Clinton)
500 West 37th St.
Manhattan, NY
877-797-1200
Cheese Shop

The **Artisanal Cheese Center** is part of Terrence Brennan's restaurant empire, which also includes **Artisanal** and original cheese mecca Picholine. The Cheese Center is mostly a wholesaler, with five cheese caves supplying Artisanal restaurant (and many other top places) with the finest fromages. There's also a cheese classroom for lessons with cheese celeb Max McCalman, which can also be reserved for parties. To buy retail cheese, Artisanal restaurant has a sales counter.

Order from the Artisanal Cheese Center online at www.artisanal cheese.com

CHEESE DANISH

Ceci-Cela (Soho)
55 Spring St.
Manhattan, NY
212-274-9179
French Café

Chiffon Bakery (Brooklyn)
1373 Coney Island Ave.
Midwood, Brooklyn, NY
718-258-8822
Eastern European Jewish Bakery

College Bakery (Brooklyn)
239 Court St.
Carroll Gardens, Brooklyn, NY
718-624-5534
Bakery

Leske's Bakery (Brooklyn)
7612 5th Ave.
Bay Ridge, Brooklyn, NY
718-680-2323
Danish Bakery

Stork's Pastry Shop (Queens)
12-42 150th St.
Whitestone, Queens, NY
718-767-9220
Bakery

Sullivan Street Bakery (Clinton)
533 W. 47th St.
Manhattan, NY
212-586-1626
Italian Bakery

Sullivan Street Bakery (Soho)
73 Sullivan St.
Manhattan, NY
212-334-9435
Italian Bakery

Among a certain generation of unrepentant New Yorkers, it's always singular: "A cheese danish," "Two cheese danish." That generation is fading, and their cheese danish fade with them, but there are still a few points of highly caloric light out there.

There always seem to be Danish grandmas (or at least older Danish women) presiding over cheese Danish at **Leske's Danish Bakery. College Bakery** makes Danish with a crumb topping (though crullers and crumb cake are their most famous offerings, you MUST get the crullers early in the morning; they're terrible later). The cheese ring at **Stork's** is essentially a giant cheese Danish . . . and a steal at $6.75. **Chiffon's** is an old-fashioned Jewish bakery (they even make potato nik!) that does make a good cheese danish. In Manhattan, **Ceci-Cela** makes a popular cheese Danish. You can also get them at **Sullivan St. Bakery**—mornings only.

○ **Ceci-Cela:** *see also* **pp. 96, 201.**
○ **Sullivan Street Bakery:** *see also* **p. 22, 36, 244.**

CHEESECAKE

Andre's Hungarian Strudels
(Queens)
100-28 Queens Blvd.
Forest Hills, Queens, NY
718-830-0266
Hungarian Bakery

Cafe Mozart
(Upper West Side)
154 W. 70th St., #1
Manhattan, NY
212-595-9797
Central/Eastern European Café

Cascon Cheesecake (Queens)
7-04 149th St.
Whitestone, Queens, NY
718-767-5700
Bakery

Ciao Bello Ristorante & Bar
(Somerset County)
156 N. Gaston Ave.
Somerville, NJ
908-704-8444
Italian

Downtown Atlantic Restaurant
and Bakery (Brooklyn)
364 Atlantic Ave.
Flatbush, Brooklyn, NY
718-852-9945
Eclectic New American

Eileen's Cheesecakes
(Little Italy)
17 Cleveland Pl.
Manhattan, NY
212-966-5585
Bakery

Ennio & Michael Restaurant
(Greenwich Village)
539 Laguardia Pl.
Manhattan, NY
212-677-8577
Italian

Fortunato Bros. (Brooklyn)
289 Manhattan Ave.
Williamsburg, Brooklyn, NY
718-387-2281
Italian Café

La Flor Bakery & Cafe (Queens)
53-02 Roosevelt Ave.
Woodside, Queens, NY
718-426-8023
Mexican/American

La Locanda dei Vini (Clinton)
737 9th Ave.
Manhattan, NY
212-258-2900
Italian

L'Ecole (Soho)
462 Broadway
Manhattan, NY
212-219-3300
New American/French

Margaret Palca Bakes (Brooklyn)
191 Columbia St.
Red Hook, Brooklyn, NY
718-643-3507
Bakery

Martha Frances Mississippi
    Cheesecake (Upper East Side)
1707 2nd Ave.
Manhattan, NY
212-360-0900
Bakery

Peter Luger (Brooklyn)
178 Broadway
Williamsburg, Brooklyn, NY
718-387-7400
Steak House

Peter Luger (Nassau County)
255 Northern Blvd.
Great Neck, NY
516-487-8800
Steak House

Porgy & Bass Seafood (Harlem)
321 Malcolm X Blvd.
Manhattan, NY
212-531-0300
Southern/Seafood

S & S Cheesecake (Bronx)
222 W. 238th St.
Bronx, NY
718-549-3888
Bakery

Vida (Staten Island)
381 Van Duzer St.
Staten Island, NY
718-720-1501
New American

Yujin (East Village)
24 E. 12th St.
Manhattan, NY
212-924-4283
Japanese/New American

Cheesecake has splintered into so many stylings that it's more a quantum field than a class of pastry. But whether it's ricotta-based, lemon-tinged Italian cheesecake, yuppied-outshticky cheesecake, or old-fashioned traditional New York cream cheese cheesecake, chowhounds, as ever, only care about sussing out the best and brightest. The following are some sources that have especially fascinated lately.

Supersleuth *Aki* reports incredible unadvertised pumpkin cognac cheesecake on the back of a shelf at **Cafe Mozart**. He raves that the texture is so silky, it's almost like a pumpkin puree, and so subtle with the cheese that it's much more like a pumpkin mousse than a pumpkin cheesecake. Very, very, subtle cognac flavor is perfectly balanced, not overpowering. There is a very thin layer of fresh whipped cream; this makes all of the flavor and texture really stand out. The cake's charms are so delicate that it must be had absolutely fresh and eaten immediately for optimum deliciousness. Getting it to go is out of the question.

S&S cheesecake is a great secret mysterious choice raved about by several hounds and is theorized to be the cheesecake served at several restaurants known for their cheesecake (e.g., maybe The Palm). Urhound *Pete Feliz* offers advice: The bakery lurks behind an iron door. Buzz if locked. Get small plain, and try to buy frozen (serve just at the point of thaw). If you must get a fresh cake, hurry and eat it, as it has no shelf life at all.

Cascon Cheesecake formerly sported an industrial look but has now morphed into a warmer bakery/café. They've extended their menu but still offer reliable cheesecake. The extremely friendly owner will happily bake a pumpkin pie upon request (in only an hour!), and even served *Big V* free cake and coffee as the pie cooled.

Margaret Palca makes world-class cheesecake-type desserts and rugelach; **Fortunato Bros.** makes memorable cheesecake, and chowhound *shortstop* recommends **Ennio and Michael's** ricotta cheesecake (it's a restaurant, so get it to go).

Chicago Mike has systematically tasted through many of New York's top cheescakes. Here are his notes:

- He really liked **La Flor's**, describing it as a creamy, lemony, nice lingering taste, awesome with coffee but can be nibbled on alone. A benchmark cheesecake. (Also at La Flor: good bread pudding; airy key lime pie with a sharp, interesting tartness; and terrific molten chocolate cake, which they call chocolate souffle).
- Although a bit too sweet, **Martha Frances's** cheesecake (imported from a special baker down south) is rich and enjoyable. The sweetness might work better in flavored cakes than in plain. Great banana pudding, too!
- **Andre's** makes a mild cheesecake with a faintly cottage-cheesy texture and a lemony/nutty aftertaste. It's also available by the pound.
- **Eileen's** cheesecakes offer a stronger, bolder, tangy flavor with a lingering aftertaste.

An interesting side note: Mike found that many of the cheesecakes improved with age in the fridge, possibly because fermentation brought out extra richness.

Dandy cheesecakes mentioned elsewhere in this guide (especially in our dessert roundup, Where the Good *Desserts* Live), include **La Locanda Dei Vini, Downtown Atlantic Restaurant and Bakery, Porgy & Bass, L'Ecole, Peter Luger, Vida** (for pumpkin walnut cheesecake!), **Yujin** (for Japanese yuzu cheesecake with rice cracker crust!!), and **Ciao Bello.**

- Andre's Hungarian Strudels: *see also* p. 96.
- Ciao Bello Ristorante & Bar: *see also* p. 174.
- Downtown Atlantic Restaurant and Bakery: *see also* p. 111.
- La Flor Bakery & Cafe: *see also* p. 38.
- La Locanda dei Vini: *see also* p. 170.
- L'Ecole: *see also* p. 200.
- Margaret Palca Bakes: *see also* pp. 56, 105.
- Peter Luger: *see also* pp. 51, 239.
- Porgy & Bass Seafood: *see also* p. 105.
- Vida: *see also* p. 286.
- Yujin: *see also* p. 105.

Instant CHESTNUTS

Throughout Chinatown, you can find roasted and peeled chestnuts sold in sealed foil bags. At only 99 cents for five ounces, they are an unbeatable bargain. *charliebaltimore* raves that they taste delicious, with a nutty roasted flavor and excellent consistency for soups, stuffings, desserts, or any other purpose.

CHICKEN PARMIGIANA HEROES

Buon Italia (Chelsea)
75 9th Ave., in Chelsea Market
Manhattan, NY
212-633-9090
Italian Deli

Milano Market (Upper West Side)
2982 Broadway
Manhattan, NY
212-665-9500
Italian Deli

Little Charlie's Clam Bar
    (Lower East Side)
19 Kenmare St.
Manhattan, NY
212-431-6443
Italian

Mimi's Restaurant (Midtown East)
984 2nd Ave.
Manhattan, NY
212-688-4692
Italian

Manganaro's (Clinton)
488 9th Ave.
Manhattan, NY
212-563-5331
Italian/American

Tony's (Midtown East)
817 2nd Ave.
Manhattan, NY
212-697-8848
Italian Sandwich Shop

Manganaro's Hero-Boy (Clinton)
492 9th Ave.
Manhattan, NY
212-947-7325
Italian/American

The quest is on for the absolute best chicken parmigiana hero in Manhattan!

Chicken parm sandwiches at **Buon Italia** are not your typical melted-cheese-laden mess. Freshly breaded-and-cooked chicken cutlets are topped with cooked greens, tomato sauce and cheese, or sliced eggplant (also good: meatball parm, and a prosciutto-mozzarella-arugula combination on a flat, round roll).

Little Charlie's Clam Bar (and a mysterious "green-awning stand near Forty-sixth and sixth" that nobody's ever managed to locate) are recommended, and **Milano Market** makes a great chicken parmigiana sandwich as well as excellent eggplant parmigiana. Sibling rivals **Manganaro's** and **Manganaro's Hero Boy** are mostly overpriced and underwhelming, but the former makes good chicken parmigiana sandwiches on crusty, sturdy rolls. **Tony's** makes good ones, too. **Mimi's Restaurant** is recommended emphatically . . . but only in a single uncorroborated report, so caveat eater.

○ **Tony's:** *see also* **pp. 141, 173.**

Best of **CHINATOWN**

Big Wing Wong (Chinatown)
102 Mott St.
Manhattan, NY
212-274-0696
Chinese (Cantonese)

Big Wong (Chinatown)
67 Mott St.
Manhattan, NY
212-964-0540
Chinese (Cantonese)

Central Buffet (Chinatown)
195 Centre St.
Manhattan, NY
212-226-2905
Chinese

Chinatown Ice Cream Factory
   (Chinatown)
65 Bayard St.
Manhattan, NY
212-608-4170
Chinese/American Ice Cream or
   Gelato

Congee Village (Lower East Side)
100 Allen St.
Manhattan, NY
212-941-1818
Chinese (Cantonese)

Deluxe Food Market (Chinatown)
79 Elizabeth St.
Manhattan, NY
212-925-5766
Chinese

Dim Sum Go Go (Chinatown)
5 E. Broadway
Manhattan, NY
212-732-0796
Chinese (Dim Sum)/
   Chinese (Hong Kong)

Doyers Vietnamese (Chinatown)
11 Doyers St.
Manhattan, NY
212-513-1521
Vietnamese

Fu Wong Restaurant (Chinatown)
100 Bowery
Manhattan, NY
212-966-2255
Chinese (Hong Kong)

Funky Broome (Lower East Side)
176 Mott St.
Manhattan, NY
212-941-8628
Chinese (Hong Kong)

Golden Unicorn (Chinatown)
18 E. Broadway
Manhattan, NY
212-941-0911
Chinese (Dim Sum)/Chinese
(Hong Kong)

HSF (Chinatown)
46 Bowery
Manhattan, NY
212-374-1319
Chinese (Dim Sum)/Chinese
(Cantonese)/Chinese
(Hong Kong)

Joe's Shanghai (Chinatown)
9 Pell St., #1
Manhattan, NY
212-233-8888
Chinese (Shanghai)

New Beef King (Chinatown)
89 Bayard St.
Manhattan, NY
212-233-6612
Chinese (Hong Kong) Store

New Green Bo (Chinatown)
66 Bayard St.
Manhattan, NY
212-625-2359
Chinese (Shanghai)

New Hao Ke Chinese Restaurant
(Chinatown)
115 Madison St.
Manhattan, NY
212-349-8088
Chinese (Fujian)

NY Noodle Town (Chinatown)
28½ Bowery
Manhattan, NY
212-349-0923
Chinese (Cantonese)

Nha Trang Centre (Chinatown)
148 Centre St.
Manhattan, NY
212-941-9292
Thai

Nha Trang Restaurant (Chinatown)
87 Baxter St.
Manhattan, NY
212-233-5948
Vietnamese

No. 1 Dumpling House
(Chinatown)
118 Eldridge St.
Manhattan, NY
212-625-8008
Chinese

Nyonya (Chinatown)
194 Grand St.
Manhattan, NY
212-334-3669
Malaysian

So Go (Chinatown)
11 Mott St.
Manhattan, NY
212-566-9888
Chinese (Taiwanese)

Sun Dou Dumpling Shop
  (Chinatown)
214 Grand St.
Manhattan, NY
212-965-9663
Chinese/Chinese (Dim Sum)

Tasty Dumpling (Chinatown)
54 Mulberry St.
Manhattan, NY
212-349-0070
Chinese

Tea & Tea (Chinatown)
51 Mott St.
Manhattan, NY
212-766-9889
Chinese Café

Tea & Tea (East Village)
157 2nd Ave.
Manhattan, NY
212-614-0138
Chinese Café

Wing Wong (Chinatown)
111 Lafayette St.
Manhattan, NY
212-274-0690
Chinese (Cantonese)

Wo Hop (Chinatown)
15–17 Mott St.
Manhattan, NY
212-267-2536
Chinese (Cantonese)

Yi Mei (Chinatown)
51 Division St.
Manhattan, NY
212-925-1921
Chinese (Fujian)

Chinatown is forever in flux. The neighborhood expands and contracts, restaurants open, restaurants close. Chefs come and go, taking quality with them. Hounds help sort out this dynamic scene by telling of the dishes that keep them coming back. The following grab bag of tips and information parallels the hugely varied nature of the Chinatown chow scene.

New Green Bo is a perennial chowhound favorite. For detailed information, see p. 000.

Big Wing Wong seems to have floated under Chowhound radar, but *dkchan* calls it the best Cantonese BBQ in Manhattan. While congee and other comfort foods are done well, the real star here is meat. Recommendations: roast duck, boiled chicken with soy sauce (be sure to ask for dark meat), *char siu,* and addictive BBQ pork ribs.

Fu Wong is known for Hong Kong–style boiled lo mein with ginger and scallions.

At New **Wing Wong**, $3 gets you a dish of rice, tender boiled chicken, and an intensely flavored green condiment of cilantro, ginger, garlic, and oil.

Big Wong is the granddaddy of Cantonese BBQ places, and its kitchen was the training ground for the chefs at Big Wing Wong, Fu Wong, New Wing Wong, and many others. Some say it's been in decline for a few years, but hounds still go there for beef *chow fun* and congee with pork, beef, and squid.

Golden Unicorn, another old standby, remains an excellent choice for dim sum. Carts circulate frequently, and they have helpful signs. The staff's friendly, but you need to get their attention for water or anything not on a cart. Lots of seafood, and all of it very fresh, reports *e212*, who says clams in black bean sauce (a whole lot of great smallish clams in a very tasty sauce) and lightly fried shrimp (in their shells with heads in place) garnished with jalapenos are among the highlights. Steamed dumplings needed dipping sauce, and deep-fried rolled bacon is fatty enough without the dipping mayonnaise provided. Don't miss the mango pudding dessert.

Lots of Vietnamese dishes at the two **Nha Trang** restaurants deserve mention: *mi ga cary* (chicken and rice noodle curry soup); crispy squid spring rolls; salt and pepper shrimp; soft shell crabs; BBQ beef; BBQ pork over rice vermicelli (the pork pieces are tender, charred in the right places, with a very subtle caramelized sweetness. Mmmm, so good, says *Muk*).

At **Central Buffet**, $4 gets you four items (very authentic, but sitting in a steam table) over rice, plus soup. While the soup is mostly an afterthought, *Iron Frank* says this is a good place to explore items you might not order if working off a poorly translated menu or paying for a full serving. Tripe is tender; tofu and egg white satisfying; and a baked tofu, jalapeño, and tiny salted fish stir-fry is overwhelmingly spicy but still delicious. Really excellent white rice if you get it fresh.

Piney says **New Hao Ke's** Foo Chow–style dumpling with soup could be called a tasty choking hazard. The dumplings are perfectly round and the diameter of a fifty-cent piece. Outside wrappers are very sticky and have a consistency closer to a wet Tanjin-style steamed bun. Lychee pork on rice is notable for the balance between ingredients.

Deluxe Food Market is a huge Chinese supermarket with a food court at the Elizabeth Street end serving Peking duck rolls with scallions, cucumber, and hoisin sauce for a buck (!). It's not the best Peking duck in town, but *Aki* says the meat portion is decently sized . . . and you can't beat the price! The small kitchen to the right of the entrance makes fresh fish-ball soup from scratch to order right in front of you for $2.75. They also serve very sweet peanut dessert soup from a pot kept simmering for hours. It's really hot, with complex Chinese herb flavors. Super-cheap, steam-table, three-dish-plus-rice plates. Dragon beard candy (sort of like cotton candy), and high-quality meat products, too. Really mobbed on weekends.

HSF garners praise for hot, fresh dim sum (for example, slippery noodles, pork buns, turnip cakes, and shumai).

Dim Sum Go Go gets generally middling comments *except* for two consistent winners: chicken with fried garlic shoots and spicy eggplant claypot with chili.

So Go serves Taiwanese foods like stewed pork shoulder with an earthy, herbal quality and clams with basil and chicken stewed in a casserole with soy, garlic, ginger and basil.

Boiled dumplings are good at **Sun Dou Dumpling Shop**, while fried dumplings get the nod at **Tasty Dumpling**, where spicy noodles with meat sauce and noodle soup with fish balls, shrimp, wontons, or whatever are popular.

Steamed dumplings and sesame pancakes (with or without beef) at **No. 1 Dumpling House**.

At **Congee Village**, scallion pancakes and jellyfish appetizer are praised, and *Abbylovi* says she could eat their pork belly casserole with preserved vegetables every day of her life.

Roast pork wonton and roast duck noodle soups stand out at **NY Noodletown**. Also recommended: roast baby pig; salt-baked crab; and duck, pork, or fish with flowering chives.

Joe's Shanghai is probably best known for its soup dumplings, but pork shoulder (in brown sauce), crispy noodles with vegetables, and pea shoots with garlic also draw praise.

Funky Broome for marinated goose intestines and stir-fried Norwegian fish filet (with minced pork and shredded snow peas).

Yi Mei offers three choices plus soup for $2.75, and *anil* says the food is much better than you'd expect for the price.

Wo Hop: roast pork or shrimp chow fun.

New Beef King: dried spicy beef and pork.

Doyers Vietnamese: shrimp and string beans in black bean sauce and roast shrimp with rice noodles.

Nyonya: roti canai, beef rendang, and mango chicken.

After all that food, two other treats stand out: hot black milk tea with ginger from the two **Tea & Tea** stores, and ice cream (mango, almond cookie, ginger, red bean, green tea, et al) at **Chinatown Ice Cream Factory**.

See also Chinatown Beef *Jerky*, and all restaurants indexed under "Chinatown" in nabe index.

○ **New Beef King:** *see also* p. 188.
○ **New Green Bo:** *see also* pp. 83, 228.
○ **NY Noodle Town:** *see also* p. 250.
○ **Nyonya:** *see also* p. 209.
○ **Sun Dou Dumpling Shop:** *see also* p. 83.

CHINATOWN VENDORS

DAU-fu FA Ladies (Chinatown)
Around Canal and Grand Sts.
Manhattan, NY
Chinese Street Cart/Truck

Fish-Ball Soup Lady (Chinatown)
79 Elizabeth St., in front of
　Deluxe Market
Manhattan, NY
Chinese Street Cart/Truck

Mustard-Green-Sandwiches-and-
　Fried-Egg-White-Batter-Cakes
　Women (Chinatown)
Under the Manhattan Bridge
Manhattan, NY
Chinese Street Cart/Truck

Mustard-Green-Sandwich/
　Red-Bean-Ball Woman
　(Chinatown)
Eldridge St. at Grand
Manhattan, NY
Chinese Street Cart/Truck

The following are top picks among Chinatown street vendors. Be aware that hours and locations are inherently erratic.

Several women sell sweet fresh tofu, served warm with sorghum syrup, a delicious combination called something like **DAU-fu FA**, around Canal and Grand Streets.

Women under the Manhattan Bridge sell mustard-green sandwiches (on what look like sesame bagels) for a buck. They also sell fried egg-white-batter cakes filled with stir-fried greens and beansprouts, two for $1.

Mustard-green sandwiches are also the specialty of a woman on the corner of Eldridge and Grand streets. Her second item is a red bean ball coated with sesame seeds (three for $1).

Just across from The Dragon Beard Candy Man, on the left side of the entrance of Deluxe Market, a woman sells a sixteen-ounce container of **fish-ball soup** for $2. The soup's loaded with ginger and scallions, plus squid balls, rice dumplings, and fresh lettuce. Also: sweet peanut soup that's very nutty and not cloying.

Various vendors all over the area sell leaf-wrapped rice, filled rice patties (similar to tamales) called zhong in Mandarin and jong in Cantonese, but they're meant to be warmed by steaming prior to being eaten, lest you find yourself chomping on solidified lard. You'll find versions with Chinese sausage, chicken, cubed meat, and egg yolk. Sprinkle on a little dark soy sauce and a touch of sugar, or oyster sauce and/or Worcestershire sauce.

New Jersey CHINESE

Captain Fresh Seafood
   Supermarket
   (Somerset County)
1569 U.S. Hwy. 22
Watchung, NJ
908-668-8131
Chinese, Store

Chef Ha's Duck House
   (Middlesex County)
372 North Ave.
Dunellen, NJ
732-968-8410
Chinese

China 46 (Bergen County)
88 Rte. 46 West
Ridgefield, NJ
201-313-0088
Chinese (Shanghai)/Chinese

Dragon Palace (Middlesex County)
1635 Oak Tree Rd.
Edison, NJ
732-549-7554
Chinese (Sichuan)

18 Lobster House
   (Middlesex County)
405 Rte. 18
East Brunswick, NJ
732-390-1118
Chinese

Hong Kong Supermarket
   (Middlesex County)
3600 Park Ave.
South Plainfield, NJ
908-668-8862
Chinese, Store

I-9 Seafood Plaza Restaurant
   (Middlesex County)
1021 U.S. Hwy 1
Edison, NJ
732-602-8863
Chinese

John's Shanghai Restaurant
   (Bergen County)
880 River Rd.
Edgewater, NJ
201-945-8825
Chinese (Shanghai)

Kings Village International
   (Middlesex County)
1639 Rte. 27
Edison, NJ
732-339-9858
Chinese

Shanghai Park
   (Middlesex County)
239 Raritan Ave.
Highland Park, NJ
732-247-8813
Chinese

Lotus Cafe (Bergen County)
450 Hackensack Ave.
Hackensack, NJ
201-488-7070
Chinese

Chef Ha's Duck House in Dunellen is a great place for a Chinese feast . . . the suburban sprawly location and bland exterior belie the deliciousness within. It's a favorite of *bigjeff and soopling*, who report excellent and bounteous crispy-skinned Peking duck, refined beef with bamboo shoots in an interesting XO-type sauce, Sichuan peppercorn-infused *mapo* tofu, drunken crab, shredded cold jellyfish, soup dumplings, and some extremely rich braised pork belly with sesame *sau-bing*. Also recommended: a dish of perfectly tender steamed fish known as buffalo fish or *wan-yu*. Just order red-cooked wan-yu or *hong-sau* wan-yu, and select either the tail or belly portion based upon your preference.

Pay no attention to the English menu at **Dragon Palace** in Edison. Insist on the Chinese menu. Don't read Chinese? *Brian Yarvin* recommends hot and sour soup prepared the authentic Sichuan way, and a cold dish of rabbit in chili sauce. *Alex Toledano* recommends another cold appetizer of beef and pork slices even spicier than the very spicy rabbit. Don't worry; Dragon Palace is very proud of its Chinese menu and will serve it to anyone who asks. Show interest and they'll interpret!

If you're looking for Chinese cooking ingredients, try the **Hong Kong Market** in South Plainfield or **Captain Fresh** in Watchung.

Brian Yarvin offers up a quick list of Chinese options he's found to be excellent: **Shanghai Park** (Highland Park), **King's Village** (Edison), **1–9 Seafood** (Edison), and **18 Lobster House** (East Brunswick).

Chowhound Nametag: Paul Trapani

∘○∘

Location:
Long Island, New York.

Occupation:
Computer consultant.

Cholesterol Level:
199.

Nabe Most Full of Explorable Unknown Chow:
Flushing, Queens.

Underrated by Chowhounds: Koiso (Mineola, New York). Nobody gets it but me and the old Japanese guys eating salt-grilled whole fish.

Weight Management Tip: Don't drink soda. Don't eat fast food, ever. Seriously, I lost fifteen pounds just by making these two changes.

Favorite Comfort Chow: Used to be the Terrace Diner for fries with mozzarella and brown gravy, but they changed the gravy a couple of years ago. I'm still heartbroken over it.

Guilty Pleasure:
White Castle hamburgers. Coca-Cola.

Favorite Gelato Flavor:
Stracciatella.

Favorite Mail-order Chow: The Spice House (www.thespicehouse.com) for freeze-dried sweet corn. And also their salt-free Cajun seasoning; I actually add salt to it, but I like to control how much (plus it's more cost efficient, since salt is dirt cheap).

Favorite Futile Endeavor:
Trying a slice of pizza at every pizzeria on Long Island.

∘○∘ Bergen County picks:

An impressive number of fish preparations, including several sole and salmon dishes, help separate Hackensack's **Lotus Cafe** from the jumble of suburban Chinese restaurants, so much so that *South Jersey Epicurean* says he'd gladly drive more than two hours from home to dine there again. A large serving of salmon comes planked with broccoli, carrots, mushrooms, water chestnuts, and more. Steamed dumplings (vegetable or seafood) are made with dough containing spinach, and the dipping sauce had great texture and flavor. L.O.T.U.S. delight contains julienned leeks, onions, tofu, u-shan spice, and cellophane noodles, with pork and egg—all stir-fried, topped with scrambled egg, and served with crêpes and hoisin sauce. Excellent service can get overwhelmed when the staff is very busy.

China 46 is a Shanghai restaurant in Ridgefield located inside an old diner that looks almost abandoned on the outside, and still looks like it was once a diner on the inside. But the food's great. We've had rave reports for their well-seasoned steamed juicy pork buns (aka soup dumplings, also great stuffed with both pork and crab) with a thick, rich, almost gelatinous broth; scallion pancake (thinner and crisper than the usual); fluffy pan-fried Shanghai buns; very tender Northern Chinese beef noodle soup with cilantro, big slices of garlic, some kind of pickled cabbage, and long, thick wheat noodles; fantastic Northern Chinese-style chicken (a special that's roasted so the skin's crispy, and all is permeated with a slightly smoky, subtly turmeric flavor); black mushroom with Shanghai bok choy (a large serving of very flavorful, slightly chewy fungus offset with perfectly steamed bok choy that's almost melt-in-your-mouth soft); and delicious steamed vegetable dumplings with tender-yet-resistant wrappers and fresh filling. Needless to say, avoid the part of the menu titled "Rich Tradition In America" . . . though we love restaurants with a sense of humor. Note: This place is actually on the Route 80W side of the interchange of Route 46 and routes 95S and 80W.

Paul Brodsky was the first to (tersely) tip us to China 46, and he also (tersely) recommends **John's Shanghai** in Edgewater. Since he's amply demonstrated his chow cred, we deem John's a primo lead.

See also *Edison Area* Indian . . . and More, for a couple more New Jersey Chinese tips.

Superfresh **CHINESE BUNS**

Ho Wong Coffee House
  (Lower East Side)
146 Hester St.
Manhattan, NY
212-966-5626
Chinese (Cantonese) Bakery

Mei Lai Wah Coffeehouse
  (Chinatown)
64 Bayard St.
Manhattan, NY
212-925-5435
Chinese (Cantonese)

New Green Bo (Chinatown)
66 Bayard St.
Manhattan, NY
212-625-2359
Chinese (Shanghai)

Sammy's Noodle Shop
  (Greenwich Village)
453 Ave. of the Americas
Manhattan, NY
212-924-6688
Chinese

Sun Dou Dumpling Shop
  (Chinatown)
214 Grand St.
Manhattan, NY
212-965-9663
Chinese/Chinese (Dim Sum)

Sun Say Kai (Chinatown)
220 Canal St.
Manhattan, NY
212-964-7256
Chinese

If a shop in Chinatown refers to itself as a "bakery" or "coffeeshop" it usually will sell buns either baked (brown) or steamed (white), and with various fillings. **Ho Wong** sells particularly good taro buns. Outside Chinatown, **Sammy's Noodle Shop** sells a larger and slightly more expensive model.

According to *Lila*, the brown steamed pork buns at old-timey Chinatown coffee shop **Mei Lai Wah** are sweet and pretzel-y and just slightly undercooked (in a good way). Their large *dai bao* buns contain chicken, sausage, egg, and a piece of dried mushroom. *M.K.* suggests that, if you like sweets, ask for *kai yeung bao* (egg custard) or *kai mei bao* (coconut custard). These are baked, not steamed. Sausage buns are called *lop cheng bao*.

Go to **New Green Bo** at lunchtime to enjoy fresh jumbo vegetarian steamed buns. **Sun Say Kai**'s got good buns, too. And **Sun Dou Dumpling Shop** sells excellent dumplings and buns, available both frozen and heated.

- **New Green Bo:** *see also* pp. 74, 228.
- **Sun Dou Dumpling Shop:** *see also* p. 75.

Latest **CHOCOLATE** Hot Spots

Martine's Chocolates
  (Midtown East)
1000 Third Ave. Bloomingdale's
  6th Fl.
Manhattan, NY
212-705-2347
Chocolate/Candy Shop

Martine's Chocolates too
  (Upper East Side)
400 E. 82nd St.
Manhattan, NY
212-744-6289
Chocolate/Candy Shop

Ortrud Munch Carstens Haute
  Chocolature (Midtown East)
401 E. 58th St.
Manhattan, NY
212-751-9591
Chocolate/Candy Shop

Vosges Haut-Chocolat (Soho)
132 Spring St.
Manhattan, NY
212-625-2929
Chocolate/Candy Shop

Ortrud Munch is a chocolate-making artist in a league of her own. No shop, no Web site, she only does custom orders, and she's sometimes booked months in advance, says*Trish Untrapped*.

Those seeking instant chocolate gratification should check out **Martine's** inside Bloomingdale's (or at their uptown shop). *Trish Untrapped* raves that their stuff is melt-in-your-mouth bliss with full flavors—especially the chocolates containing fresh cream.

With flavors like dark chocolate-wasabi and black sesame seed-ginger, chocolate bars from **Vosges Haut Chocolat** are clearly aimed at adults. Their naga bar (Belgian milk chocolate with sweet curry powder and coconut flakes) is very tasty and not at all spicy, says *philtersweet*. For more traditional palates, we hear great things about their milk chocolate hazelnut-almond praline bars.

Serious **CHOCOLATE CAKE**

Amy's Bread (Chelsea)
75 9th Ave., in the Chelsea
   Market
Manhattan, NY
212-462-4338
Bakery

Amy's Bread (Clinton)
672 9th Ave.
Manhattan, NY
212-977-2670
Bakery

Amy's Bread (Upper East Side)
972 Lexington Ave.
Manhattan, NY
212-537-0270
Bakery

Blue Smoke (Gramercy)
116 E. 27th St.
Manhattan, NY
212-447-7733
Barbecue/American

Boerum Hill Food Company
   (Brooklyn)
134 Smith St.
Cobble Hill, Brooklyn, NY
718-222-0140
New American

Cake Man Raven Confectionery
   (Brooklyn)
708 Fulton St.
Fort Greene, Brooklyn, NY
718-694-2253
Southern Bakery

Good Enough to Eat
   (Upper West Side)
483 Amsterdam Ave.
Manhattan, NY
212-496-0163
American

Ruby Foo's Times Square
   (Theater District)
1626 Broadway
Manhattan, NY
212-489-5600
Pan-Asian Fusion

Two Little Red Hens
   (Upper East Side)
1652 2nd Ave.
Manhattan, NY
212-452-0476
Bakery

Jim Leff wasn't in the mood for clever chocolate cake, stupid chocolate cake from a mix, or trendy variations (chocolate mousse cake, etc., etc.). Just plain old regular honest chocolate cake. Hounds recommended the following cakes to make him happy.

Ruby Foo's of Times Square seems an unlikely place for it, but

Camille G insists their cake is enormous, yummy, and home-made tasting (rich chocolate with chocolate frosting), and *Clarissa* concurs. At **Blue Smoke**, it's just a huge piece of good old chocolate cake. Nothing fancy, but there's real—not plastic—flavor, says *Mara*. **Good Enough to Eat's** chocolate cake is available whole or by the slice, to stay or to go, and *jake pine* thinks it's great (same for their coconut cake). Three-layer chocolate cake with rich chocolate frosting in between is what you'll find at the Clinton and Upper East Side locations of **Amy's Bread**. (It's not sold at the Chelsea Market location. Excellent Brooklyn black-out cake at **Two Little Red Hens** wins a rave from *shortstop*. It's all that chocolate cake should be: moist and just the right sweet-ness to balance all that chocolate. A small cake, just right for two portions, runs $11, or go for a good-sized chocolate cupcake for $4. **Cake Man Raven** in Brooklyn *only* makes honest, nontrendy cakes—the kind you might find at a southern church bake sale, writes *Abbylovi*. Chowhound *budino* loves the amazing dense chocolate fudge cake at **Boerum Hill Food Company**. Nothing fancy, and $4.25 gets you a huge slice, but call ahead to make sure they have it that day.

- Amy's Bread: *see also* pp. 21, 238.
- Blue Smoke: *see also* p. 207.
- Good Enough to Eat: *see also* p. 42.

CHOCOLATE CHIP COOKIES

Bagel Basket (Upper West Side)
2415 Broadway
Manhattan, NY
212-721-1800
Bagel Shop

Levain Bakery
  (Upper West Side)
167 W. 74th St.
Manhattan, NY
212-874-6080
Bakery

Ruby et Violette (Clinton)
457 W. 50th St.
Manhattan, NY
212-582-6720
Bakery

The "big mama square chunks of chocolate in each cookie" at the **Bagel Basket** cause *amy t.* to melt. **Levain Bakery** bakes a fabulous chocolate chip cookie, and **Ruby et Violette** makes a number of yummy chocolate chip cookie variations. Crispy chocolate cookie lovers need to try a nameless deli right near West End Superette (273 W. 72nd St.), but you must arrive early because they sell out fast. According to *miltk*, they're excellent, not overloaded with with chocolate chips—just enough to make them tasty. They're crispy and light, 2.5 inches in diameter, and burnt at the edges (in a good way).

○ **Levain Bakery:** *see also* p. 35.

CHURCH CAFETERIA Lunch

Interchurch Center (Upper West Side)
475 Riverside Dr.
Manhattan, NY
212-870-2200
American

The cafeteria at the **Interchurch Center** is open to the public during office hours and is popular with Columbia University staff and students. About $5 gets you a complete meal that *Tim H.* calls remarkably good for what it is. Best: sandwich bar and daily specials (salads leave much to be desired).

Piping Hot Crunchy CHURROS

Buenos Aires Bakery (Queens)
90-09 Roosevelt Ave.
Corona, Queens, NY
718-672-4046
Argentinian Bakery

The Doughnut Plant
  (Lower East Side)
379 Grand St.
Manhattan, NY
212-505-3700
Bakery

Pipa (Union Square)
38 E. 19th St., in ABC Carpet
Manhattan, NY
212-677-2233
Spanish

Tasty churros, sort of thin, fried Mexican crullers, are available from vendors in many major subway stations. But where can you go for a piping hot, freshly made one?

If you hit the **Doughnut Plant** at the right time, you may score a warm batch of their churros. Beware, though, that they're hideous after sitting a while. *Jen Kalb* reports hot, crisp, and corny churros at the **Buenos Aires Bakery** in Queens. And, as a hopeful note, **Pipa** every great once in a while has offered dessert churros with three dips. (including chocolate and *dulce de leche*). All join hands in prayer that this happens again one day.

- **Buenos Aires Bakery:** *see also* **p. 38.**
- **The Doughnut Plant:** *see also* **p. 110.**

CLAM SHACKS on the CT Shore

Lenny & Joe's Fish Tale
   Restaurant (Middlesex County)
86 Boston Post Rd.
Westbrook, CT
860-669-0767
Seafood

Lenny & Joe's Fish Tale
   (New Haven County)
1301 Boston Post Rd.
Madison, CT
203-245-7289
Seafood

Lenny's Indian Head Inn
   (New Haven County)
205 S. Montowese St.
Branford, CT
203-488-1500
Seafood

Sea Swirl Restaurant
   (New London County)
30 Williams St.
Stonington, CT
860-536-3452
Seafood

A few real good ones:

Lenny's Indian Head Inn has been in business for decades and looks it, but their lobster rolls haven't gotten lazy; they contain little mayo or celery filler and their fried clams are awesome, says *Amy Mintzer*, who notes they're made with whole clams. The Madison location of **Lenny and Joes's Fish Tale** (a different Lenny) has the most seating but no table service. You order at the counter and wait for your number to be called to pick up your order. **Sea Swirl**, near Mystic, is a clam shack with yummy clams, reports *Zina*.

○ **Lenny's Indian Head Inn:** *see also* p. 41.

Cold Weather **COMFORT FOOD**

Salt (Soho)
58 MacDougal St.
Manhattan, NY
212-674-4968
New American

As the temperature drops, the comforting food at **Salt** gets even more attractive, says *sonja*, who carries fond memories of risotto. *Jim Fallon* says crab/shrimp dumplings and pea and asparagus risotto appetizers are very good, and chicken with pureed cauliflower and Brussels sprouts, and roast cod with shrimp are surprisingly tasty and inexpensive. The menu's ever changing, though, so stay loose if you go.

Western **CONNECTICUT:**
Chowhound Mecca

American Pie (Fairfield County)
29 Route 37 Ctr.
Sherman, CT
860-350-0662
American Café

Banana Brazil Luncheonette
    (Fairfield County)
91 Main St.
Danbury, CT
203-748-5656
Brazilian

Bantam Bread Co.
    (Litchfield County)
853 Bantam Rd.
Bantam, CT
860-567-2737
Bakery

Blue Colony Diner
    (Fairfield County)
Church Hill Rd., near Exit 10 off
    1-84
Newtown, CT
203-426-0745
Diner or Coffee Shop

Bountiful Board
    (Fairfield County)
68 Stony Hill Rd (Rte. 6)
Bethel, CT
203-790-6522
Store

Carminuccio's Pizza
    (Fairfield County)
76 S. Main S.
Newtown, CT
203-364-1133
Italian/Pizza

Carriage House Cafe
    (Fairfield County)
80 Rte. 39
New Fairfield, CT
203-746-4125
American

Chuck's Steak House
    (Fairfield County)
20 Segar St.
Danbury, CT
203-792-5555
Steak House

Dr. Mike's Ice Cream Shop
    (Fairfield County)
158 Greenwood Ave.
Bethel, CT
203-792-4388
Ice Cream or Gelato

The Egg and I Pork Farm
    (Litchfield County)
355 Chestnut Land Rd.
New Milford, CT
860-354-0820
Farm or Farm Stand

Elliot Seafood (Litchfield County)
Parks on Rte. 7
New Milford, CT
Street Cart/Truck

First & Last Cafe
   (Fairfield County)
2 Pembroke Rd.
Danbury, CT
203-790-8662
Italian

Gail's Station House Restaurant
   (Fairfield County)
378 Main St.
Ridgefield, CT
203-438-9775
Diner or Coffee Shop

Ganga Haute Cuisine Of India
   (Fairfield County)
41 Wall St.
Norwalk, CT
203-838-0660
Indian

The Goodie Shoppe
   (Fairfield County)
1 Brush Hill Rd.
New Fairfield, CT
203-746-7279
Bakery

Goulash Place (Fairfield County)
42 Highland Ave.
Danbury, CT
203-744-1971
Hungarian

Hopkins Inn of Lake Waramaug
   (Litchfield County)
22 Hopkins Rd.
New Preston, CT
860-868-7295
Austrian

JB Barbecue (Fairfield County)
2 Lake Ave. Extension,
   across from Ethan Allen Inn,
   off I-84, Exit 4
Danbury, CT
203-743-1919
Barbecue

Jim Barbaries Restaurant
   (Fairfield County)
47 Padanaram Rd.
Danbury, CT
203-743-3287
Seafood

Lakeside Diner (Fairfield County)
1050 Long Ridge Rd., just north
   of Merritt Pkwy, Exit 34
Stamford, CT
203-322-2252
Diner or Coffee Shop

Log House Restaurant
   (Litchfield County)
110 New Hartford Rd.
Barkhamsted, CT
860-379-8937
Diner or Coffee Shop

Marbella (Fairfield County)
1479 Barnum Ave.
Stratford, CT
203-378-6702
Spanish/Italian

Mecca (Fairfield County)
44 Main St.
Norwalk, CT
203-831-8636
Spanish

Meigas (Fairfield County)
10 Wall St.
Norwalk, CT
203-866-8800
Spanish

Mina's Carne & Deli
   (Fairfield County)
36 Osborne St.
Danbury, CT
203-797-9800
Brazilian

New Milford Farmer's Market
   (Litchfield County)
On the green
New Milford, CT
Farmers' Market

Oliva (Litchfield County)
18 E. Shore Rd.
New Preston, CT
860-868-1787
Italian

Phillip's Diner (Fairfield County)
740 Main Street South
Woodbury, CT
203-263-2516
Diner or Coffee Shop

Portofino Restaurant & Pizza
   (Fairfield County)
88 Rte. 37
New Fairfield, CT
203-746-3604
Italian/Pizza

Roti International (Fairfield County)
210 W. Main St.
Stamford, CT
203-967-8318
Trinidadian

Sprinkles Homemade Ice Cream
   (Fairfield County)
28 Rte. 39
New Fairfield, CT
203-746-1484
Ice Cream or Gelato

Stroble Baking Co
   (Litchfield County)
14 S. Main St.
Kent, CT
860-927-4073
American Bakery

The Sycamore
   (Fairfield County)
282 Greenwood Ave.
Bethel, CT
203-748-2716
Diner or Coffee Shop

Theo & Gretchen's
   (Fairfield County)
125 Main St N., in Northwood
   Village
Woodbury, CT
203-263-6767
Diner or Coffee Shop

Two Steps (Fairfield County)
5 Ives St.
Danbury, CT
203-794-0032
American

Widow Brown's (Fairfield County)
128 Federal Rd.
Danbury, CT
203-743-7021
American

Looking for a getaway chow vacation? This section of Connecticut (Fairfield and Litchfield counties) is a supremely underrated chow mecca, and even locals fail to realize the splendor that surrounds them. Believe it or not, the following is merely the tip of the chowberg. We've excluded a slew of highly praised places (just because opinions are a bit dated), including, just in Danbury alone, The Sesame Seed and Hanna's (both Middle Eastern), Thang Long (Vietnamese), House of Yoshida (Japanese), Sunderban (Indian), Rocco's (Italian and pizza), Los Andes (Ecuadorian), and Turkish Kebab house. Here's a tour of top picks, grouped mostly by town, but with some rundowns at the end that you won't want to miss.

Danbury/Bethel

Goulash Place (Danbury) serves soulful Hungarian food in a large annex built onto the house of owner/hostess Magda and husband/chef John. Both are real characters, and their prices are from another era. Eschew the salad bar, the bread, the wine list, the desserts, the TV, and the paper napkins at Goulash Place and delight in everything else, which is tear jerkingly delicious and evocative. *Jim Leff* suggests ordering a stuffed cabbage appetizer and chicken paprikash or goulash (or the "special plate") as an entrée. Be sure to take home incredible soup.

All in Danbury: **Jim Barbaries** is good (but, some reports indicate, inconsistent) for New England clam chowder, lobster, and traditional shore dinners. **Chuck's Steak House** is a busy, fun place with good food. **Widow Brown's** for a leisurely weekend lunch. **Two Steps**, primarily a bar, cooks good southwestern food. A few Brazilian venues cluster around the south end of Main Street in Danbury, including **Banana Brazil** and **Mina's Carne & Deli**. As at any Brazilian place, look for cashew fruit juice (*caju,* pronounced "kah ZHU," like a Brazilian sneeze) and also cheese bread (*pão de quijo,* pronounced "pow dzhuh KAYzho") if you arrive early enough in the day.

Bountiful Board (Bethel) makes memorable fancy sandwiches (much loved by *Jim Leff*).

New Milford

In New Milford, **The Egg and I** sounds like a breakfast place, but is a source of terrific pork sausages, ham, pork loin and more.

The mysterious **Elliot Seafood** truck (we're not sure of its exact name or location) drives down from Maine with fresh and smoked fish and shellfish and parks somewhere on Route 7 in New Milford. It's not that big a town; just ask around).

New Milford's green becomes a farmers' market on Saturday mornings, selling good organic peas, tiny new potatoes, local blueberries, and a very nice raspberry-blueberry pie for $10.

Norwalk

At the Spanish restaurant **Meigas**, *SJ* recommends *escabeche*, made with marinated bluefin tuna. Also olive oil ice cream (sounds bizarre but tastes great!) with crabmeat, tomato and scallion, and crispy potatoes. Wood-roasted piquillo peppers stuffed with braised oxtail, crispy chickpeas, and marinated anchovies on crispy toast with black olive tapenade and salmon roe are also great choices.

Mecca is a less formal Spanish restaurant with a fine selection of one-dish meals. What Mecca lacks in style is more than made up for by the quality of the food, says *Chris G*. Good list of reasonably priced Spanish wines.

There's no pretense at **Ganga** Indian Restaurant. The wood-paneled decor might remind you of a basement home office, but that lets you concentrate on the flavors. *Spetcram* reports excellent tandoori chicken and spiced chickpeas at prices very moderate by Fairfield County standards.

Various Towns

The beery atmosphere at **Carriage House Cafe** (New Fairfield) ain't great, says *TrishUntrapped*, who recommends getting their exceptional burgers with grilled onions to go.

There are about a dozen ways to fill your roti at **Roti International** (Stamford), including curry chicken, stew chicken, beef, goat, shrimp, conch, and vegetables. Other fillings are called buss-up-shut and phoulorie (we're stumped, too). Also patties (beef or chicken), fruit juices, and traditional Jamaican drinks like Irish moss. According to *cteats*, the roti bread has great texture, and the fillings are well spiced and flavorful.

Gail's Stationhouse Cafe (Ridgefield) has good egg dishes served in cast-iron skillets with delicious hash browns. They also carry very good baked goods, reports *Ehilts*, who also likes lunch and dinner here.

Our sole report on **Marbella** (Stratford) is very positive. Steamed octopus is killer, as are codfish croquettes and marinated salmon layered with crisp pasta. Halibut with green sauce on rice is equally good, says *sophia's mom*.

Oliva (New Preston) has outdoor seating overlooking a lake and tasty Mediterranean and Italian food wonderfully prepared with fresh ingredients, says *christian*. BYOB. Also in New Preston, we have mixed news about **Hopkins Inn**, as *susabelle* had all sorts of disappointing food there, but wiener schnitzel is really terrific, as is their Toblerone sundae. And who doesn't crave weiner schnitzel and ice cream?

American Pie (Sherman) and **Stroble** (Kent) are both primarily bakeries, but also serve lunch. Stroble makes sandwiches, salads, and soups, which you can eat at one of three small tables inside, in one of the nearby state parks or on one of the benches outside. *Gioia* loves their incredible crab po' boys on freshly baked baguette (full of crab and perfectly flavored) and soft, moist, flaky scones loaded with blueberries.

Roundups

PIZZA options include **Portofino's** (New Fairfield), which also serves good Italian food, **First & Last Cafe** (Danbury) for wood-fired pizza with fresh mozzarella, and **Carminuccio's Pizza** for classic thin-crust pies.

The DINERS up here are great. Don't miss **The Sycamore** in Bethel, a real 1950s drive-in (with stellar burgers and homemade root beer), **Blue Colony Diner** in Newtown (home of the $1.50, ten-inch apple turnover), and **Phillip's Diner** in Woodbury (specializing in doughnuts). The incredibly homey and picturesque **Lakeside Diner** in Stamford serves "to drive for" banana pancakes and house-made sugar-cinnamon doughnuts. Its name is inspired by the diner's large picture window overlooking a pond. **Theo & Gretchen's** (Woodbury) serves breakfast all day (Tuesday through Friday, 6:00 a.m.–2:30 p.m., Saturday and Sunday; 7:00 a.m.–2 p.m.; closed Mondays) including freshly made crispy corned beef hash that's the best *Uncledave* has had in a long time. Terse but passionate, *Greg Minsky* reports a great breakfast, some of the best pancakes ever, at **Log House Restaurant** in Barkhamsted.

As for DESSERTS AND BAKERIES . . . **Bantam Bread Co.** (Bantam) has a serious selection of well-made breads, rolls and pastries, but prices can be steep. **The Goodie Shop** in New Fairfield is another serious place for specialty breads. **Sprinkles**, an ice-cream stand (New Fairfield), is one of the unknown chow meccas of Fairfield, Connecticut. *TrishUntrapped* says ice creams, ices, and sorbets are first rate, and the proprietors give delightful service. With live music in the summer, it's a real community gathering spot. **Dr. Mike's Ice Cream** (Bethel) has excellent taste and texture, and they're most famous for their chocolate lace and cream flavor, ribboned with rich, crunchy hard candy. This place is not as good it once was, but it's very relaxing in summertime to lick ice cream cones around their picnic tables. (Great for kids.)

CRAB NAAN

Curry in a Hurry (Murray Hill)
119 Lexington Ave.
Manhattan, NY
212-683-0900
Indian/Pakistani

Chowhound opinion of **Curry in a Hurry** ranges from average to solid. But everyone loves their crab naan. *Tolstyak* raves that it's undeniably wicked, though he's never even seen this in India. Much goodness for only $4.50.

Buttery, Blissful CROISSANTS

Andre's Hungarian Strudels
    (Queens)
10028 Queens Blvd.
Forest Hills, Queens, NY
718-830-0266
Hungarian Bakery

Balthazar (Soho)
80 Spring St.
Manhattan, NY
212-965-1414
French Bistro

Ceci-Cela (Soho)
55 Spring St.
Manhattan, NY
212-274-9179
French Café

City Bakery (Gramercy)
3 W. 18th St.
Manhattan, NY
212-366-1414
Café

Delices De Paris (Brooklyn)
321 9th St.
Park Slope, Brooklyn, NY
718-768-5666
French Bakery

Fauchon (Upper East Side)
1000 Madison Ave.
Manhattan, NY
212-570-2211
French Café

Greenwich St. Greenmarket
   (Tribeca)
Greenwich St., just north of
   Chambers
Manhattan, NY
Farmers' Market

Jacques Torres Chocolates
   (Brooklyn)
66 Water St.
DUMBO, Brooklyn, NY
718-875-9772
Chocolate/Candy Shop

J'Adore French Bakery & Cafe
   (Gramercy)
2 W. 23rd St.
Manhattan, NY
212-620-0388
French Sandwich Shop

La Bergamote Pastries
   (Chelsea)
169 9th Ave.
Manhattan, NY
212-627-9010
French Café

Margot Patisserie
   (Upper East Side)
1212 Lexington Ave.
Manhattan, NY
212-772-6064
French Bakery

Margot Patisserie
   (Upper West Side)
2109 Broadway
Manhattan, NY
212-721-0076
French Bakery

Patisserie Claude
   (Greenwich Village)
187 W. 4th St.
Manhattan, NY
212-255-5911
French Bakery

Silver Moon Bakery
   (Upper West Side)
2740 Broadway
Manhattan, NY
212-866-4717
Bakery

On Wednesdays and Saturdays at the Greenwich Street Greenmarket, a man sells large, American-style croissants made by his
brother-in-law, a La Varenne-trained baker. They're very buttery and have a nice crust, *epicure-us* says, though they're
sometimes a little underdone. (The same guy also sells garlicky
Chinese eggplant buns.) Croissants at Ceci-Cela are very light
(try their cheese danish, too). La Bergamote's croissants are fresh

and buttery, and their chocolate croissants are the closest you'll find to Parisian ones in New York, says *aab*. Good hot chocolate, too. At **Patisserie Claude**, croissants and *pain au chocolat* share praise with little apricot tarts, almond tarts, and cookies. At **Balthazar** the croissants are chewier and must be had early in the morning. Some think whole wheat croissants weird, but *scrittric* raves about the ones at **City Bakery**. **J'adore** is a tiny place with good sandwiches in addition to great croissants, says *higgins*. **Silver Moon Bakery** makes lovely croissants. And croissants are terrific at **Margot Patisserie's** West Side location. (No word yet about the East Side branch.) Besides regular croissants, **Fauchon** turns out excellent almond croissants, pain au chocolat, and "this tasty round hazelnut thingie that's also worth trying," suggests *Clarissa*.

Outer Borough croissant hot spots include **Delices De Paris**, whose croissants may not look beautiful, but are very buttery and crisp, says *Ann*. The chocolate croissants at **Jacques Torres** are *Jim Leff*'s favorites in New York City (try their Mexican spiced hot chocolate, too). At **Andre's Hungarian** Bakery, chocolate is mixed into the croissant dough, instead of being added later, and swirls through the pastry. It's best right out of the oven, when the chocolate's hot and melty.

○ **Andre's Hungarian Strudels:** *see also* p. 68.
○ **Balthazar:** *see also* pp. 35, 41, 104, 238.
○ **Ceci-Cela:** *see also* pp. 67, 201.
○ **City Bakery:** *see also* pp. 161, 207.
○ **Fauchon:** *see also* pp. 136, 161.

Forty Years of Tasty **CUBAN**

Victor's Cafe (Midtown West)
236 W. 52nd St.
Manhattan, NY
212-586-7714
Cuban

Cuban food was almost unknown in New York when **Victor's** first opened forty years ago. Hounds recommend roast suckling pig (be sure to ask for an extra bit of the crispy skin); an appetizer of ground pork with sweet plantains; oxtail stew (*rabo*); and black bean soup. Shrimp and lobster preparations are also good.

Hot tip: they'll even prepare a Cuban sandwich to take home, though it's not on the menu.

A Collection of **CUBAN SANDWICHES**

Cafe Habana (Soho)
17 Prince St.
Manhattan, NY
212-625-2001
Cuban

Cibao Restaurant
    (Lower East Side)
72 Clinton St.
Manhattan, NY
212-228-0703
Cuban

Clinton Restaurant
    (Lower East Side)
293 E. Houston St.
Manhattan, NY
212-982-3222
Dominican

El Castillo de Jagua
    (Lower East Side)
113 Rivington St., 1st Fl.
Manhattan, NY
212-982-6412
Dominican

Havana Chelsea (Chelsea)
190 8th Ave.
Manhattan, NY
212-243-9421
Cuban

IPN Deli (Tribeca)
350 Greenwich St.
Manhattan, NY
212-766-0085
Cuban

Sophie's Cuban Cuisine
    (Lower Manhattan)
205 Pearl St.
Manhattan, NY
212-269-0909
Cuban

Sophie's Cuban Cuisine
    (Lower Manhattan)
106 Greenwich St.
Manhattan, NY
212-385-0909
Cuban

Sophie's Cuban Cuisine
  (Lower Manhattan)
18 Maiden Ln.
Manhattan, NY
212-513-1998
Cuban

Spanish American Food
  (East Village)
351 E. 13th St.
Manhattan, NY
212-475-4508
Cuban

Sophie's Cuban Cuisine
  (Lower Manhattan)
75 New St.
Manhattan, NY
212-809-7755
Cuban

New York is blessed with lots of places for a good Cuban Sandwich (aka Cubano). Each of the following is recommended by at least one hound. Great ingredients (typically: roast pork, ham, swiss cheese, mustard, a pickle, and a soft Cuban roll) are a must, but *Michelle C.* notes that technique and presser are just as important.

At **El Castillo De Jagua**, very large Cubanos are only $3.25. They slice the pickle a bit too thick, but their *pernil* (roast pork) is tender and succulent; also, they toast the bread perfectly, says *elvislives*, who finds all their other fare excellent as well.

Sophie's Cuban Cuisine is a growing empire downtown. The newest location, on Chambers Street, is spotlessly clean, while the others seem more lived in. Daily specials are big enough for two. Closed on Sundays.

Other quick tips: They don't press and toast the bread at **Clinton Restaurant**, but some hounds say the Cubanos there are nonetheless very good. **Cafe Habana's** Cubanos are also not pressed, but are heated on a grill—which toasts the bread and leaves grill marks. Great people watching, too. Cubanos at **Havana Chelsea** are reportedly very large and very delicious. **Spanish American Food** is a tiny lunch counter with lots of good Cuban cooking, including sandwiches. **Cibao** is also reported to do a pretty mean Cubano. **IPN Deli** makes 'em and is convenient to the Pier 25 recreation area.

○ **Cibao Restaurant:** *see also* p. 64.
○ **Clinton Restaurant:** *see also* p. 64.

○ El Castillo de Jagua: *see also* p. 64.
○ Spanish American Food: *see also* p. 65.

CUCHIFRITOS Defined and Scouted

Abuela's Cocina
  (Upper East Side)
1758 1st Ave.
Manhattan, NY
917-492-1790
Puerto Rican

Cuchifritos (Spanish Harlem)
168 E. 116 St.
Manhattan, NY
212-876-4846
Puerto Rican

Delicioso Restaurant (Bronx)
423 E. 149th St.
Bronx NY
718-665-3336
Puerto Rican

El Molino Rojo II (Bronx)
101 E. 161 St., just down
  the block from the Yankee
  Stadium subway stop
Bronx, NY
718-538-9642
Puerto Rican/Dominican

La Isla (Brooklyn)
1439 Myrtle Ave.
Bushwick, Brooklyn, NY
718-417-0668
Puerto Rican

La Parada (Brooklyn)
341 Broadway
Williamsburg, Brooklyn, NY
718-963-1944
Puerto Rican/Dominican

Cuchifritos **is a blanket** term for Dominican or Puerto Rican fried stuff. *Mark DiBlasi* says most cuchifritos places carry fried codfish fritters (*bacalaitos*), fried meat pies (*pastellitos*), fried potato balls stuffed with ground meat (*papa relleños*), fried stuffed cassava fingers (*alcapurrias*) plus a variety of sauced innards like pig ears in tomato gravy (*orejas*) and pork liver. You'll often find rotisserie chicken, sweet plantains stuffed with chopped meat, blood sausages, and *mofungo* (hypergarlicky plantain mash). Also fruity fountain drinks (try *ajonjolí*, a sesame drink that tastes like liquified Lucky Charms marshmallows, but in a *good* way). A meal of these things can be had for five to six bucks. Quality depends on the freshness of the oil and how recently stuff was cooked.

The following are all highly recommended: **Molino Rojo**, near Yankee Stadium, which will freshly fry items on request. **Delicioso**, which you can smell from the 149th and Third Avenue subway station; *mryc* reports fine chicken and baccalao as well as the standard cuchifritos. **La Isla**, like many **cuchifritos** places, is open twenty-four hours a day. *Mark DiBlasi* says Cuchifritos on 116th Street rocks. **La Parada**/Chicken Q is mostly known for barbecue, but they also sell a few cuchifritos—very fresh and very delicious. The elusive **Abuela's Cocina** ("grandmother's kitchen") is almost always shuttered. But on those rare occasions when they open . . . watch out. The best!

- ○ **El Molino Rojo II:** *see also* p. 340.
- ○ **La Parada:** *see also* p. 252.

CURRIED CHICKEN ROTI Rave

Caribbean Spice (Clinton)
402 W. 44th St.
Manhattan, NY
212-765-1737
Jamaican

"The curry chicken has lots of big chunks of chicken so tender they fell apart when I put my fork to it (dish was almost all chicken and curry—lots of white meat, with a little bit of potato). Curry was slow cooked and rich in flavor with deep yellow/ almost green color. Had a bit of oil on top that I poured off. The roti was excellent, freshly made, crisp around edges, very flavorful—with layer/dusting of coarsely ground chickpea flakes and spices," writes *elvislives* about a delivery from **Caribbean Spice**.

Chowhound Nametag: Aki

∘◯∘

Location:
New York/Manhattan/East Village.

Occuptation:
Tour guide for Japanese tourists. I'm Japanese.

Cholesterol Level: Very low. I take poly- and monounsaturated fat as much as possible.

Number of Visits to McDonald's in Past Decade: Million times, but *only* for the grilled chicken sandwich without mayo.

Farthest out of the Way Traveled Just for Chow: New York!! I'm from Tokyo, Japan. It's really far, far away. And was it worth it? It's great!!

Nabe Most Full of Explorable Unknown Chow:
Anywhere.

Top Chinatown Pick: Kam Hing (119 Baxter Street, Manhattan; 212-925-0425). They have the greatest sponge cake in the world for sixty cents.

Underrated by Chowhounds: John's Twelfth Street. True classic American Italian. The best spaghetti meatballs.

Weight Management Tip: Three days of weight training, three days of cardio exercise in a week. For the cardio, I do kick boxing. I also jog thirty minutes, three days in a week. Eat low fat, low carb, high fiber, lots of water, good supplement. I don't drink alcoholic beverages and soda.

Favorite Gelato Flavor:
Ricotta.

Where the Good **DESSERTS** Live

Balthazar (Soho)
80 Spring St.
Manhattan, NY
212-965-1414
French Bistro

Blue Hill (Greenwich Village)
75 Washington Pl.
Manhattan, NY
212-539-1776
New American

Blue Ribbon Bakery
   (Greenwich Village)
33 Downing St.
Manhattan, NY
212-337-0404
American

Bright Food Shop (Chelsea)
218 8th Ave.
Manhattan, NY
212-243-4433
Mexican/American/East
   Asian/Eclectic

Cafe Sabarsky (Upper East Side)
1048 Fifth Ave. at 86th St., in
   the Neue Galerie
Manhattan, NY
212-288-0665
Austrian

Chikalicious Dessert Bar
   (East Village)
203 E. 10th St.
Manhattan, NY
212-995-9511
New American/Japanese Café

Etats-Unis Restaurant
   (Upper East Side)
242 E. 81st St.
Manhattan, NY
212-517-8826
New American/French

Gramercy Tavern (Gramercy)
42 E. 20th St.
Manhattan NY
212-477-0777
New American

Home Restaurant
   (Greenwich Village)
20 Cornelia St.
Manhattan, NY
212-243-9579
American

Kitchenette (Tribeca)
80 W. Broadway
Manhattan, NY
212-267-6740
American/Diner or Coffee Shop

Kitchenette Uptown (Harlem)
1272 Amsterdam Ave.
Manhattan, NY
212-531-7600
American/Diner or Coffee Shop

Le Monde (Upper West Side)
2885 Broadway
Manhattan, NY
212-531-3939
French Bistro

CURRIED CHICKEN ROTI

Margaret Palca Bakes (Brooklyn)
191 Columbia St.
Red Hook, Brooklyn, NY
718-643-3507
Bakery

Noho Star (Greenwich Village)
330 Lafayette St.
Manhattan, NY
212-925-0070
New American/Chinese

NYC ICY (East Village)
21 Avenue B
Manhattan, NY
212-979-9877
Ice Cream or Gelato

O.G. (East Village)
507 E. 6th St.
Manhattan, NY
212-477-4649
Pan-Asian Fusion

Payard Patisserie & Bistro
   (Upper East Side)
1032 Lexington Ave.
Manhattan, NY
212-717-5252
French Bistro/French

Porgy & Bass Seafood (Harlem)
321 Malcolm X Blvd.
Manhattan, NY
212-531-0300
Southern/Seafood

Teany (Lower East Side)
90 Rivington St.
Manhattan, NY
212-475-9190
Vegetarian

Village (Greenwich Village)
62 W. 9th St.
Manhattan, NY
212-505-3355
French Bistro

Yujin (East Village)
24 E. 12th St.
Manhattan, NY
212-924-4283
Japanese/New American

Chowhounds always feel an overwhelming need to maximize their deliciousness. When tons of calories enter the equation, it's that much more urgent that only greatness be ingested. Hounds share their favorite fail-safe desserts.

Chikalicious offers a three-course (plus, believe it or not, *amuse*) $12 prix-fixe dessert menu! You choose an "entrée" from a choice of about a half dozen, but the house sets the first and third courses. Portions are very small and flavors are intense and well matched, reports *Toot and Puddle*. *Eva L.* says corn ice cream is surprisingly good, but cheesecake has the texture of cottage cheese.

Porgy & Bass is a fried fish place, but don't miss their signature bread pudding with bourbon sauce, added after you order to prevent sogginess. Apple crumb cheesecake is amazing, says *Aki*, who reports great sweet potato cheesecake, chocolate cake, and red velvet cake, too. Oh, and also peach cobbler.

The Mexican-Asian fusion stylings of **Bright Food Shop** are also apparent in their desserts. *Susan J* recommends their popular key lime tart, ginger cake with sauce, rice pudding with unusual additions, and an extremely intense *piñon* cake with heady caramelized dark crust and rich dips of caramel, cherry compote, and fresh whipped cream (all necessary because the cake itself is a bit dry).

Then there's Japanese-American fusion desserts at **Yujin**, e.g. Japanese yuzu cheesecake with rice cracker crust or molten chocolate cake with caramel sauce. (Sushi here, by the way, is decent, but don't miss perfect Scottish salmon in miso with broccoli rabe.)

Pudding lovers should check out date pudding at **Etats-Unis** (not fancy, just scrumptious, says *dkchan*), chocolate bread pudding at **Blue Hill**, chocolate pudding at **Home**, and banana walnut and chocolate chip bread puddings—big enough for two—at **Blue Ribbon Bakery**. *Jim Leff* loves chocolate pudding (Friday nights only) at **Noho Star**.

Margaret Palca's rugelach are treasured, but she also bakes Eastern European pies, brownies, and fruit tarts. Apple pie and multiberry tarts garner high praise, as do muffins available for breakfast (she opens very early). Serious cheesecake, too, and fondant-topped cupcakes, decorated to order. Margaret's husband prepares elegant gourmet food gift baskets. Worth a pilgrimmage to Brooklyn.

Check out the apple tart at **Balthazar**. "To die for!!! Sooo yummy!!! I'm going back just so I can have this tart again," exults *Rachael*.

Chowhound *catcat* says apple tarts at **Village** are thin, crisp, and the apples are just perfect.

O.G. has five-spice chocolate cake.

Teany: collapsed chocolate souffle, strawberry-rhubarb pie, and chocolate-peanut-butter bomb cake (like decadent homemade "Funny Bones," reports *CB*). Also over a hundred blends of tea. Recording artist Moby is an owner.

Cafe Sabarsky: Viennese *klimttorte* and apple strudel.

A large variety of homey cakes, pies and cupcakes at **Kitchenette's** two locations.

Payard has cases of things like *réligieuses* and other stuff you'd find at nicer patisseries in Paris.

Le Monde is pretty pedestrian until it comes to desserts. The pastry chef makes artful rounds of various fruit, chocolate, or coffee mousses, and delightful crêpes (especially the raspberry).

And what would dessert be without ice cream? **Gramercy Tavern** serves fanciful parfaits (and excellent desserts all around), while **NYC Icy** serves unusual flavors like ginger apricot.

See also What to Get at Manhattan *Bakeries* and all listings under "bakeries" and "dessert cafes" in the cuisine index.

- **Balthazar:** *see also* **pp. 35, 41, 96, 238.**
- **Blue Ribbon Bakery:** *see also* **pp. 42, 266, 272.**
- **Gramercy Tavern:** *see also* **pp. 139, 250.**
- **Home Restaurant:** *see also* **p. 42.**
- **Kitchenette:** *see also* **pp. 42, 151, 205, 240, 280.**
- **Margaret Palca Bakes:** *see also* **pp. 56, 69.**
- **Noho Star:** *see also* **pp. 43, 233.**
- **Payard Patisserie & Bistro:** *see also* **p. 267.**
- **Porgy & Bass Seafood:** *see also* **p. 69.**
- **Yujin:** *see also* **p. 69.**

DI FARA Pizzeria: The Legend Continues

Di Fara Pizzeria (Brooklyn)
1424 Avenue J
Midwood, Brooklyn, NY
718-258-1367
Pizza/Italian

The pizza at **Di Fara's** is always mind blowingly great, because the legendary Domick DeMarco always makes it. Back in the kitchen, three chefs revolve. Dom's daughter is a magician, as is one of his sons, with prepared dishes (pastas, entrées, heroes), but a second son (the grouchy taciturn one—he's hard to miss) doesn't apply the same care. Learn the cast of characters in order to strategize when to stick to pizza. Though the artichoke slices (with fresh, beautiful, sautéed artichokes) have been much touted, *Nina* points out that if you order them on a slice, you're missing the prime experience. Since the topping has been mounted atop a precooked slice, which is then reheated, you don't enjoy the essential synergy of both pie and topping cooked together. You've *got* to order a whole pie fresh from the oven, as it's intended to be eaten.

For those who don't know, Di Fara's, an old-fashioned Brooklyn pizzeria, is one of the most-loved destinations for chowhounds. It's mobbed weekend late afternoons and evenings, but no matter how impatient the crowd, Mr. DeMarco never loses his cool, placidly crafting perfect works of pizza art in a state of deep Zen-like absorption.

○ **Di Fara Pizzeria:** *see also* p. 1.

Rule #1 at **DI PALO**

Di Palo Fine Foods (Little Italy)
206 Grand St.
Manhattan, NY
212-226-1033
Store

"I've come to the realization that anything on the counter at **Di Palo's** is delicious and without question should be grabbed. Olives, marinated artichokes, wax cow figurines, whatever. Just get it because no doubt you'll wonder how you lived your life without it," says *Abbylovi*, who discovered delicious homemade meat stromboli there. And look for *pizza rustica*, like a crustless, creamy ham and salami quiche, available only around Easter.

○ **Di Palo Fine Foods:** *see also* pp. 53, 290.

DIM SUM and More in Williamsburg

M Shanghai Bistro & Den
  (Brooklyn)
129 Havemeyer St.
Williamsburg, Brooklyn, NY
718-384-9300
Chinese (Shanghai)/Chinese
  (Dim Sum)

Oslo Coffee Co. (Brooklyn)
133 Roebling St.
Williamsburg, Brooklyn, NY
718-782-0332
Vegetarian

Din Sum and Williamsburg are not two words you normally hear in the same sentence. **M Shanghai Bistro** changes that with its brunch menu, which includes delicious steamed juicy pork buns, spicy wonton, and a steamed red-bean paste bun with a perfect balance of salty and sweet. As a bonus, a free drink (bloody mary, mimosa, beer) comes with every dim sum plate. For those who can't face heavy Shanghai dumplings weekend mornings, nearby **Oslo** serves excellent espresso, macchiato, hot chocolate, and more. (Look for its unusual wrought-iron door and window treatment.)

Uptown Upscale DOMINICAN

Don Pedro's (Upper East Side)
1865 2nd Ave.
Manhattan, NY
212-996-3274
Cuban/Puerto Rican/
  Dominican/Spanish

DRK (Washington Heights)
114 Dyckman St.
Manhattan, NY
212-304-1717
Dominican

Food at Don Pedro's is inspired by the cuisines of Cuba, Puerto Rico, and the Dominican Republic. To further complicate things, the Dominican chef reportedly worked in Madrid and Barcelona. This place is wonderful and is a great value, reports

Kay, who recommends shrimp empanadas and says the personable owner really cares about great food. Regular entrées cost $8–$14, but specials are almost double that. Very crowded on weekends, so reservations are suggested. Don't miss their very, very garlicky *mofongo* (mashed plantain) served with sea bass with blueberry vinaigrette (when it's available as a special), or chicken with garlic sauce and rice preparations any time.

Dominican fish soup at **DRK** draws gasps; it's spectacular looking, smelling, and tasting. Various shellfish in the tomato broth lend the perfect oceanic quality, says *djk*. That's not the only uncommonly tasty standard Latin American item; ceviche arrives in a three-dish combo with shrimp in spicy tomato sauce and octopus in a sprightly green sauce. Outstanding *arepas* come plain or with braised short ribs. Desserts include churros with chocolate and guava dipping sauces and excellent *dulce de leche*. Good wine list and a champagne lounge upstairs.

Outstanding **DOUGHNUTS** (and Apple Fritters)

Amish Market (Clinton)
731 9th Ave.
Manhattan, NY
212-245-2360
Store

Amish Market East
  (Grand Central)
240 E. 45th St.
Manhattan, NY
212-370-1761
Store

Cupcake Cafe (Clinton)
522 9th Ave.
Manhattan, NY
212-465-1530
American Café

The Donut Pub (Chelsea)
203 W. 14th St.
Manhattan, NY
212-929-0126
American Café

The Doughnut Plant
  (Lower East Side)
379 Grand St.
Manhattan, NY
212-505-3700
Bakery

The Donut Pub makes gaily decorated doughnuts in unusual flavors. Their cake doughnuts are superior to their raised ones. And even though their blueberry doughnuts probably contain more Jiffy muffin mix-style fruit than anything resembling an actual blueberry, they're still great in their own tawdry way. Also good: Boston cream doughnuts and anything filled with whipped cream. They also sell apple fritters. Opinion on **The Doughnut Plant** is divided. Some swear by their creations (both conventional and nouveau), while others find them decent but overly hyped. Their pear doughnuts—made only occasionally—have developed a cult following. In spite of its name (and reputation for items that look better than they taste), **Cupcake Cafe** makes excellent doughnuts, and while the **Amish Markets** are not highly regarded by chowhounds, we've heard rumors you can get real West Coast-style apple fritters at either branch.

○ **Cupcake Cafe:** *see also* p. 240.
○ **The Doughnut Plant:** *see also* p. 87.

DOWNTOWN ATLANTIC:
Undreckish Cupcakes and Much More

Downtown Atlantic Restaurant and Bakery (Brooklyn)
364 Atlantic Ave.
Boerum Hill, Brooklyn, NY
718-852-9945
Eclectic New American

The cake is lighter than air, and the frosting is pure butter cream yet doesn't sit in your stomach like a chunk of lard-infested cheapo bakery dreck. This is how *Dipsy*, in her distinctive way, lauds the cupcakes at **Downtown Atlantic**. They come in either vanilla or chocolate cake with vanilla or chocolate icing, topped in sprinkles or coconut. Simple and divine. Other baked goods include cakes, cheesecakes, tarts, and cookies, all made on the premises. Food in the restaurant is fantastic, interesting and reasonably priced. While some say pastas are best avoided, we've heard raves for their tagliatelle, as well as penne in tomato cream sauce with sausage. Also good: mussels, crab cake, scallops with spinach and couscous, rib-eye steak, and desserts. Live jazz every weekend.

○ **Downtown Atlantic Restaurant and Bakery:** *see also* **p. 68.**

DUCK TONGUE (So Hard to Find Good!)

Ping's (Chinatown)
22 Mott St.
Manhattan, NY
212-602-9988
Chinese (Hong Kong)

There are two duck tongue dishes at **Ping's,** and *cabrales* says the lightly deep-fried one is best. "The ducks' tongues arrived— fattier than I had ever experienced them; not as gelatinous as usual. I liked the feel of extracting the flesh from the bit of hard substance (bone? cartilage?) toward the center of the duck's tongue." *The Rogue*, however, finds them tough, flavorless, and a hassle to eat.

DUMPAKHK . . . or Something Like That

Joy Indian Restaurant (Brooklyn)
301 Flatbush Ave.
Prospect Heights, Brooklyn, NY
718-230-1165
Indian

Dumpakhk (we're not certain of spelling or pronunciation) is an Indian cooking technique where the pot is sealed with dough—basically a flour-and-water paste—to keep in moisture. It has been adapted by **Joy Indian**, among others, as an Indian potpie with a fluffy bread topping. *Dipsy* says the rendition here is divine. Note that this place also makes an especially great chicken tikka masala (spiced on the sweet side, but they'll bring it up to your requested heat level), and nice *chana chat* and veggie samosas.

EDISON AREA Indian . . . and More

Aangan (Monmouth County)
3475 Rte. 9, in the Chester
   Lighting Shopping Mall
Freehold, NJ
732-617-9200
South Indian

Atithi Restaurant
   (Middlesex County)
214 Worth St.
Iselin, NJ
732-750-8845
South Indian

Edison Noodle House
   (Middlesex County)
775 US Hwy. 1 and Old Post Rd.,
   in the Shop Rite shopping
   center
Edison, NJ
732-572-0600
Korean

Healthy Tofu (Middlesex County)
560 Old Post Rd.
Edison, NJ
732-287-3353
Korean

Igloo Tea House
   (Middlesex County)
1784 Rte. 27
Edison, NJ
732-339-9889
Chinese

Ming Far Eastern Cuisine
   (Middlesex County)
1655-185 Oak Tree Rd.
Edison, NJ
732-549-5051
Indian/Chinese

Moghul (Middlesex County)
1655-195 Oak Tree Rd., in lower
   section of Oaktree Shopping
   Center
Edison, NJ
732-549-5050
Indian

Swagath Gourmet
(Middlesex County)
1700 Oak Tree Rd., in the Cherry
Tree Mall
Edison, NJ
732-549-2626
South Indian

Wonder Seafood
(Middlesex County)
1984 Rte. 27
Edison, NJ
732-287-6328
Chinese (Hong Kong)/Chinese
(Dim Sum)

The environs of Edison, New Jersey, host one of the country's largest concentrations of South Asians. Indian restaurants abound, many of them centered around Oak Tree Road. But Edison is more than just Indian! Few realize that a much more diverse Asian population is starting to arrive, and restaurants are popping up to cater to them.

Swagath Gourmet's South Indian food earns raves from *Murghi*, who particularly likes rice dishes and *dosas*—better than anything he had in India.

Moghul's food is very good, though a bit pricey (be sure to reserve).

Outside Edison proper, **Atithi Restaurant** has done the unthinkable: They stuff dosas (the apotheosis of Brahmin vegetarianism) with meat. This is reportedly the cheapest buffet in the area.

Down the road from Atithi, **Aangan** is a large, attractively decorated restaurant with a Thursday night $15 buffet dinner offering generous selections.

Wonder Seafood is a newish Hong Kong–style seafood restaurant with dim sum from carts on weekends (à la carte—i.e., not on carts!—during the week) and what *Susan* describes as amazing seafood preparations, including a fish-head soup declared serious by her Shanghainese friend. Sautéed squid with Chinese scallions, taro, and delicately fried fish that is so fresh you can almost taste the sea exploding in your mouth. There's a broad range of frog dishes, as well as more traditional stuff.

Healthy Tofu serves delicious soft tofu stews, reports *Val G*.

Edison Noodle House specializes in *ja-jang myun,* a Korean/Chinese noodle dish with black bean sauce with pork and onion to which seafood and various meats can be added. But the large menu has a full range of purely Korean dishes. Television screens show the noodle maker at work. ("The combination of seeing the TV image and feeling the bang of the dough is twenty-first-century technology at its best," says *Brian Yarvin*.) Dumplings are small but very tasty, and portions are generous.

Ming's bridges all of Asia, serving Indian/Chinese, the intensely spiced and delicious cuisine developed by Chinese restaurateurs to please the Indian palate. Get payaya salad for an appetizer and also an unnamed cauliflower dish. Good entrées include fish in a clay pot, divine stuffed eggplant, and bamboo rice. All the Manchurian-sauced dishes are excellent. Try to intersperse the superspicy dishes with a couple of milder items so that you can truly distinguish flavors. BYOB.

Igloo Tea House serves Asian and Western desserts plus tea drinks.

Happening EGGPLANT PARM HEROES

Amici Deli (Brooklyn)
520 Henry St.
Carroll Gardens, Brooklyn, NY
718-522-3663
Italian Deli

Carlo's Grocery (Brooklyn)
1983 52nd St.
Borough Park, Brooklyn, NY
718-253-0322
Italian Deli

Corona Heights Pork Store
   (Queens)
107-04 Corona Ave.
Corona, Queens, NY
718-592-7350
Italian Deli

De Fonte's of Red Hook
   (Brooklyn)
379 Columbia St.
Red Hook, Brooklyn, NY
718-855-6982
Italian Sandwich Shop

Leo's Latticini (Queens)
46-02 104th St.
Corona, Queens, NY
718-898-6069
Italian Deli

Portofino Pizza Restaurant
   (Queens)
109-32 Ascan Ave.
Forest Hills, Queens, NY
718-261-1239
Italian/Pizza

In Chicken Parmigiana Heros we sussed out the top chicken parm heroes in Manhattan. Now we go across the river for the best eggplant parm heroes in the boroughs; *hotterville-rutabaga*'s criteria for a great eggplant parmigiana hero: "Many slices of thin, non-greasy, ultra-tender breaded eggplant, preferably cut the long way. Sauce should be homemade if possible. Cheese doesn't have to be superior, pizza grade is fine, as I find that the sauce and the eggplant are the two factors which determine the quality of the overall sandwich."

That said, the **Corona Heights Pork Store** makes an amazing one, maybe the best in New York City, but be prepared to wait at least twenty minutes. There's no place to eat inside, but in nicer weather you can take your sandwich to the park across the street. Nearby **Leo's Latticini** (aka Mama's) makes good ones. If you prefer thinly sliced eggplant, try Portofino's, which uses a multitude of thin layers, says *jmui*.

Moving over to Brooklyn, another takeout-only slow food pick is **Carlos Grocery**, where everything is made caringly to order. **De Fonte's in Red Hook** is a real old-time sandwich shop using wonderful mozzarella, and **Amici's** is a top eggplant parm pick in Carroll Gardens.

○ **De Fonte's of Red Hook:** *see also* **pp. 30, 56.**

The Best **ESPRESSO** in Town?

Brown (Lower East Side)
61 Hester St.
Manhattan, NY
212-254-9825
Café

Leonidas (Lower Manhattan)
3 Hanover Sq.
Manhattan, NY
212-422-9600
Belgian

Higher Grounds Cafe
  (East Village)
700 E. 9th St.
Manhattan, NY
212-358-9225
Diner or Coffee Shop

The best espresso in town can be found at **Higher Grounds**, proclaims *David the Burninator*. **Leonidas** makes a nice espresso using Illy brand beans, and you get a chocolate with every coffee! Brown brews a smooth cup of espresso with a nice *crema* (and they, too, offer chocolate squares).

ETHIOPIAN . . . Such as It Is

Aida's Ethiopian Cafe
   (Hudson County)
739 Broadway
Bayonne, NJ
201-436-9593
Ethiopian or Eritrean

Awash (Upper West Side)
947 Amsterdam Ave.
Manhattan, NY
212-961-1416
Ethiopian or Eritrean

Ghenet Restaurant (Soho)
284 Mulberry St.
Manhattan, NY
212-343-1888
Ethiopian or Eritrean

Meskerem Ethiopian Cuisine
   (Greenwich Village)
124 MacDougal St.
Manhattan, NY
212-777-8111
Ethiopian or Eritrean

Meskerem Ethiopian Restaurant
   (Clinton)
468 W. 47th St.
Manhattan, NY
212-664-0520
Ethiopian or Eritrean

Queen of Sheba (Clinton)
650 10th Ave.
Manhattan, NY
212-397-0610
Ethiopian or Eritrean

Zula Café (Upper West Side)
1260 Amsterdam Ave.
Manhattan, NY
212-663-1670
Ethiopian or Eritrean

We don't know why, but while each of the Ethiopian restaurants in town has occasional moments of glory, none are consistently outstanding. The best seems to be out of town (see hot tip at bottom).

Both **Meskerem** restaurants have been popular with hounds for dishes of collard greens, yellow split peas, and samosas, but *Hellkatte* reports the injera quality at the 47th Street location has been on a steady, persistent decline. **Queen of Sheba** serves bargain-priced Ethiopian food. Enormous lunch specials, and all dinner specials are under $13. Hounds report that you often see Ethiopians dining at **Awash,** and **Zula,** even farther uptown, has its fans.

Ghenet gets general praise, but some say the food is not worth the relatively high prices. *JackS* did better, reporting that one particularly spicy dish was so good it practically gave him hallucinogenic visions. Waiter, make ours a double . . .

But here's the hot tip: There's a joint in Bayonne called Aida's with a limited menu that's as close to home-cooked Ethiopian as you are likely to find, says *Bond Girl*. Rent a car!

○ **Queen of Sheba:** *see also* p. 254.

Flipping over **FELIDIA** (Pear Ravioli, Spinach-topped Veal Chops, et al)

Felidia Ristorante (Upper East Side)
243 E. 58th St.
Manhattan, NY
212-758-1479
Istrian/Italian

Steve R. flipped over dinner at **Felidia**, describing a veritable showcase of excellent food and service. Pear ravioli seemed to be the best ravioli ever, with a hint of pear changing it from simplicity to memorable ambrosia. An appetizer of duck foie gras, duck carpaccio, and goose terrine had great texture and flavor. Spinach-topped veal chops seemed simple but revealed complex flavors. Sommelier service was outstandingly gracious and knowledgeable. Really extensive pasta selection.

Rockland County **FILIPINO**

Filipino Fiesta (Rockland County)
580 Rte. 303 South
Blauvelt, NY
845-365-1969
Philippine

Filipino Fiesta is a caterer offering takeout and lunch buffet with just a couple of tables. The self-serve buffet (12:00–2:00 p.m.) includes a choice of three entrees, rice, and vegetable. *Deven Black* thought it looked a bit tired, but he'd arrived very late. So he opted for a takeout order of goat caldereta—a real winner. He raves that the nicely spiced goat was falling off the bone but still had some chaw. The place seems to be a family-run operation doing real home cooking.

FIRST for Ambitious Pub Food

First (East Village)
87 1st Ave.
Manhattan, NY
212-674-3823
American

Good ambitious bar-style food at **First** makes up for horrendous service. Recommended dishes include tuna au poivre, chicken wing lollipops, fried oysters, and the BLT. Salmon cones appetizer is salmon tartar in an ice-cream cone topped with crème fraiche and salmon roe. First's burgers (White Castle–style sliders on steroids) have their fans as well as their detractors, and fries garner praise, as do tiny tinies (minicocktail plus shaker for refills) from the bar. Be sure to save room for make-your-own s'mores for dessert.

When to Visit FISH on Bleecker

Fish (Greenwich Village)
280 Bleecker St.
Manhattan, NY
212-727-2879
Seafood

Weekdays offer the best selection at Fish; they don't seem to be able to replenish supplies on weekends. (It's admirable that they don't simply overstock, at the expense of Sunday freshness!) Mix-and-match oyster options get high praise, as do catfish po' boys (hard to find good ones in New York), cole slaw, fries, and Caesar salad.

FISH SANDWICHES

A Salt and Battery (East Village)
80 2nd Ave.
Manhattan, NY
212-254-6610
British

A Salt and Battery
   (Greenwich Village)
112 Greenwich Ave.
Manhattan, NY
212-691-2713
British

Famous Fish Market (Harlem)
684 St. Nicholas Ave.
Manhattan, NY
212-491-8323
Southern

Heartland Brewery
   (Midtown West)
1285 Ave. of the Americas
Manhattan, NY
212-582-8244
Pub

Heartland Brewery (Union Square)
35 Union Sq. W.
Manhattan, NY
212-645-3400
Pub

Heartland Brewery Chop House
   (Theater District)
127 W. 43rd St.
Manhattan, NY
646-366-0235
American

Hole-in-the-Wall Fish Place
   (Harlem)
SE corner of 125th and Lenox
Manhattan, NY
Southern/Seafood

Houston's Restaurant (Gramercy)
378 Park Ave. S.
Manhattan, NY
212-689-1090
American

Houston's Restaurant
   (Midtown East)
153 E. 53rd St.
Manhattan, NY
212-888-3828
American

Mary's Fish Camp
  (Greenwich Village)
64 Charles St.
Manhattan, NY
646-486-2185
Seafood

Pearl Oyster Bar
  (Greenwich Village)
18 Cornelia St.
Manhattan, NY
212-691-8211
Seafood

Pearl Oyster Bar's pan-fried fish sandwich with shoestring fries is popular. Get it with grouper, says *Dave Feldman*.

The fish sandwich selection changes daily at **A Salt and Battery's** two locations (and you can finish your meal with deep-fried Mars bars).

Mary's Fish Camp serves cod sandwiches daily at lunch.

Loeb recommends **Famous Fish Market** and another hole-in-the-wall fish place at the SE corner of 125th and Lenox (might be A Taste Of Seafood, 50 East 125th St., 212-831-5584, which is actually at Madison), two tiny Harlem fried-fish joints where you can get a tasty fish sandwich served briskly but pleasantly for under $4.

Houston's two locations serve tasty fish sandwiches. Check out their shoestring fries.

Heartland Brewery can be touristy and crowded, but *Michelle* says they serve a highly enjoyable crispy, fresh cod sandwich (not thickly breaded) with fries and slaw.

FISH TACOS

Cafe el Portal (Soho)
174 Elizabeth St.
Manhattan, NY
212-226-4642
Mexican

Green Cactus
  (Nassau and Suffolk Counties)
www.greencactusgrill.com/
  main-location.htm
Mexican

El Rey del Sol (Greenwich Village)
232 W. 14th St.
Manhattan, NY
212-229-0733
Mexican

Miracle Grill (East Village)
112 1st Ave., #2a
Manhattan, NY
212-254-2353
American

Pampano Taqueria (Midtown East)
805 3rd Ave., bottom floor of
  Crystal Pavilion
Manhattan, NY
212-751-5257
Mexican

Radio Mexico Cafe
  (Lower Manhattan)
259 Front St.
Manhattan, NY
212-791-5416
Mexican

Fish tacos are a treat from the Baja peninsula in Mexico and are just starting to make an impact on New York menus. They're still rare, since most immigrants (and restaurateurs) in the area are from Puebla, and Pueblans don't know from fish tacos. Here are some exceptions:

Pampano Taqueria makes surprisingly creditable fish tacos using red snapper. The fish is good quality, thanks to an affiliation with the high-end Mexican seafood restaurant Pampano. Good shrimp tacos and snapper tortas, too.

Cafe El Portal is a family-owned, very inexpensive place that tends to get very crowded. Whereas much of the food's Americanized, *mynyc* says fish tacos are very close to ones he's had in Baja.

Radio Mexico's tacos are made with unbreaded fish, usually moist and flavorful marinated mahimahi. A large order is $10.

Though not at all "authentic," the catfish taco appetizer at **Miracle Grill** is really delicious.

El Rey Del Sol serves fish tacos.

On Long Island, the **Green Cactus** restaurants serve fish tacos very much like those in Baja for under $3 each, says *jesse*. They're battered fried fish with shredded cabbage and a spicy slightly creamy sauce. The Rockville Center branch is right across from the train station. But there is a report of poorly prepared food at the Wantaugh location.

○ **Miracle Grill:** *see also* **p. 151.**

FLAPJACK Faves

Cafe Luluc (Brooklyn)
214 Smith St.
Cobble Hill, Brooklyn, NY
718-625-3815
French Bistro

Fairway Market (Upper West Side)
2127 Broadway
Manhattan, NY
212-595-1888
Store

good Restaurant
   (Greenwich Village)
89 Greenwich Ave.
Manhattan, NY
212-691-8080
New American/Latin American

Mitchel London Foods (Clinton)
458 9th Ave.
Manhattan, NY
212-563-5969
American

Mitchel London Foods
   (Upper East Side)
22 E. 65th St.
Manhattan, NY
212-737-2850
American

Sarabeth's East (Upper East Side)
1295 Madison Ave., in the
   Whitney Museum
Manhattan, NY
212-410-7335
American

Sarabeth's West
   (Upper West Side)
423 Amsterdam Ave.
Manhattan, NY
212-496-6280
American

Shopsin's (Greenwich Village)
54 Carmine St.
Manhattan, NY
212-924-5160
Eclectic Diner or Coffee Shop

Tom's Luncheonette (Brooklyn)
782 Washington Ave.
Prospect Heights, Brooklyn, NY
718-783-8576
Diner or Coffee Shop

Zoe Restaurant (Soho)
90 Prince St.
Manhattan, NY
212-966-6722
New American

Hounds sure are passionate about their favorite flatcakes! And
lemon ricotta pancakes are a burgeoning trend.

How's this sound: citrus-ricotta pancakes with blueberry
compote and crème fraîche? They make 'em at **Zoe**. You get a
stack of three pancakes with the warm blueberry compote and
crème fraîche swirled together melting onto the plate. A small
pitcher of maple syrup is served on the side. The mixture of the

Chowhound Nametag: Caitlin Wheeler

○◯○

Location: Manhattan, New York, New York.

Occupation: Corporate attorney and amateur food writer (livejournal.com/users/amuses).

Cholesterol Level: I don't actually know, but my doctor hasn't been complaining.

Number of Visits to McDonald's in Past Decade: I really can't count (sometimes I want fries or a sausage biscuit—and ten years is a long time).

Farthest Out of the Way Traveled Just for Chow: About thirty-five miles (I live in Manhattan, where everything is within twenty blocks—so that's impressive) from Pasadena to Malibu for lunch at Tavrna Tony, some of the best Greek food I've had in the United States. And it was fabulous.

Top Chinatown Pick: Viet Nam Banh Mi So 1.

Underrated by Chowhounds: Otto—it gets a lot of discussion, but the pizza isn't bad—it's just a different style from New York pizza. It tastes a lot like pizza I've had in France.

Favorite Comfort Chow: French onion soup at Les Halles, or pho from Anh.

Guilty Pleasure: Deep-fried zucchini blossoms.

Favorite Gelato Flavor: Olive oil at Otto. Or rum raisin ice cream (not gelato) from Wentworth's in Hamden, Connecticut.

Favorite Mail Order Chow: Dark and white *panforte* from www.igourmet.com (the closest I've found to authentic Sienese panforte) and Fortnum and Mason Queen Anne tea (unfortunately no longer available in the United States, but you can get it online at www.fortnumandmason.com).

Chowhounding Rule of Thumb: Order something you wouldn't make at home—you won't be tempted to say, "I could make better."

Favorite Afternoon Snack: Hobnobs (British wheatmeal cookies/biscuits) with sharp cheddar cheese.

compote, crème fraîche, and syrup with the lighter than air texture of the pancakes is wonderful, says *raw60*, who admits the $11.50 price tag is steep, but says the pancakes are well worth it.

Pancakes "should be light, delicate and soft and have a quality that could best be described as smooth, inside and out," insists *Clarissa*. "The syrup should grace the outside with enough absorption to enhance without soaking." Such are the plain, buttermilk pancakes at **Sarabeth's**. Chowhound *adam* loves Sarabeth's lemon-ricotta pancakes—delicate as air, good syrup, and a grace note of fresh blackberries.

It seems like nobody makes a wider variety of pancakes than **Shopsins**, but feelings persist that the old Shopsins was better than the current incarnation. Recommended: Slutty Pancakes and Mac and Cheese Pancakes.

Lemon ricotta pancakes and also gingerbread pancakes with sour cream, walnuts, and bananas are recommended at **good**. Check out their cheesy arepas (sort of Colombian corn pancakes), too.

The pancakes at **Mitchel London Foods** are terrific, and (Clinton location only), your order is bottomless. The cakes are small, light, fluffy, and creamy says *yumyam3* (also nice sandwiches, macaroni and cheese, and baked goods). Mitchel London also provides the food for **Fairway Market's** dining room.

Pancakes at **Cafe Luluc** in Brooklyn win a rave from *mm* "Slightly crispy, buttery, moist and the perfect balance between fluffy/dense. And wonderful flavor, not too sweet, not too starchy, just purely yummy. So delicious!"

Lemon ricotta pancakes at **Tom's Luncheonette**, also in Brooklyn, are very tasty (and the warmth and generosity of the service are unsurpassed).

○ **Fairway Market**: see also p. 53.
○ **good Restaurant**: see also p. 42.
○ **Sarabeth's**: see also p. 22.

Three Food Stands in
FLUSHING

AA Plaza (Queens)
Main St. next to LIRR station,
    south of 40th Rd.
Flushing, Queens, NY
Chinese

Octopus Man (Queens)
38–18 Prince St., in front of
    Laifood
Flushing, Queens, NY
Chinese

Fresh Noodle Soup Stand (Queens)
40–48 Main St., in Mayflower
   Plaza Food Court
Flushing, Queens, NY
Chinese

All courtesy of *Eric Eto*:

Don't be put off by the lack of English signage at the **fresh noodle soup stand** in the Mayflower Food Court, where noodles look oh-so-inviting. Beef noodle soup is really satisfying. The noodles are the best part, slightly chewy and about the width of thick linguine, and stewed beef chunks are tender and not overpowered with five-spice, as in other places. The broth is just slightly lacking, but all together, a good bowl of noodles. Check out the other stands in that same food court, including a Taiwanese noodle shop, an attractive buffet, two Sichuan stands, an ice dessert and tea stand, and a sushi stand.

AA Plaza is a sidewalk window/counter next to the Flushing LIRR station. There are about eight people making dumplings, fried noodles, and a few fried things for cheap and quick eating. Most appealing: steamed buns (xiao long bao), essentially a cross between a steamed bun and a soup dumpling. The wrapper is made from thick airy steamed bun pastry, but the filling is more like the pork soup dumpling. The liquid in the filling gets soaked up in the bun. Four for $1.

The **Octopus Man** has changed his corn-roasting methodology, and not for the better, either. Instead of starting with a fresh ear, he's starting to preboil them and then grill. The problem is that the corn is completely overboiled, preventing any charring on the grill, and making the kernels way too soft and mushy. But the rest of the grilled items, including octopus, are still done the same way as ever.

Exciting **FOIE GRAS** at Jean Georges . . . Informally

Nougatine (Upper West Side)
1 Central Park West at Jean Georges Restaurant in the
   Trump International Hotel
Manhattan, NY
212-299-3900
French

Foie gras (part of a five-course, $65 tasting menu) shines at **Nougatine**, the informal café housed within Jean Georges, where it's served in a very light but complex sauce that's slightly sweet, tart, and vaguely scented with cloves. The meat is a tad porky (pancetta?) tasting, and is a tad crispy outside and tender inside, reports *Faren*, whose dinner also included delicious Chilean sea bass and sliced veal with beets . . . plus opulent desserts.

FOUR SEASONS

Four Seasons (Midtown East)
99 E. 52nd St.
Manhattan, NY
212-754-9494
French/New American

Get the duck, which is a candidate for the city's best, with its crispy skin and just enough fattiness for flavor, raves *eater*. An order serves two, and comes with an ever-changing selection of fruit sauces. Final preparation's tableside.

   Also recommended: venison carpaccio with white truffles, and chateaubriand (also for two). Individual soufflés get the nod for dessert.

○ **Four Seasons:** *see also* p. 266.

FRENCH BISTROS AND BRASSERIES

Brasserie Montparnasse
(Lower Manhattan)
44 Beaver St.
Manhattan, NY
212-344-9160
French Brasserie

Café Luxembourg
(Upper West Side)
200 W. 70th St.
Manhattan, NY
212-873-7411
French Bistro

Casimir Restaurant (East Village)
103 Avenue B
Manhattan, NY
212-358-9683
French Bistro

Country Café (Soho)
69 Thompson St.
Manhattan, NY
212-966-5417
French Bistro/Moroccan

Le Gigot (Greenwich Village)
18 Cornelia St.
Manhattan, NY
212-627-3737
French Bistro

Les Halles (Gramercy)
411 Park Ave. S.
Manhattan, NY
212-679-4111
French Brasserie

Les Halles Downtown
(Lower Manhattan)
15 John St.
Manhattan, NY
212-285-8585
French Brasserie

Lucien (East Village)
14 1st Ave.
Manhattan, NY
212-260-6481
French Bistro

Seppi's Restaurant
(Midtown West)
123 W. 56th St., in the
Parker Meridien Hotel
Manhattan, NY
212-708-7444
French Bistro/Pan-Asian Fusion

Montparnasse serves solid food in a lively but uncrowded setting. Coq au vin is recommended.

Les Halles is best know for steak frites, but also serves other classic bistro fare, including great onion soup. The downtown location has a larger menu, but service has been an issue.

Country Café is quaint and casual, and their typical French café food is tasty, says *Su-Lynn*, who likes steak frites, moules frites, and duck confit.

FAB praises **Café Luxembourg's** terrific $22 grilled hanger steak with sides of mashed potatoes and string beans. The wine list isn't extensive, but it's good and inexpensive.

Tiny **Le Gigot** has a classic bistro menu and a relaxed and un-pretentious atmosphere. Try steak au poivre ($25) or their signature lamb dish.

Casimir may be in the midst of an upswing; *MICAH* reports several excellent meals here. Service is very good-natured if not always efficient.

Despite its hotel location, **Seppi's** is a comfortable and un-touristy French bistro with surprising reach: risottos, Asian touches like Vietnamese summer rolls, and an emphasis on mix-and-match small plates. Good wine, and ambience that encourages unwinding. Run by the same team that run's Raoul's, the long-running hip French bistro in Soho.

Lucien is a relaxing spot where you'll never feel rushed.

FRENCH TOAST Tips
(Both Mexican and Gringo)

La Palapa (East Village)
77 St. Marks Pl.
Manhattan, NY
212-777-2537
Mexican

Taste (Upper East Side)
1413 3rd Ave.
Manhattan, NY
212-717-9798
New American

Mexican French toast at **La Palapa** sounds like a typo, but it's not. It's extremely fluffy and rich, covered with spiced dark syrup. Everything is well balanced and delicate; *Aki* would love to have this masterpiece of French toast every weekend. Also good: omelets filled with homemade chorizo and cheese, topped with spicy sauce.

French toast at **Taste** may not be exotic, but it's excellent, says *shortstop*. This is challah French toast that almost tastes like brioche—it's that rich. They must soak it for quite some time in the egg mixture because inside it's like custard. With the sprinkling of sugar baked on top, it almost doesn't need syrup. Portion is large, and everyone at the table will be oohing and ahhing.

Idyllic Outdoor **FRENCH VILLAGE DINING**

Cassis (Lower Manhattan)
52 Stone St.
Manhattan, NY
212-425-3663
French Bistro

Cassis is more convivial than your typical French bistro, reports *djk*, who finds their mussel sauce particularly piquant, shrimp grilled to juicy perfection, pork fantastic, and wine list varied, fairly priced, and stocked with many small producers.

Stone Street is cobblestoned, closed to traffic, and surrounded by low old buildings that block views of nearby skyscrapers. To sit outside at Cassis on a nice night is as close as a Manhattanite can come to the feeling of dining in a small Provençal village.

Is **FRIED CHICKEN** an Extinct Species?

Blue Ribbon Sushi Brooklyn
    (Brooklyn)
280 5th Ave.
Park Slope, Brooklyn, NY
718-840-0404
Japanese

Bubby's Brooklyn (Brooklyn)
1 Main St.
DUMBO, Brooklyn, NY
718-222-0666
American

El Sitio Restaurant (Queens)
68-28 Roosevelt Ave.
Woodside, Queens, NY
718-424-2369
Cuban

Jack's Fifth Ave Popeyes
 (Brooklyn)
519 Fifth Ave.
Park Slope, Brooklyn, NY
718-965-8675
American

Maroons (Chelsea)
244 W. 16th St.
Manhattan, NY
212-206-8640
Southern/Jamaican

New Caporal Fried Chicken
 (Washington Heights)
3772 Broadway
Manhattan, NY
212-862-8986
American

Popeyes Chicken & Biscuits
 (Citywide)
ww.popeyes.com.
Southern

The recent decline in the quality of fat used in the local fried chicken scene has lowered your chances of finding deliciousness. Lard has been replaced by cheap oils, ranked by *Mark DiBlasi* as soybean oil (awful), canola oil (slightly less awful), or fry-max (really, really awful).

- One solution is to look upmarket to a place like **Blue Ribbon**, which can afford to use higher quality ingredients in its $24 fried chicken. The ultimate compliment: even a confirmed vegetarian like *allydee* finds their fried chicken worth breaking form for.
- You can't miss **New Caporal Fried Chicken**: its large awning has a gun-toting chicken on it. *David* says these militant birds boast a tasty Latin marinade. Open 24/7.
- Fried chicken at **Maroons** has a peppery crust. Check out their fried tomatoes.
- **Jack's Fifth Ave.,** opt for buttermilk fried chicken with tangy, perfectly crisp crust, says *Blaise*.
- Rumor has it that **Bubby's** serves very good fried chicken.
- It's not exactly American-style fried chicken, but the chicharrones de pollo at **el Sitio** might satisfy your fried poultry cravings.

Finally, it's well worth noting that while few discuss it on Chowhound, an amazing number of those profiled for this guide (and our SF one) mentioned **Popeyes Fried Chicken** as their top guilty pleasure.

- **Bubby's Brooklyn:** *see also* **p. 221.**
- **Maroons:** *see also* **p. 151.**

FRIES, Frites, Fritas, Etc.

Artisanal (Murray Hill)
2 Park Ave.; enter on 32nd St.
Manhattan, NY
212-725-8585
French

Bonnie's Grill (Brooklyn)
278 Fifth Ave.
Park Slope, Brooklyn, NY
718-369-9527
American

Café de Bruxelles
   (Greenwich Village)
118 Greenwich Ave.
Manhattan, NY
212-206-1830
Belgian

Chimichurri Grill (Clinton)
606 9th Ave.
Manhattan, NY
212-586-8655
Argentinian

The Chip Shop (Brooklyn)
383 5th Ave.
Park Slope, Brooklyn, NY
718-832-7701
British

Coffee Shop (Union Square)
29 Union Sq. W.
Manhattan, NY
212-243-7969
American/Brazilian

F & B (Chelsea)
269 W. 23rd St.
Manhattan, NY
646-486-4441
American/Belgian

Fred's at Barneys New York
   (Upper East Side)
10 E. 61st St., 9th Fl.
Manhattan, NY
212-833-2200
New American

Heights Café (Brooklyn)
84 Montague St.
Brooklyn Heights, Brooklyn, NY
718-625-5555
New American

Katz's Delicatessen
  (Lower East Side)
205 E. Houston St.
Manhattan, NY
212-254-2246
Eastern European Jewish

Le Gamin Cafe
  (Greenwich Village)
132 Houston St.
Manhattan, NY
212-673-4592
French

Pastis (Greenwich Village)
9 9th Ave.
Manhattan, NY
212-929-4844
French Bistro

Potato Republic (Queens)
70-15 Austin St.
Forest Hills, Queens, NY
718-261-4227
Eclectic

Sparky's American Food
  (Brooklyn)
135A N. 5th St.
Williamsburg, Brooklyn, NY
718-302-5151
American

'21' Club (Midtown West)
21 W. 52nd St.
Manhattan, NY
212-582-7200
New American

In the quest for exceptional french fries, chowhounds, as always, consider all levels of restaurants openmindedly. Manhattan first:

- **'21' Club's** fries are served in a white cloth napkin. Perfect french fries—not too thick, not too thin, and nary a blemish or stray skin to be found.
- At the inviting, sophisticated bar of **Café De Bruxelles**, fries are served as in Belgium: in a stainless steel cup with homemade mayonnaise. They're double fried, too— impeccably authentic. Good selection of Belgian ales.
- **Artisanal**, very popular with chowhounds for lots of good things, also serves excellent fries.
- **Katz's** deli has great steak fries. Fried dark, but cut so thick they're soft, like a baked potato inside. According to *2 slices*, who made inquiries, the counterguy confessed they're frozen . . . but they're still great!
- Fries can be ordered drizzled with truffle butter at **F & B.**
- At **Chimichurri Grill**, thin-cut fries come seasoned with garlic, salt, and parsley.
- **Pastis** serves both shoestring and thick-cut fries, with béarnaise sauce for dipping.

- At **Coffee Shop,** cheese fries come topped with Velveeta-like cheese, and they're perfect when you're tipsy at 3:00 a.m., says *jacinthe*.
- Also good: **Le Gamin** and **Fred's**.

In Brooklyn:

- **Bonnie's Grill** has the best fries under the sun (not Belgian-style, but nonetheless megadelicious, says *jt*).
- **Heights Cafe** has supernal fries, best with their equally excellent burger.
- When you name your place **"The Chip Shop,"** your fries better be good. Try them with malt vinegar.
- **Sparky's American Food** serves freshly cut, crispy fries with perfect flavor.

In Queens:

- **Potato Republic** (aka Papal Republic) is a Belgian-style frites shop offering a host of toppings including curry, cheese, mayo, and more. Near 71st/Continental stop on the E, F.

○ Artisanal: *see also* **pp. 32, 66, 207, 266.**
○ Pastis: *see also* **p. 43.**

GARDEN CAFE: Romantic, Delicious, and Refined

Garden Cafe (Brooklyn)
620 Vanderbilt Ave.
Prospect Heights,
Brooklyn, NY
718-857-8863
New American

The **Garden Cafe** serves a frequently changing menu of supremely delicious food, well presented, in a romantic environment. It's small (only nine tables) but not cramped, with a refined atmosphere that makes it feel like you're dining in someone's house. The cooking is of the "over" school: *Faren* swoons over their foie gras with fresh currants and onion compote, lightly cooked scallops over lentils, rib lamb chops over pureed white beans, and sliced duck breast over sweet potatoes with grilled cabbage.

Louise reports delicious red snapper (poached with truffles in butter and served over bok choy) and tender rack of venison (over a bed of mashed sweet potato, with an overly sweet berry reduction sauce). Midweek they offer a three-course prix fixe dinner for just $25.

GELATO in Ossining

Sapori D'Italia (Westchester County)
181 Croton Ave. (Rte. 133)
Ossining, NY
914-923-0501
Italian

Sapori D'Italia makes the best gelato *Josh Mittleman* has had this side of Rome—and he's been searching for real gelato ever since he returned from Italy. Pistachio tastes like pistachios rather than sugar. Blueberry tastes like blueberries. Pineapple to die for.

GELATO AND SORBET IN MANHATTAN

Ambrosia Cafe (Grand Central)
158 E. 45th.
Manhattan, NY
212-661-1717
French/Italian Café

Bussola Annex (East Village)
65 4th Ave.
Manhattan, NY
212-254-1940
Italian Ice Cream or Gelato

Fauchon (Upper East Side)
1000 Madison Ave.
Manhattan, NY
212-570-2211
French Café

Il Laboratorio del Gelato
  (Lower East Side)
95 Orchard St.
Manhattan, NY
212-343-9922
Italian

In the middle of a heat wave, anything frozen tastes great. But hounds say these places deliver the goods even when the weather's less beastly.

Pistachio gelato at **Il Laboratorio del Gelato** is an earthy color, much closer to that of green tea than the usual Day-Glo green. *Iron Frank* says it's the truest pistachio flavor he's ever tasted in a gelato. The bits of ground pistachio provided the ideal extra bit of textural contrast.

Check out marsala-flavored gelato at **Bussola Annex**. *Aki* finds it overly sweet, but the texture is just right and it has full flavor of marsala. Every gelato is great here, especially having them with the cannoli shell!

Fauchon has a host of unusual sorbet flavors, and large single scoops are a bargain at just $1.50. *mt* reports mango-ginger finishes nicely with a fresh ginger taste, while raspberry-chile's fruit is juicy and thick—and the chile tastes like roasted serrano, but without the heat. Other flavors include peach-lavender, curry-mango, rose petal and crème brûlée.

We've heard raves for the gelato at **Ambrosia Cafe**. *ChowLad* describes it as impeccably rich and creamy yet also soft and light, with intense, clean, fresh flavor.

○ **Fauchon:** *see also* **pp. 97, 161.**

Venerable Queens **GERMAN**

Celtic Gasthaus (Queens)
64-04 Myrtle Ave.
Ridgewood, Queens, NY
718-456-8341
German

Forest Pork Store (Queens)
6639 Forest Ave.
Ridgewood, Queens, NY
718-497-2853
German

Gebhardt's (Queens)
65-06 Myrtle Ave.
Ridgewood, Queens, NY
718-821-5567
German

Karl Ehmer Quality Meats
  (Queens)
63-35 Fresh Pond Rd.
Ridgewood, Queens, NY
718-456-8100
German

Von Westernhagen Restaurant
  (Queens)
7128 Cooper Ave.
Ridgewood, Queens, NY
718-821-8401
German

Zum Stammtisch (Queens)
6946 Myrtle Ave.
Ridgewood, Queens, NY
718-386-3014
Austrian/German

German-born *knoedel* is horrified at how badly many chow-hounds report ordering at legendary **Zum Stammtisch** restaurant and has set us straight. Avoid sauerbraten, which is both too sweet and too sour, he says. Stay away from jaegerschnitzel as well. Instead, try steak tartar (a southern German variation), *schsenmaul salat* (sliced tongue), *bayrische bauern platte* (an assortment of great items like smoked pork chops and leberkaese, "grilled" camembert—actually breaded and fried), and the Westphalian ham sandwich (request the ham sliced thinly). In general, avoid anything with gravy, as it's terribly generic. The home fries are pretty greasy, but you can substitute potato dumplings. For dessert, stick with the strudel or *eier eis* (ice cream topped with egg liquor). If you enjoy schnitzel but want to avoid that gravy, *Wayne* recommends off-menu Wiener schnitzel a la Holstein. Also good: cucumber salad.

If you somehow still find yourself craving meat after dinner, stop for some cuts and wursts at **Forest Pork Store** or **Karl Ehmer**.

Other German restaurants in the area to check out include the long-forgotten **Von Westernhagen**, and **Gebhardt's**, which has great food but lacks the charming ambience of Zum Stammtisch. And then there's **Celtic Gasthaus**, formerly Hans Gasthaus, where Irish have taken over—hence that inexplicable name—but the old German chef remains (dinners only). The place used to be known for rouladen, but for all we know, it's gone corned beef.

- ○ **Forest Pork Store:** *see also* **p. 260.**
- ○ **Karl Ehmer Quality Meats:** *see also* **p. 260.**

GHANAIAN Food Primer

Abay (Bronx)
2364 Jerome Ave., just south of
    Fordham Rd. 4 train station
Bronx, NY
718-220-1300
Ghanaian

Giftanco (Queens)
97-09 57th Ave.
Corona, Queens, NY
718-760-3897
Ghanaian

Kowus African Carribean (Bronx)
3396 3rd Ave.
Bronx, NY
718-401-6232
Ghanaian/Caribbean

Unnamed store in the basement
    of Lefrak City (Queens)
9608 57th Ave.
Corona, Queens, NY
Ghanaian

None of the city's Ghanaian restaurants have menus. You have to know what you're looking for, though you'll find Ghanaians generally friendly and glad to help you appreciate their cuisine. All the restaurants are open late to accommodate Ghanaian cab drivers and hospital workers.

Abay has bulletproof glass but is otherwise a cheery, well-lit space. You might get special help if you speak to owner Rama, and tell her Jill sent you. (We know her as *JH Jill* . . . and she's the source of all this info.) There's no glass at Kowus, so communication's easier, but the seating area is drearier.

Both restaurants serve the staple soups, usually a spicy light one and an earthy groundnut one. At **Kowus**, add fish or goat to the soup. Go for beef or chicken (or a combination) at Abay. Eat the soups (using your right hand, as with all African dining), and accompany with *fufu* (plantain, yam, or cassava paste), *banku* (fermented plantain paste), or, at Kowus, a ball of rice. Other add-ins: okro-spinach (adds a slimy texture), *waatchie* (spicy rice-bean mixture), *gari* (sauteed cassava meal).

Kenke is a very popular Ashanti meal not for the faint-hearted: a boiled, fermented corn tamalelike ball wrapped in corn husk, quite fragrant, served with fish or sardines from the can, some fresh *shito* (very hot sauce), and, at Kowus, some pureed ginger. This is all eaten with the hand, right only, please.

Giftanco and, across the street, the **shop in the basement of Lefrak City** (just enter the basement commercial area and go to the right) are both retail shops with a very strong smell from the smoked fish piled around. Ask the clerks or other customers to help you pick out choice African yams to buy. Also: fufu flour, kenke (either the corn-husk or Fante-style one wrapped in banana leaf—get the handmade ones), shito, *dzomi* (palm oil), sardines, as well as stomach remedies like Alafia bitters. You'll also find some British goods like Horlick's malted milk powder, ginger cookies, and digestive biscuits.

○ **Kowus African Carribean:** *see also* p. 281.

The Plumpest and Most Tender
GNOCCHI

'Cesca (Upper West Side)
164 W. 75th St.
Manhattan, NY
212-787-6300
Italian

Gramercy Tavern (Gramercy)
42 E. 20th St.
Manhattan, NY
212-477-0777
New American

Lupa Restaurant
  (Greenwich Village)
170 Thompson St.
Manhattan, NY
212-982-5089
Italian

Peasant (Little Italy)
194 Elizabeth St.
Manhattan, NY
212-965-9511
Italian

Pepolino Restaurant (Soho)
281 W. Broadway
Manhattan, NY
212-966-9983
Italian

Piccola Venezia Restaurant
  (Queens)
42-01 28th Ave.
Astoria, Queens, NY
718-721-8470
Italian/Istrian

Queen Italian Restaurant
(Brooklyn)
84 Court St.
Brooklyn Heights, Brooklyn, NY
718-596-5954
Italian

Savoia Pizzeria (Brooklyn)
277 Smith St.
Cobble Hill, Brooklyn, NY
718-797-2727
Italian

According to *doc*, gnocchi are deceptively simple to make, requiring only a couple of ingredients but masterful technique to make them light enough. His standout: gnocchi in gorgonzola sauce served at **Piccola Venezia**. The gnocchi at **Lupa** are fresh, delicious, and generally incredible, raves *J.D.*. *M.K.* sampled some top-notch gnocchi as part of a tasting menu at **Gramercy Tavern**. Brooklyn hounds should head to **Queen Restaurant** for gnocchi with choice of sauce. **Pepolino** makes great gnocchi, and the ones at **Peasant** are reliably good. Gnocci at **'Cesca** and **Savoia** are highly praised in reports elsewhere in this guide.

- **'Cesca:** see also p. 61.
- **Gramercy Tavern:** see also pp. 104, 250.
- **Peasant:** see also p. 250.
- **Queen Italian Restaurant:** see also p. 170.
- **Savoia Pizzeria:** see also p. 270.

Inexpensive **GRAND CENTRAL AREA LUNCHES**

Bel Paese Italian Deli
(Grand Central)
459 Lexington Ave.
Manhattan, NY
212-697-4736
Italian Deli

Cafe Zaiya (Murray Hill)
18 E. 41st St.
Manhattan, NY
212-779-0600
Japanese

Chez Laurence (Murray Hill)
245 Madison Ave.
Manhattan, NY
212-683-0284
French

Evergreen Shanghai (Murray Hill)
10 E. 38th St.
Manhattan, NY
212-448-1199
Chinese (Shanghai)

Masa's (Grand Central)
89 E. 42nd St.
Manhattan, NY
212-972-3688
Japanese

Menchanko-Tei Restaurant
  (Grand Central)
131 E. 45th St., 1st Fl.
Manhattan, NY
212-986-6805
Japanese

Milant's Gourmet Sandwiches
  (Murray Hill)
158 E. 39th St.
Manhattan, NY
212-682-0111
Sandwich Shop

Tony's (Midtown East)
817 2nd Ave.
Manhattan, NY
212-697-8848
Italian Sandwich Shop

Trini-Pak Boyz (Midtown West)
43rd St. and 6th Ave.
Manhattan, NY
Pakistani/Trinidadian

Yagura Market (Grand Central)
24 E. 41st St.
Manhattan, NY
212-679-3777
Japanese

Hounds aren't thrilled with the Grand Central Food Court, but there are inexpensive lunch options in the neighborhood around the terminal. It's a tough area to crack, though, so bear in mind that many of the following places are good-not-great (we figure that those who must eat locally will be glad for even marginal improvement!). Sushi at **Masa's** is consistently outstandingly fresh and delicious, reports *Dan Sonenberg*, who particularly likes their heavenly little *inari zushi* (sweet rice wrapped in bean curd). They also make a fab seaweed salad that's a sensational bargain. **Trini-Pak Boyz** is a hot spot for much-loved curry chicken (or lamb) over rice ($4.50 for the large size chicken, $6 for the lamb). **Milant's Gourmet Sandwiches** makes really good soup, sandwiches, and coffee. *Jeremy Osner* recommends three-bean soup, pesto chicken with sun-dried tomatoes and mozzarella, fine baba ghanoush. **Tony's** has incredible food at very low prices, says *Mike V*, who recommends chicken parm hero or plate with a side of pasta for $6. Meatball parm and sausage parm sandwiches also rock, though you may want to forgo the inferior cheese. Fridays, it's calamari or shrimp with pasta. **Cafe Zaiya** makes good karaage chicken sandwiches and curry doughnuts, but some say the place is overpriced. **Bel Paese Italian Deli** does good hot and cold Italian subs. **Evergreen Shanghai** is a reliable standby for Shanghai food. Good soup dumplings, and a lunch special with ribboned tofu, pork, and preserved vegetables. **Menchanko-Tei's** inexpensive Berkshire pork tonkatsu ramen is consistently terrific. **Yagura Market** is a Japanese market and lunch counter with really cheap, competent food. They serve oden in cool weather. And **Chez Laurence** makes a real good weekend brunch.

See also Grab Something to Eat in *Bryant Park*.

Plus see the nabe index for other nearby choices.

- **Chez Laurence:** *see also* p. 42.
- **Menchanko-Tei Restaurant:** *see also* p. 179.
- **Tony's:** *see also* pp. 72, 173.
- **Trini-Pak Boyz:** *see also* p. 58.
- **Yagura Market:** *see also* p. 48.

GRAND SICHUAN

Grand Sichuan International
  (Clinton)
745 9th Ave.
Manhattan, NY
212-582-2288
Chinese (Sichuan)

Grand Sichuan NY (Murray Hill)
227 Lexington Ave.
Manhattan, NY
212 679-9770
Chinese (Sichuan)

Grand Sichuan International East
  (Midtown East)
1049 2nd Ave.
Manhattan, NY
212-355-5855
Chinese (Sichuan)

Chowhounds love the Grand Sichuan restaurants, and constantly try to track what's best at each. The situation (like most chow phenomena) is ever changing, but here are two of our more recent reports:

Huo guo is a spectacularly spicy hot-pot dish regularly available only on the menu written in Chinese at the Lexington Avenue location of Grand Sichuan International, but it can be had at the Clinton branch if you phone ahead. It comes in white and red varieties, and red is the spicy one. *Minna* says various veggies and meats (especially kidneys) are good to dip into the broth.

The Second Avenue branch of Grand Sichuan International has added to its menu four pages of new-school Sichuan cooking not available anywhere else in the city. Chong qing spicy and aromatic chicken is an overflowing mass of small hot peppers, with some plump chunks of chicken thrown in for good measure. The chicken picks up a bit of heat and a lot of flavor from the chilis. The more blackened peppers are addictively hot and the others are incendiary. Also great: new-style Sichuan orange beef that's tender, spicy, and a bit sweet—just perfect, says *Iron Frank*. But avoid soup dumplings with tough wrappers and a lack of juice. Not everything is consistently delicious, so try ordering a variety of items and eat selectively.

○ Grand Sichuan International: *see also* p. 254.

Crispy, Sweet GRASSHOPPERS

Taka (Greenwich Village)
61 Grove St.
Manhattan, NY
212-242-3699
Japanese

Along with sushi served on pottery made by the restaurant's owner, Taka serves a special of crispy, sweet grasshoppers, $3 for ten. They crunch when you bite into them, reports *daniel*, and have a sweet sake taste.

Chowhound Nametag: the fedex guy

○◯○

Neighborhood:
Maspeth.

Occupation:
I deliver for FedEx in Jackson Heights.

Cholesterol Level:
On the high side.

Nabe Most Full of Explorable Unknown Chow: I wanna go to Williamsburg; I think they have tons of new places, cool food and atmosphere. So far I've only tried Vera Cruz on Bedford Avenue for Mexican. I liked it—get roasted corn on cob.

Top Chinatown Pick: I like Wo Hop (downstairs only, cuz I remember the upstairs suckin').

Underrated by Chowhounds: Nina's Italian in Greenpoint, on Kingsland and Meeker Aves, real Italian—great chick francese, $11 . . . as well as fresh fish. Also really love King Wah Chinese, in Jackson Heights on Northern Blvd. between Sixty-ninth and Seventieth Streets, across from Wendy's: awesome boneless ribs. Been goin' there since high school, 1985.

Weight Management Tip:
Drink vodka with cranberry and OJ instead of soda.

Chowhounding Rule of Thumb: Ask waitress (youngest one in restaurant) what is good or fresh—what was made today. The generic answer you always get is "everything." I follow up with "what is *really* good;" then they tend to open up.

Inner Borough **GREEK**

Ethos (Murray Hill)
495 3rd Ave.
Manhattan, NY
212-252-1972
Greek

Molyvos (Midtown West)
871 7th Ave
Manhattan, NY
212-582-7500
Greek

Pelagos (Upper West Side)
103 W. 77th St.
Manhattan, NY
212-579-1112
Greek

Pylos (East Village)
128 E. 7th St.
Manhattan, NY
212-473-0220
Greek

Snack Taverna
  (Greenwich Village)
63 Bedford St.
Manhattan, NY
212-929-3499
Greek

Thalassa (Tribeca)
179 Franklin St.
Manhattan, NY
212-941-7661
Greek

Trata Estiatorio
  (Upper East Side)
1331 2nd Ave.
Manhattan, NY
212-535-3800
Greek

As Astoria diversifies via an influx of new immigrant groups, and the once-vaunted Greek restaurants flounder, their quality declining, Manhattan, of all places, is looking more and more like the place for good Greek food.

David Lerner proclaims **Pylos** the best country-style Greek restaurant since Ithaka left the Village. It's run by cookbook author Diane Kochilas and her husband. Try the eggplant dip, complemented by top-notch pita; *saganaki*; spicy goat filo wrap appetizer (one of a trio of filo fillings); and very tender clay-baked pork medallions in mushroom and wine sauce. There's a selection of Greek wines to match.

Ethos started out as an Italian place but has busted out as a Greek restaurant serving great, generously portioned fish and meat dishes. Excellent meze include terrific Greek salad, feta spiked with fresh jalapeños, and well-spiced tzatziki, all accompanied by fresh, toasty bread. Fresh branzini, red snapper, flounder, sea bass, striped bass, St. Pierre fish, and sardines are displayed on ice, priced by the pound, cooked to simple perfection with olive oil, and served with lemon wedges. Everyone seems to particularly love Ethos' grilled octopus. Meat dishes are equally good. Moussaka and lamb stew are delicious and beautifully presented in attractive clay pots. Wait staff is very polite and attentive, and happy to fillet and debone.

At **Pelagos**, *newsjoke* praises grilled octopus, salads, and pan-fried smelts as absolutely delicious. You just put the whole little fish in your mouth, bones and all, chew it a bit and swallow— kind of like eating a particularly tasty plate of French fries. Avoid grilled fish, sold by the pound; reportedly bland and not worth the cost.

A fabulous starter of meaty, salty assorted olives at **Snack Taverna** is your first indication of the deliciousness to follow. Large and lemony *dolmades* (stuffed grape leaves), cracklingly fresh *horiatki* (Greek salad), and a dish of tender shrimp and calamari atop a bed of shredded, pickled beets are among the best mezes. A rich and tasty lamb shoulder makes for a great main course, and delicious desserts include a complex dish of extra-creamy rice pudding with traces of sour cranberry, and poached figs in wine with manouri cheese and pistachios. All-Greek wine list.

Grilled octopus at **Thalassa** is tender and firm without being rubbery, and traditional Greek dips (served with slightly charred pita) are light, fluffy and flavorful, reports *mark*, who says cubed beets served with the dips provide good counter-point.

The menu at **Trata Estiatorio** revolves around fresh fish, grilled with lemon and a little oil, deboned when served and priced by the pound. *Cliff* thinks it's good, though it can't possibly live up to similar fish he's eaten, cooked within an hour of being caught, in Greece. But there are certain things he really, really, likes, such as perfect tarama—rich but light, producing sea reveries he'd previously experienced only with top-notch *uni*. Saganaki is salty, as usual, but full of flavor, and crisp on the outside, oozing inside. Grilled shrimp are amazingly tender, not overcooked at all. Paper-thin, crisp flash-fried zucchini rounds are served with the most luxurious, garlicky tzatziki, a meal in itself.

Terrific appetizers at **Molyvos** (e.g. olives and cheese, stuffed grape leaves, and marinated fluke). But one diner reports saganaki with too much ouzo, and lamb *yuvetsi* underflavored and disappointing. Pop back in for dessert; *antivic69* says the fritters in honey are tasty, but the baklava is totally out of control . . . in a good way, of course.

For more Greek tips, see the cuisine index.

○ **Molyvos:** *see also* p. 267.

The State of Astoria **GREEK**

Athens Cafe (Queens)
32-07 30th Ave.
Astoria, Queens, NY
718-626-2164
Greek

Central (Queens)
20-30 Steinway St.
Astoria, Queens, NY
718-726-1600
Greek

Christos Hasapo-Taverna
  (Queens)
41-08 23rd Ave.
Astoria, Queens, NY
718-777-8400
Greek

Elias Corner (Queens)
24-02 31st St.
Astoria, Queens, NY
718-932-1510
Greek

Kolonaki (Queens)
33-02 Broadway
Astoria, Queens, NY
718-932-8222
Greek

Omonia Cafe (Queens)
32-20 Broadway
Astoria, Queens, NY
718-274-6650
Greek

Romano Famous Pizza (Queens)
32-21 Broadway
Astoria, Queens, NY
718-626-5292
Greek

S'agapo Taverna Ouzeri
  (Queens)
34-21 34th Ave.
Astoria, Queens, NY
718-626-0303
Greek

Stamatis Restaurant (Queens)
31-14 Broadway
Astoria, Queens, NY
718-204-8964
Greek

Taverna Kyclades (Queens)
33-07 Ditmars Blvd
Astoria, Queens, NY
718-545-8666
Greek

Telly's Taverna (Queens)
28-13 23rd Ave.
Astoria, Queens, NY
718-728-9056
Greek

The best strategy for Greek food in Astoria might be a progressive dinner, trying one dish here, another there, as no one place does everything well. Here's the fantasy version, assuming infinite appetite:

- Start at **S'Agapo** for drinks and mezes like tzatziki and skordalia and a great grape leaf dip, plus fish (especially striped bass).
- **Telly's Taverna** does a good job with standard Greek salads and dips, but their specialty's grilled fish. Grilled octopus is amazing: sufficiently charred, tender, full of flavor and oh-so-fresh, raves *Kenzi*.
- Next stop, **Taverna Kyclades** for swordfish kebabs or steaks. If they offer free *galaktoboureko,* have dessert early.
- **Stamatis** is another stop for grilled seafood.
- If you're looking for meat, the lamb chops at **Central** are some of the best in New York City, reports *Natasa Sevoleva*, who says avgolemono soup and steaks are also wonderful (and the lunch-only 'tost' of haloumi loudza is surpassed only by the version at **Athens Cafe**).
- **Christos Hasapo-Taverna** is the place to go for steaks.
- **Romano's** is known for excellent gyros and good souvlaki platters, lamb, tzatziki, french fries, individual pizzas, and serious diner-style burgers. Mixed reports on Greek salad.
- **Kolonaki** and **Omonia** are cafés good for a quick bite. Get spinach pie at Kolonaki and eggs at Omonia.
- **Elias Corner** for dessert: hot honey-cinnamon doughnuts. Other than that, most hound comments are fairly negative on this tourist magnet, but *Katherine Bridges* says if you order in Greek, you might get better food.

Around **GREENPORT, LI**

Bruce's Cafe & Cheese Emporium
(Suffolk County)
208 Main St.
Greenport, NY
631-477-0023
American

Claudios (Suffolk County)
111 Main St.
Greenport, NY
631-477-0627
Seafood

Cliff's Elbow East
(Suffolk County)
Kenneys Rd. & N. Sea Dr.
Southold, NY
631-765-1203
Southern/Steak House

Hellenic Snack Bar
(Suffolk County)
5145 Main Rd.
East Marion, NY
631-477-0138
Greek

The Loft (Suffolk County)
48 Front St.
Greenport, NY
631-477-3080
American

The Seafood Barge
(Suffolk County)
150 Old Main Rd., in Port of
Egypt Marina
Southold, NY
631-765-3010
Seafood

The Loft is atop a deli, and *chrisl* reports outstanding veal meatloaf with grilled zucchini and a terrific shrimp appetizer there. Service has been accommodating toward his noncarb-eating wife, and there's outdoor seating. **Cliff's Elbow East** (aka Cliff's Elbow Room) has good lobster, shrimp, and marinated steaks. **Hellenic Snack Bar** has very tasty Greek food. **Bruce's** is a good place to pick up casual snacks and sandwiches. Solid deli and decent cheese selection. As the name implies, the **Seafood Barge** has a good selection of fish and seafood. **Claudio's** boasts beautiful views of the harbor and a great old bar, though the kitchen staff (and thus quality) varies from season to season.

Dairy Overload (**GRILLED CHEESE + MILK SHAKES?**)

Be-Speckled Trout
  (Greenwich Village)
422 Hudson St.
Manhattan, NY
212-255-1421
Ice Cream or Gelato

Ray's Candy Shop (East Village)
113 Avenue A
Manhattan, NY
Ice Cream or Gelato

Original New York Milkshake
  Company (East Village)
37 St Marks Pl.
Manhattan, NY
212-505-5200
Ice Cream or Gelato

Original New York Milkshake Company is not for the lactose intolerant. The entire menu is shakes, malts, waffle ice cream sandwiches, egg creams . . . and grilled cheese sandwiches. (Oddly, they don't serve ice cream.) Shakes (made from Double Rainbow ice cream from San Francisco) come in flavors like espresso bean, green tea, and ginger. Despite the mall-like look, the malteds are good—the vanilla is thick and satisfying—says *bryant*. *Jim Leff* finds the milk shakes just ok, but loves their grilled cheeses, which come in about a half-dozen varieties. *ThorNYC* agrees, finding them sublime. The girls behind the counter wear matching orange and yellow uniforms and paper hats, all of which match the bright decor.

Other milk shake advice:

Jim Leff vastly prefers milk shakes at **Ray's Candy Shop**, and, even better, malteds. Ray's egg creams are famous, but Leff doesn't love them. But he finds their shakes and malteds superb.

Be-Speckled Trout is the milk shake mecca for the vast majority of chowhounds. The place itself is a time-machine recreation of an old-fashioned soda fountain, complete with malteds and milk shakes the way they used to be. The place is, in a word, unbelievable, says *Faren*. Their chocolate malted is the real thing, made with Horlicks Malted Milk crushed by the owner, who's a real purist (gets his milk from a special source to ensure it has the right amount of fat in it, makes his own sauces, syrups, and so on). And we don't know of any other place serving sour cherry milk shakes. Also: lots of penny candies, four varieties of licorice, and homemade chocolates. There's no menu. If you crave something, they'll make it for you. In cold weather, they make a nice creamy/milky hot chocolate. The big caveat on Be-Speckled Trout is to only order prepared-to-order stuff like shakes when the man's there, since the older woman doesn't make them nearly as well.

Kissable **GRITS**

Jerry's (Soho)
101 Prince St.
Manhattan, NY
212-966-9464
New American

Kitchenette (Tribeca)
80 W. Broadway
Manhattan, NY
212-267-6740
American/Diner or Coffee Shop

Kitchenette Uptown (Harlem)
1272 Amsterdam Ave.
Manhattan, NY
212-531-7600
American/Diner or Coffee Shop

Maroons (Chelsea)
244 W. 16th St.
Manhattan, NY
212-206-8640
Southern/Jamaican

Miracle Grill (East Village)
112 1st Ave., #2a
Manhattan NY
212-254-2353
American

The Pink Tea Cup
   (Greenwich Village)
42 Grove St.
Manhattan, NY
212-807-6755
Southern

Virgil's Real BBQ
   (Theater District)
152 W. 44th St.
Manhattan NY
212-921-9494
Barbecue

While many Northerners just don't see the point of grits, Southerners get cravings.

Shrimp and grits, available at brunch at **Maroons**, are slow cooked with cream and served with a fiery combination of hot pepper, onion, and tomato. **Virgil's BBQ** has amazing cheese grits, with good texture and sharp cheese flavor, reports *elvislives*, who also likes the interestingly seasoned large-grained grits at **Miracle Grill**. Large-sized grits are cheesy at **Jerry's**.

Grits can be added to any of the artery-clogging breakfasts at the **Pink Tea Cup** (take in the wall-mounted photos of luminaries ranging from soap stars to leaders of the civil rights movement in the 1960s). *Jim Leff* recommends their cheese grits. Chowhound fave **Kitchenette** also serves grits.

- **Kitchenette:** *see also* **pp. 42, 103, 205, 240, 280.**
- **Maroons:** *see also* **p. 131.**
- **Miracle Grill:** *see also* **p. 121.**
- **The Pink Tea Cup:** *see also* **p. 280.**

The Last Place You'd Look for Good **GUACAMOLE**

Bar @ Etats-Unis (Upper East Side)
247 E. 81st St.
Manhattan, NY
212-396-9928
French/New American/Wine Bar

French wine bar Etats-Unis is the last place in the world you'd expect to find amazing guacamole (outside of, maybe, a Chinese takeout in Reykjavik), but a couple of hounds say they've got the goods. The Mexican kitchen staff makes it to order, and *Eddie Bennet* says it has a perfect blend of lime juice and cilantro and heat. Besides the guac, he recommends their wine list and chocolate soufflé.

End-of-the-Line **GUYANESE**

Foo On Chinese Restaurant (Queens)
183-04 Hillside Ave.
Jamaica, Queens, NY
718-297-1287
Guyanese/Chinese

At the last stop on the F train in Queens there's a restaurant run by a Guyanese woman (who cooks West Indian) and a Chinese cook (who cooks Chinese). Chowhound *queue* enjoyed falling-off-the-bone chicken curry, cut into small pieces in a deep-dark curry sauce reminiscent of Japanese curries. Other diners have been spotted enjoying the house's most popular dish, chicken fried rice.

Unlikely **HASH BROWNS**

Izakaya Riki (Grand Central)
141 E. 45th St.
Manhattan, NY
212-986-5604
Japanese

World Famous Ray's Pizza
  (Greenwich Village)
595 Ave. of the Americas
Manhattan, NY
212-620-4181
Italian/Pizza

CKOne says hash browns at **Izakaya Riki** would make her Iowa grandmother proud. Alas, this restaurant serves them not for breakfast but at dinner only. Of course, they're not called hash browns. Order *hosogiri no potato bata* (thin-sliced potatoes in butter), and they'll come perfectly seasoned and crispy on both sides. No scrambled eggs, unfortunately.

The following is the unlikeliest tip in this entire guide: **Famous Ray's Pizza**, a conventional pizza joint, doesn't leap to mind as a breakfast place (and we wouldn't eat pizza there if guns were held to our heads), but the following report is so weirdly intriguing that we couldn't resist throwing it in:

Sean says pretty good omelets ($3.25 and up) come with what he calls the best home fries he's ever eaten. "They peel and slice the potatoes the night before and soak them in water, garlic and onion overnight (I had to ask the guy one time). Then, the next morning they DEEP fry them (again, in garlic and onion), so by the time they get to your plate, they're moist, and taste like they were cooked in butter and have loads of flavor." No one's ever taken him up on it (and lived to report back). So . . . caveat eater!

○ **Izakaya Riki:** see also p. 181.

Pumping Up **HEALTHY**

The Pump (Midtown West)
40 W. 55th St.
Manhattan, NY
212-246-6844
Vegetarian

The Pump (Murray Hill)
113 E. 31st St.
Manhattan, NY
212-213-5733
Vegetarian

With its myriad options, clearly stated preparation times for each food item, and suggested ordering times for fastest service, the **Pump's** menu has always made for an entertaining read ("the Dr. Bronner's of takeout menus," according to *Jim Leff*). The trouble is figuring out what to actually order from among the massive choices at this health food-oriented minichain. Try yummy turkey burgers (especially with tomato sauce and fat-free mozzarella, advises *Muk*), vegetarian salad platters, soups, veggie chili, baked falafel with hummus, and "the Baseball," which comes with chicken (or tofu, turkey breast, or turkey burger) baked with tahini sauce and served over spinach and brown rice.

HERALD SQUARE for Lunch

Chandni
  (Herald Sq/Garment District)
11 W. 29th St.
Manhattan, NY
212-686-4456
Pakistani

Mandoo Bar
  (Herald Sq/Garment District)
2 W. 32nd St.
Manhattan, NY
212-279-3075
Korean

Salumeria Biellese (Chelsea)
376 8th Ave.
Manhattan, NY
212-736-7376
Italian

Chowhounds know Salumeria Biellese as a place to get *guanciale* (a bacon made by drying the meat from a hog's jowls), but it also serves tasty sandwiches from house-made sausages. Chicken sausage loaded with white meat is removed from its casing, pressed flat, and grilled before being combined with apricots in one sandwich. According to *eatzealot*, they just keep ladling sausages and peppers onto the rolls. Takeaway only.

Steam-table dishes change daily at **Chandni**, where little is labeled and the staff is mostly noncommunicative (though queasy folks may want to know if brain or cows' feet are on the menu). Curried chicken stew is a frequent feature and is reported to be good. Chicken or goat with spinach is better. *Chana dal* (chickpeas) and a heavy eggplant-and-potato dish are also praised. Lunch specials are around five bucks.

Mandoo Bar serves house-made dumplings and cellophane noodles. We've had mixed reports about most things there, but *Deb Van D* singles out really tasty translucent potato noodles with beef and vegetables; she says the noodles have an amazing texture.

There are tons of Korean places nearby; check the cuisine index for tips. And check the nabe index for many other choices in the area.

HERRING from Heaven

Russ and Daughters (Lower East Side)
179 E. Houston St.
Manhattan, NY
212-475-4880
Eastern European Jewish

Russ and Daughters is more than a Lower East Side neighborhood treasure. To some hounds, it's the ultimate appetizing store, and favorite items are gushed over. Chopped herring is highly delicious, says *middlesister*, whose all-time fave is the *matjes* herring with onions, which she says is the closest thing to being in the Netherlands. Other favorites: a huge dried fruit selection; smoked peppered mackerel; many cured salmon varieties, including smoked wild Alaskan belly lox, smoked scotch nova or lox, and others. Holland herring arrive late spring, reminds *Patricia C Goldberg*. They sometimes carry a variety of herring whose name we're not clear on. *galleygirl* calls them North Bay herring, and they're basically raw: flash-frozen as required by law, then ever so lightly salted. No marinade, no pickling brine. Whatever their name, they're the whole dressed (sans head and skin) fish in among the various fillets, and they're killer. They don't have the chewy texture (not that that's a bad thing!) we associate with pickled herring; the flesh melts on your tongue like the fattiest sashimi. There's also none of the pungent sweetness (not that that's a bad thing, either!) associated with pickled herring—only the lightest sweetness from the freshest of flesh, barely any salt, and no strong flavor at all.

The Mighty (Tasty) **HIMALAYAS**

Himalayas (Middlesex County)
1296 Centennial Ave., in Piscataway Towne Center
Piscataway, NJ
732-562-0099
South Asian

Chowhound *piney* thinks that Pakistani/North Indian **Himalayas** (a nondescript-looking restaurant in a nondescript shopping center on a nondescript street in the nondescript town of Piscataway, NJ) might be a spicy hidden gem. A weekend buffet included *aloo gobi*, lamb *sagwala*, vegetable biryani, vegetable vindaloo, and a dish labeled simply "fish curry." Dishes are distinguished by a clearly higher level of spiciness (heatwise) than most South Asian buffets. The extra spiciness, though, doesn't overwhelm. Quite the contrary, the chef's deft hand ensures that each ingredient clearly sings its own melody. Just avoid South Indian items, like dosas.

HISPANIC Long Island

Brisas del Valle
(Nassau County)
199 W. Sunrise Hwy.
Freeport, NY
516-623-9445
Colombian

Chuzos Y Mas (Suffolk County)
1680 Islip Ave. (Rte. 111)
Brentwood, NY
631-952-5100
Colombian

El Rinconcito Salvadoreno
(Nassau County)
976 Front St.
Uniondale, NY
516-564-1003
Salvadoran

Genesis Restaurant
(Nassau County)
48 Guy Lombardo Ave.
Freeport, NY
516-377-0258
Salvadoran

Guantanamera (Suffolk County)
117 W. Jericho Tpk.
Huntington Station, NY
631-547-6818
Cuban

Gusto Latino Pizzeria
(Nassau County)
129 W. Sunrise Hwy.
Freeport, NY
516-546-0066
Honduran/Salvadoran/
Italian/Pizza

La Cubanita II (Suffolk County)
183 Bay Shore Rd.
Deer Park, NY
631-667-8533
Cuban

La Finca Restaurant
(Nassau County)
170 Broadway
Hicksville, NY
516-935-0951
Colombian

Freeport's Salvadoran restaurants set an aberrantly high chow standard, reports *Jim Leff*. The keystone of Salvadoran food is *pupusas*: highly craveable fried corn cakes stuffed with pork cracklings (*chicharron*), cheese (*queso*), or meat and cheese (*revuelta*). They're crisp, satisfying snacks usually eaten with beer and always with *curtido*, mildly pickled shredded cabbage.

Genesis Restaurant, the first of the trio on our Freeport Salvadoran radar, is a well-lit deli with informal seating and an extensive array of steam-table offerings. Their pupusas are lively and interesting, with very tangy cheese and rich corn flavor, and the cabbage and red sauce are consummately fresh. Other tasty options: crisp yet juicy fried chicken, fine-grained pork tamales, and fried mushy beans.

Don't be put off by the dreary interior at **Taco Grill**. *Tamales de elote*, made from fresh corn, are properly heavy and tender, and contain no discernible added sugar. Pupusas de loroco (an edible flower) are quiet wonders, made with extramild cheese. Curtido here is extra tangy, very fresh and crunchy, a true companion to the excellent pupusas.

Gusto Latino is a pizza place where slices and calzones fly out the door. Skip them. Also skip the small menu of Salvadoran stuff. Opt instead for the sub-sub menu of a few Honduran dishes: *tacos catrachos* (Honduran tacos); *casamiento* (eggs, cheese, avocado, and yellow plantain); and *baliada* (beans, cheese, and cream). Also *mariscada catracha*, a coconut milk-based seafood soup with fresh lobster, crab, shrimp, clams, and mussels; and *sopa de caracol*: snail soup Honduran style.

From the outside, Uniondale's **El Rinconcito Salvadoreno** looks like an unassuming, decrepit mess, but don't let that deter you because you'd miss out on some very tasty items. Cuajada cheese is hard but crumbly, like goat cheese but creamier and milder, and it's made in-house. *TastyLlama* says while items here have familiar names, they taste better because of the care the chef/owner puts into his creations. Highlights include earthy, grainy tortillas, very spicy chicken tamales, really good casamiento (here a mixture of rice, beans and a few vegetables, with an underlying corned beef hashiness) and, of course, the cheese. Be sure to try the quesadilla for dessert. It's a pastry made from rice, cheese, and sour cream that's an inch-thick slice of light brown cake sprinkled with sesame seeds that's an entirely new taste sensation: chewy, and sweet, with a very pleasant aftertaste from the cheese.

The Cuban sandwiches at Deer Park's **La Cubanita II** are the best around, says *johnknoesel*. Sometimes they run an after-lunch special of $2 Cubanos Mondays through Wednesdays. Check out their steam-table selection, as well.

Guantanamera in Huntington Station is Cuban and primarily a takeout place (there's one table), and not much English is spoken. Lots of daily specials, often including *rabo en vino rojo* (oxtail in red wine). Cubanos are $4.75, as are pork, chicken, and turkey sandwiches. Everything is tasty, *herb056* says.

Colombian restaurants keep popping up on Long Island, and a good starting point is **Chuzos Y Mas** in Brentwood, where all the food has a nice home-cooking quality, and the place is like being in someone's kitchen in Colombia, reports *Paul Trapani*. *Papas chorreradas* are boiled potatoes with a special sauce containing scallions, butter, and curryish spice. The friendly women behind the counter say this isn't typical restaurant food; it's the kind of thing Colombians make at home when there's nothing in the cupboard but some potatoes and some scallions. Trapani says the potatoes are perfectly boiled and make for a satisfying dish.

Colombian **Brisas del Valle** in Freeport is worth further exploration, judging by the *calentado con huevos perico* *Paul Trapani* tried. It's rice mixed with beans and pieces of blue potatoes, served with eggs scrambled with peppers and tomatoes. Normally a breakfast dish, they'll make it at lunch upon request.

At **La Finca**, in Hicksville, yet another Colombian, Sunday is all about hen. Other days, this small Colombian restaurant serves a different soup with rice and an arepa for about $6. Shredded beef empanadas are made with orange cornmeal dough that's crispy outside and chewy inside. *Paul Trapani* says expertly fried chicharron (pork skin) had large pieces of baconish meat attached. Hearty breakfasts are served from 9:30 a.m. until noon.

HONDURAN BREAKFAST

Honduras Maya (Brooklyn)
587 5th Ave.
Park Slope, Brooklyn, NY
718-965-8028
Honduran

Breakfast at Honduras Maya seems to be a set piece. There are no menus. The table gets a bowl of *crema* and a basket of chewy flatbread for scooping, while individuals receive a plate with a dollop of refried beans, a scoop of sweet plantains, scrambled eggs, and a credit-card sized sliver of dense, salty, white cheese. Everything's delicious, says *at203*, and the medium-sized portions are quite adequate.

HOPE AND ANCHOR: Red Hook's First On-Map Chow?

Hope and Anchor Diner (Brooklyn)
347 Van Brunt St.
Red Hook, Brooklyn, NY
718-237-0276
Eclectic New American

When last we heard, Ken Munz (formerly of Jean Georges) had settled in running the kitchen, and **Hope and Anchor** seemed solidly on the upswing after a period of sharp decline. Entrées like orange-glazed salmon with onion rings, red Chinese roast pork, and Vietnamese beef salad, along with homemade desserts like banana cream pie and coconut custard tart, are drawing crowds. Expect to wait for a table at weekend brunch.

Red Hook's long been a nabe many have expected to "up and come," but this is one of the few major chow signs of life.

Top **HOT CHOCOLATES**

City Bakery (Gramercy)
3 W. 18th St.
Manhattan, NY
212-366-1414
Café

Fauchon (Upper East Side)
1000 Madison Ave.
Manhattan, NY
212-570-2211
French Café

La Maison du Chocolat
  (Midtown West)
30 Rockefeller Plaza
Manhattan, NY
212-265-9404
French

La Maison du Chocolat
  (Upper East Side)
1018 Madison Ave.
Manhattan, NY
212-744-7117
Chocolate/Candy Shop

MarieBelle (Soho)
484 Broome St.
Manhattan, NY
212-925-6999
Café

The hot chocolate at **La Maison du Chocolat** might be the most delicious *and* expensive in town. Seven different types of chocolate are distilled into one small cup of potent cocoa elixir. The result is intense and bitter and unlike any other hot chocolate *reina-de-fideo* has tasted, though the $7 price tag is a bit steep to enjoy to go in a paper cup. So savor it in the café in the back of the Madison Avenue location—properly in a china cup and saucer (and with, but of course, a bit of chocolate on the side).

Clarissa has enjoyed the superrich hot chocolate at **Fauchon**.

The **City Bakery** throws a much-anticipated Hot Chocolate Festival each winter, with different flavors each day. Info and flavor calendar (don't miss chili pepper) at www.hot-chocolate-festival.com

MarieBelle is a hot spot for intensely flavored hot chocolate. Intensely thick, too; this is hot chocolate you can almost eat with a fork. Think chocolate sludge with chunks of heaven, describes *brad kaplan*. It comes in intriguing flavors like Aztec and spicy (which is spiked with chili, chipotle, and cinnamon), and they serve both European style (in small espresso cups) and also a thinner American version (made with milk, not water) in a mug. Brad bought some powder and reports that it's 95 percent as good at home as in the café, and calling it a "powder" is not quite true, as there are more bits and pieces than granules. Divine stuff, maybe not to everyone's tastes, but amazing.

○ **City Bakery:** *see also* **pp. 96, 207.**
○ **Fauchon:** *see also* **pp. 97, 136.**

Eastern Queens **HYBRIDS**

Bariloche Bakery (Queens)
132-13A 14th Ave., in the
  Whitepoint Shopping Center
College Point, Queens, NY
718-746-4956
Argentinian/Italian

European Corner Deli (Queens)
199-02 32nd Ave.
Bayside, Queens, NY
718-631-2873
Central/Eastern European

Bariloche serves Argentine and Italian goods, with some Colombian items thrown in. Cheese bread (*pan de bono*), milk bread (*pan de leche*), and wonderful chocolate-covered meringue cookies come recommended by *billyblancoNYC*, who says even the fat-free muffins taste good.

As you'd expect, **European Corner** is on a corner and specializes in European goods, ranging from German puddings to Macedonian packaged soups to Swiss chocolates. Lots of hard-to-find items. The deli counter carries German pork loin, a variety of salamis, headcheese, and a bunch of stuff *billyblancoNYC* couldn't identify. He says the owners, a family from Transylvania, are very helpful.

Downtown Down Under
ICE CREAM

Australian Homemade Premium Ice Cream & Chocolates (East Village)
115 St. Marks Pl.
Manhattan, NY
212-228-5439
Ice Cream or Gelato

Ice creams at **Australian Homemade Premium Ice Cream & Chocolates** are made in very small batches in the back room, so they often run out of popular flavors. It's frustrating, yes, but it means everything's fresh. *Iron Frank* insists that this is a whole different class of ice cream, really dense and creamy and extremely true of flavor. Pistachio is the essence of the nut. Hazelnut Almond is actually hazelnut ice cream with perfectly distributed almond and hazelnut chunks throughout. They have fresh fruit sorbets, tasty chocolates, and grown-up flavored sodas, too.

IL BUCO'S Current Chef Delivers the Goods

Il Buco (East Village)
47 Bond St.
Manhattan, NY
212-533-1932
Italian

Il Buco went through a downswing a while ago, but current chef Jeremy Griffiths is, we hear, a stickler for fresh ingredients and knows how to use them. Intriguing appetizers include grilled octopus over a chickpea, parsley, red onion, and chopped olive salad, and cod fritters with sweet red pepper puree. Roast suckling pig gets high praise, as do perfectly cooked and seasoned steaks. Service is gracious.

West Side **INDIAN** Find

Bengal Express (Clinton)
789 9th Ave.
Manhattan, NY
212-489-8036
Bangladeshi

Bengal Express is a tiny restaurant cooking up big flavors, says *offbalance*, who raves about vegetable samosas that burst with flavor, chicken curry, and *chana gosht*, which sent him "to food nirvana on a cloud of perfectly seasoned sauce." Prices are inexpensive, but the dining room's empty, unfortunately, despite a brisk takeout business.

INDONESIAN SPICE Hunt

Hong Kong Supermarket
   (Chinatown)
109 E. Broadway, #1002
Manhattan, NY
212-227-3388
Chinese

New York Supermarket (Queens)
82-66 Broadway
Jackson Heights, Queens, NY
718-803-1233
East Asian

Top Line Meat Market (Queens)
81-37 Broadway
Jackson Heights, Queens, NY
718-458-5505
Indonesian

There are, unfortunately, no great Indonesian restaurants in New York City as of this writing. And it's even hard to find provisions to make your own. Here's where to go:

Lemon basil leaves can be found at any markets carrying Thai or Vietnamese herbs, such as the two Asian markets on

Mulberry north of Bayard. The small one on the east side of Mulberry Street carries many Southeast Asian herbs, while the larger on the west side (with sign reading: "Thai, Philippines, Indonesia") stocks a good array of Indonesian items, including a great selection of sambals. Another off-radar place, a small Indonesian grocery on Mott and Bayard (two doors down from Häagen-Dazs), stocks Indonesian spices such as Klepon. **Hong Kong Supermarket** sells long sheaves of pandan leaf in the frozen foods department. **Top Line** is a small Queens grocery stocking Indonesian spices. Nearby **New York Supermarket** carries many Indonesian products as well.

INTERNATIONAL Food Warehouse

International Food Warehouse (Bergen County)
370 Essex St.
Lodi, NJ
201-368-9511
Store

It's tough to walk through International Food Warehouse, an enormous multinational supermarket above a National Wholesale Liquidator store on Rte. 17 in Jersey, without wanting to buy maniacally. Choices are overwhelming, and you could spend hours wandering the aisles, gazing at interesting packages and deciphering foreign labels. The key is to be selective and avoid impulse buying, says *elvislives*, who offers this additional advice: avoid bulk/large quantity items that are very cheap. (All our "misses" fell in this category, e.g. large tubs of jam from Poland for $3, but we could have been smarter—the experience and cute packaging took over our senses). And while there is an incredible range of worldwide foods, note that some hard-to-find American items can also be found at great prices.

Here are some top finds there, reported by *elvislives*, to offer a sense of the stunning range:

- Mors Original Wonder Berry (Russia)—$2.99 for a large carton. A delicious fruit juice made only out of the fruits of the Russian forest: cranberries, blueberries, and blackberries. Rich, tart, and fruity with a subtle earthy taste of the forest (as the label promises). I'd have to go back for this alone if nothing else!
- Lazzaroni Bittersweet Chocolate bar with Amaretti di Saronno Crumbles (Italy)—$1.39 for a large 3.2-ounce bar of excellent dark chocolate with crushed amaretto cookies (for a slight almond flavor and delicate crispy texture, like a gourmet Nestle's Crunch!).
- La Baleine Sea Salt (France)—$2.47 for the large 25.5-ounce container.
- Sylvia's Flapjack batter—$.99. An *excellent* pancake batter; just add water!
- Toschi Sour Cherry Syrup (Italy)—$4.59 for a 19-ounce bottle. Beautiful package. A splash in seltzer makes fantastic cherry soda.
- Dried apricot paste from Damascus, Syria (like a giant fruit roll up)—$1.97 for 17.5 ounces, or about 1 foot by 2 feet when unfolded. Great packaging, simple ingredients, and nice bright apricot flavor with a soft/but chewy texture. Ingredients are apricots, sugar, glucose, olive oil, and sulfur dioxide for preservative. (U.S. dried apricots always contain this.
- Vanilla/Plain Malt Flavor Ovaltine—have not seen this in twenty years! $3.29 for large.
- Apollo Tyropita (cheese filo frozen appetizers—$3.97 for a package of twelve). Very good crisp filo; not oily, tasty cheese inside, would serve at party.
- Gundelsheim Choucroute au Vin Blanc—$1.47 for a 10.5-ounce can. Sauerkraut with wine, from Germany, the best canned sauerkraut ever, very thinly sliced, crisp and a wonderful flavor. Ingredients listed as "sauerkraut and wine."
- Hengstenber Mustard (Germany)—$2.77 for medium-sized jar. A yellow, sharp, German mustard (very simple/basic ingredients), but the kicker is that it comes in a very nice white ceramic crock with a stencil in green of the town of Hengstenber going around the entire jar!
- Cortas Pomegranate concentrate (Lebanon)—$2.57 for a

10-ounce bottle. Excellent concentrated pomegranate syrup. Very tart and flavorful, a little like tamarind only tastier. Good in drinks or sauces. Ingredients are pomegranates.

ISRAELI Flavors in an Israeli Atmosphere

Azuri Cafe (Clinton)
465 W. 51st St.
Manhattan, NY
212-262-2920
Sephardic/Israeli

Bissaleh (Brooklyn)
1922 Coney Island Ave.
Gravesend, Brooklyn, NY
718-998-8811
Sephardic/Israeli

Carmel Grocery (Queens)
64-27 108 St.
Forest Hills, Queens, NY
718-897-9296
Sephardic/Israeli

Hoomoos Asli (Lower Manhattan)
100 Kenmare St.
Manhattan, NY
212-966-0022
Sephardic/Israeli

Mabat (Brooklyn)
1809 E. 7th St.
Gravesend, Brooklyn, NY
718-339-3300
Sephardic/Israeli

Olympic Pita Corp. (Brooklyn)
1419 Coney Island Ave.
Midwood, Brooklyn, NY
718-258-6222
Sephardic/Israeli/Iraqi

Pick-A-Pita
  (Herald Sq/Garment District)
247 W. 38th St.
Manhattan, NY
212-730-7482
Sephardic/Israeli

Serious Israeli food. Brooklyn first . . . of course:

   Bissaleh's *malawah* (Yemenite pan bread) is flaky, crispy, buttery, and chewy; and one of them can easily feed two, reports *Miss Needle*, who says they serve several stuffed versions but she prefers plain. Closed Friday night and Saturday (like most, if not all, of the following).

Chowhound Nametag: djk

○○○

Neighborhood: Flatiron.

Occupation: Lighting designer for gardens and homes.

Cholesterol Level: Average.

Number of Visits to McDonald's in Past Decade: Actually, none.

Farthest Out of the Way Traveled Just for Chow: Jumped on a plane to Barcelona for three days because I missed Cal Pep (tapas bar) and it was worth it. Fantastic.

Top Chinatown Pick: It would probably have to be on a dish-by-dish basis . . . but for simple and always good, Dumpling House on Eldridge Street.

Underrated by Chowhounds: Mr. Dennehy's on Carmine Street; New York Noodletown in Chinatown.

Favorite Comfort Chow: It changes but . . . Bongo Lounge for lobster roll/oysters and a martini, Petrosino for their inzimino or trennette with truffle oil and cheese, plus their bufala mozz cheesecake.

Guilty Pleasure: City Bakery—macaroni and cheese.

Favorite Gelato Flavor: Fig or coffee.

Favorite Mail Order Chow: Tuna from www.tunaguys.com, various salts from www.salttraders.com, various Italian products (oils, bottarga) from www.esperya.com.

Chowhounding Rules of Thumb:
1. always check out the crowd—percentage of specific ethnicity in same ethnic restaurant;
2. look of zeal on all faces as they eat;
3. wafting smell;
4. how inviting does each dish look;
5. do servers seem proud;
   . . . but mostly I rely on my intuition.

Everyone's Israeli at **Mabat**, where grilled items are featured. Excellent baby chicken shish kebab, *meurav Yerushalmi* (mixed grill, Jerusalem style), and hummus, reports *Nina W.*.

Olympic Pita is a terrific shwarma parlor. On first bite you'll know this is an entirely different species of sandwich. The meat is tender and perfectly spiced, the crunchy pickles, salads, and sauces all pile up in a tower of flavor. The turkey is so peppery it tastes almost like pastrami, and the warm, dense freshly baked tandoori bread elevates the whole thing to perfection, says *Iron Frank* of a shawarma on *lafah* (a huge sesame-dotted, pita-ish bread). They also have fantastic falafel, kebabs, and salads.

Back in Manhattan, **Pick-A-Pita**, a bargain-priced Israeli joint, is open only Monday through Friday, 9.00 a.m. to 6.00 p.m., and you have to go through a loading dock to find it. Persevere and you'll find a kitchen, four or five tables, and a humming drinks cooler. Enjoy kosher shwarma that's glistening with fat and reeking of cloves, as well as very good falafel, hummus, baba ghanoush, and other Middle Eastern treats. Also hot peppers and cukes pickled on premises.

Falafel at **Azuri Cafe** comes with a mind-boggling variety of eggplant and other salads, pickles, slaws, relishes, sauces, and dips—all piled into your pita or piled in greater quantities on your combo plate. *Jen* says everything is very fresh, and the selection of toppings gives the sandwich a combination of spicy and fruity flavors. A very generous sandwich is $4. Mainly take-out, but there are some tables. Owner is notoriously brusque.

The entire staff at **Hoomoos Asli** and most of the customers are Israeli, so the *avirah* (atmosphere) is much more "there" than here. Falafel is flattened (not balls), baba ghanoush is less smoky than some, and cholent is perfect for taking a chill off. Hoomoos (aka hummus) rocks, of course.

Carmel, not far from the LIE in Forest Hills, Queens, has lusciously tasty hummus, reports *Hungryphil*. They make all the spreads sold and even roast their own coffee.

Lesser-Known **ITALIAN**

Cantinella (East Village)
23 Avenue A
Manhattan, NY
212-505-2550
Italian

Crispo (Chelsea)
240 W. 14th St.
Manhattan, NY
212-229-1818
Italian

Dominic (Tribeca)
349 Greenwich St.
Manhattan, NY
212-343-0700
Italian

Giorgione (Soho)
307 Spring St.
Manhattan, NY
212-352-2269
Italian

La Locanda dei Vini (Clinton)
737 9th Ave.
Manhattan, NY
212-258-2900
Italian

Monte's Trattoria Ltd.
    (Greenwich Village)
97 MacDougal St.
Manhattan, NY
212-674-9456
Italian

Papazzio (Queens)
39-38 Bell Blvd.
Bayside, Queens, NY
718-229-1962
Italian

Parma (Upper East Side)
1404 3rd Ave.
Manhattan, NY
212-535-3520
Italian

Paulding Porto Cervo Restaurant
    (Bronx)
1024 Morris Park Ave.
Bronx, NY
718-430-9423
Italian

Queen Italian Restaurant
    (Brooklyn)
84 Court St.
Brooklyn Heights
Brooklyn, NY
718-596-5954
Italian

Salpino's (Nassau County)
3463 Merrick Rd.
Wantagh, NY
516-221-4991
Italian

Volare (Greenwich Village)
147 W. 4th St.
Manhattan, NY
212-460-5073
Italian

Some of the following relatively obscure Italian restaurants are better known than others, but none get the recognition hounds think they deserve.

La Locanda Dei Vini's extensive menu of salads and pastas makes it hard to decide what to order, says *antivic69*, who praises extra large, fresh rigatoni with stewed meat sauce topped with ricotta, and a salad with apparently fresh anchovies and shaved parmesan. Eggplant in tomato-based sauce is smoky, and ricotta cheesecake is fabulous. Moderate prices and fun atmosphere. Not to be confused with the Brooklyn restaurant with a very similar name.

A former chef and beverage manager from Scalinatella on the Upper East Side opened **Cantinella** in the East Village. The kitchen prepares a long list of specials each night but is also open to cooking whatever you please. Recommended dishes include grilled veal chops, baby octopus grilled so that they're crispy yet tender inside, homemade papardelle with porcini mushrooms and truffle oil, chicken and sliced sausage served in a reduction of red wine vinegar and stock, and, for dessert, mixed berries topped with fresh zabaglione cream.

Crispo gets consistently solid marks for tasty Italian preparations. Their spaghetti carbonara is delicious. They put a poached egg on top so you can break the yolk and mix it in with the pasta, says *Martini*, who also praises their ham and cheese appetizer as a great blend of flavors and textures. Another hound says veal ravioli verde with mushrooms is very rich, and so, so good. Bread is very average, though.

Giorgione (a wider-known choice among lesser-knowns) garners serious praise for simple but deliciously prepared Italian dishes. In season, start with their special heirloom tomato salad of five varieties. And a large and fresh oyster selection. The risotto sotto bosco, consisting of porcini mushrooms, rosemary, sage, and blueberries, is the best risotto *daniel*'s ever eaten and, for dessert, a roasted pear in a honey sauce served with a side of fresh ricotta cheese and rice pudding served with a plum sauce are both brilliant. The pizza oven burns both gas and wood, giving the crust extra flavor. Most entrées are in the $15 to $25 range, but watch out for higher-priced specials.

The Portuguese restaurant formerly known as Pico has been converted into Italian **Dominic**. It's much friendlier, more informal, and less expensive than Pico ever was, and feels more spacious with all of the banquettes removed. Each night three pastas are available in appetizer, entrée, or family-serving sizes. *Wurstle* had fantastic agnolotti filled with duck ragout (and permeated with exotic North African undertones). Suckling pig remains from Pico's menu. Zeppoles, fried dough coated in powdered sugar, are served street-fair style in a paper bag.

Volare, Monte's, and Parma are three unapologetic old-school red sauce bastions that many don't know about. Volare may have a menu, but you'll never see it. The waiters usually come to the table and just ask what you feel like. Try to feel like osso bucco and gnocchi—both are spectacular, says *barbara*. Great ambience and a long colorful history can add a lot to standard red sauce Italian-American fare. Monte's has lots of ambience to lend atmosphere to very good food, reports *Cullen Dickey*. And while there's nothing fancy about Parma, the food is solid, albeit pricey.

At Brooklyn's Queen Italian Restaurant, *wannabechef* reports homemade mozzarella to die for, served as one "loaf," with roasted peppers, olives, and grilled asparagus. It's got exactly the right creamy/chewy texture, and salting's perfect, too. Grilled portobello mushrooms with melted goat cheese and pesto sauce also earn raves. But chicken parmagiana is merely good, nothing special. Desserts look fine, but servings are so large no one ever seems to try them. Generally, order from the specials side of the menu.

Food quality, service, and very moderately priced wine list are all pluses for Papazzio in Bayside, Queens. Veal with capers and lemon butter sauce is outstanding, and is made with great sauce and fantastic paper-thin, butter-tender veal, reports *billyblancoNYC*. Fettuccini Alfredo is more creamy than cheesy.

Entrées are massive at Paulding's in the Bronx, and salads and sides come family style. Veal parmigiana is a huge portion of delectable, melt-in-your-mouth veal, and sauce and cheese are perfect, says *Flori*. There's not a lot of ambience to go with the food, but wait staff is friendly and attentive.

Somebody in the kitchen at Salpino's really knows what they're doing. Expect excellently balanced and presented dishes with meats and sauces cooked perfectly. For example, mussels are amply portioned (like everything here), gritless and cooked in a sauce of tomato, basil, and soft garlic, says *Uncledave*, who notes that Salpino's brines their pork chops for a few days to produce a slightly cured hammy flavor. They're broiled nice and juicy.

○ **Dominic:** *see also* p. 250.
○ **La Locanda dei Vini:** *see also* p. 69.
○ **Queen Italian Restaurant:** *see also* p. 140.

ITALIAN SUBS

Alidoro (Soho)
105 Sullivan St.
Manhattan, NY
212-334-9530
American/Italian Sandwich Shop

Faicco's Pork Store
  (Greenwich Village)
260 Bleecker St.
Manhattan, NY
212-243-1974
Italian Deli

Lamazou (Gramercy)
370 3rd Ave.
Manhattan, NY
212-532-2009
Italian Deli

Lenny's Gourmet
  (Upper West Side)
489 Columbus Ave.
Manhattan, NY
212-787-9368
Italian Sandwich Shop

Parisi Bakery (Little Italy)
198 Mott St.
Manhattan, NY
212-226-6378
Italian Bakery

Tony's (Midtown East)
817 2nd Ave.
Manhattan, NY
212-697-8848
Italian Sandwich Shop

- Does an Italian sub have to be made by an Italian to be good? At **Lenny's Gourmet** the owner is Asian and the sandwich maker Hispanic, but *Jake Pine* says they turn out great sandwiches stocked with shredded lettuce, thin-sliced tomatoes, spicy peppers, good meat, cheese, and bread. There are other branches of Lenny's, but we haven't had reports on them.
- **Faicco's Pork Store's** reputation is built on high-quality meats, but it might be the mozzarella that distinguishes sandwiches here. Ask for the Italian special with roasted peppers. It comes piled high with meat and fresh mozzarella for $10. Leave the meat off and it's only $5.

- **Lamazou** has high-quality meats and cheeses, and makes an amazing prosciutto di Parma sandwich.
- **Parisi's** has Italian owners who've been at it a long time and turn out excellent sandwiches.
- **Tony's** makes huge tasty Italian subs for $6.
- **Alidoro** is next to a small park—a nice setting to enjoy one of the best Italian subs in the city.

○ Tony's: *see also* **pp. 72, 141.**

Jersey **ITALIAN**

Ciao Bello Ristorante & Bar (Somerset County)
156 N. Gaston Ave.
Somerville, NJ
908-704-8444
Italian

Zuppa di vongole at **Ciao Bello** is superb, and stocked with garlic and very fresh clams and a rich and heady sauce. Minestrone is incredibly fresh and hearty and filled with tender vegetables (including some al dente escarole) and beans, reports *Sethy*. For entrées, a huge serving of gnocchi comes in excellent, subtle, sweet, meaty, hearty, rich bolognese sauce. Shrimp are perfectly cooked, but spicy arrabbiata sauce lacks depth, and veal is tough and bland. Sautéed spinach with garlic is flawless. For dessert, go for the light, fluffy cheesecake.

○ **Ciao Bello Ristorante & Bar:** *see also* **p. 68.**

JACKSON HEIGHTS Taste Treats

Churros vendor (Queens)
Roosevelt Ave. at 85th St.
Jackson Heights, Queens, NY
Mexican Street Cart/Truck

Dimple Indian Fast Food (Queens)
7231 37th Ave.
Jackson Heights, Queens, NY
718-458-8144
Indian/South Indian/Vegetarian

Hornado Ecuatoriano (Queens)
7618 Roosevelt Ave.
Jackson Heights, Queens, NY
718-205-7357
Ecuadorian

Inti Raymi Restaurant (Queens)
8614 37th Ave.
Jackson Heights, Queens, NY
718-424-1938
Peruvian

Kabab King Diner (Queens)
7301 37th Rd.
Jackson Heights, Queens, NY
718-457-5857
Pakistani

La Casa de Pollo Peruano
    (Queens)
8707 Roosevelt Ave.
Jackson Heights, Queens, NY
718-397-1910
Peruvian

La Nueva Bakery (Queens)
8610 37th Ave.
Jackson Heights, Queens, NY
718-507-2339
Latin American Café

La Picada Azuaya (Queens)
8419 37th Ave.
Jackson Heights, Queens, NY
718-424-9797
Ecuadorian

Laureles (Queens)
7617 Roosevelt Ave.
Jackson Heights, Queens, NY
718-899-8529
Colombian

Los Arrieros (Queens)
7602 Roosevelt Ave.
Jackson Heights, Queens, NY
718-898-3359
Colombian

Maharaja Sweets and Snacks
    (Queens)
7510 37th Ave.
Jackson Heights, Queens, NY
718-505-2680
South Indian

Miracali Bakery (Queens)
7604 Roosevelt Ave.
Jackson Heights, Queens, NY
718-779-7175
Colombian Bakery

Rice Avenue (Queens)
7219 Roosevelt Ave.
Jackson Heights, Queens, NY
718-803-9001
Thai

Shahi Snack (Queens)
3738 72nd St.
Jackson Heights, Queens, NY
718-457-7766
Pakistani Bakery

Tamale vendors outside Pacific
    Market (Queens)
7501 Broadway
Jackson Heights, Queens, NY
Mexican

Tibetan Yak (Queens)
7220 Roosevelt Ave.
Jackson Heights, Queens, NY
718-779-1119
Tibetan

Villa Colombia Bakery (Queens)
4042 82nd St.
Jackson Heights, Queens, NY
718-476-3500
Colombian

Jackson Heights, Queens (easily accessible by many subway lines), is the most diverse neighborhood on earth, and that means tons of good eating. Hounds quickly point out some of their faves:

- **Tibetan Yak** is New York's best Tibetan. Don't miss the homemade noodles in the soup, homemade ricey sausages, and great desserts (but don't sweat the buttered tea, which is complementary but noncompulsory). Much of the cooking is fairly mild, but if you ask for your food served spicy, they can really lay on the pepper.
- **Shahi** Foods does fresh ultrahandmade Pakistani parantha and roti.
- **Rice Avenue** Thai is a stylish, friendly Thai café, best for rice dishes (especially green curry rice), but northern non-Thais must beg for spice.
- Look for the tamale vendors outside **Pacific Market.**
- **Dimple** and **Maharaja Sweets and Snacks** are South Indian vegetarian. Get *pani poori* at the former, and chat at the latter.
- **Kabab King Diner** is a Pakistani spot for kebabs and surprisingly good baba ghanoush.
- **Laureles** and **Los Arrieros** are good for homestyle Colombian (e.g. *platos montañeros*).
- **Hornado Ecuatoriano** is your venue for all things pork. **La Picada Azuaya,** also Ecuadorian, makes good tripe.
- **Miracali Bakery** is a Colombian bakery specializing in pan de yucca (best when warm, especially with coffee), buñuelos (basically doughnut holes) and chorizo. Competitor **Villa Colombia Bakery** excels at guava pastries. A third Columbian bakery, **La Nueva Bakery,** is good for fried empanadas (especially chicken), guava and cheese pastelillos, really good buñuelos, and the puffy cheesy little Colombian rolls called pan de bono.

- **La Casa de Pollo Peruano** makes good cheap Peruvian chicken combos.
- **Inti Raymi** is a venerable, much-respected Peruvian restaurant that's closed Monday through Wednesday.
- Look for the **churros vendor** on Roosevelt at Eighty-fifth. As *JH Jill* says, hot, crispy churros are one of life's great guilty pleasures and these guys make 'em just right.

See also Encyclopedic Roosevelt Ave Area *Mexican* Roundup.

○ La Nueva Bakery: *see also* p. 38.
○ Rice Avenue: *see also* p. 304.
○ Tamale vendors outside Pacific Market: *see also* p. 299.

Open-Minded **JAMAICAN** Spots

Rug-B (Brooklyn)
1310 Cortelyou Rd.
Kensington, Brooklyn, NY
718-284-0024
Caribbean/Barbecue

Stir It Up (Brooklyn)
514 Atlantic Ave.
Boerum Hill, Brooklyn NY
718-643-3716
Jamaica

Stir It Up is a Jamaican place that is for some reason really into stir fries. They're good, made to order. The standard steam-table items are good, too. Some complain that their goat is too refined and not gamy enough. But fish cakes—fried battered chunks of cod—are unquestionably terrific, says *bosshog*. They're beautifully done with a perfect balance between the onion, green pepper, and scallion flavors. Caution: Salads come with Wishbone dressing.

Another open-minded Brooklyn Jamaican, **Rug B**, offers a Caribbean menu during the week (most chicken dishes are good, but avoid boneless chicken breast specials), but BBQ Sundays feature tasty beef ribs and live music in their garden. The regular menu offers generous children's portions for $5.

JAMAICAN/TRINI VEGGIE

Caribbean Delicacy (Brooklyn)
575 Lincoln Pl.
Crown Heights, Brooklyn, NY
718-778-7558
Vegetarian Jamaican

HIM Vegetarian Restaurant
   (Bronx)
2130 White Plains Rd.
Bronx, NY
718-239-7146
Vegetarian Jamaican

Imhotep (Brooklyn)
734 Nostrand Ave.
Crown Heights, Brooklyn, NY
718-493-2395
Vegetarian

I'Qulah Vegetarian & Seafood
   Restaurant (Queens)
164-07 89th Ave.
Jamaica, Queens, NY
718-523-4636
Jamaican

Singh's Roti Shop (Queens)
13118 Liberty Ave.
Jamaica, Queens, NY
718-323-5990
Trinidadian

Uptown Juice Bar (Harlem)
54 W. 125th St.
Manhattan, NY
212-987-2660
Southern Vegetarian

Veggie Castle (Brooklyn)
2242 Church Ave.
Flatbush, Brooklyn, NY
718-703-1275
Jamaican Vegetarian

Singh's is a Chowhound hot spot known for huge killer roti containing shrimp, chicken, etc. And even though Singh's isn't known as a vegetarian haven, *JC* is nonetheless bowled over by their divine veg offerings, such as pumpkin (a spicy, slightly sweet puree), creamy spinach, and green beans. The bread itself is good enough to forget about fillings. "Doubles" are two tender slabs of bread—fluffier than roti, simultaneously delicate, soft, and chewy—filled with curried chickpeas and various hot sauces. Try yeast-raised coconut bread, too. Beware: The hot sauce is fierce!

JC's other top picks for veg-friendly Caribbean are: **Veggie Castle, Imhotep, Caribbean Delicacy, I'Qulah,** and **Uptown Juice Bar** (more like veggie soul food than pure Caribbean) . . . and the elusive and unlisted Ras Diggi, serving awesome lo mein, dumpling soup, and not much else—described as a block or two north of Nostrand, a long, long avenue, and we're not sure of the cross street. Good luck!

HIM Vegetarian serves Jamaican-style vegetarian. The veggie chicken is a particular highlight. Order a combo plate to sample a bit of everything (but the flavors tend to blend together). The 2 train Pelham Parkway, stop is about a block away.

Locate a roti shop near you at www.rotishops.com.

- Imhotep: *see also* p. 323.
- Veggie Castle: *see also* p. 323.

JAPANESE Noodle Soups

Ise Japanese Restaurant
   (Midtown West)
58 W. 56th St.
Manhattan, NY
212-707-8702
Japanese

Ise Restaurant (Lower Manhattan)
56 Pine St.
Manhattan, NY
212-785-1600
Japanese

Ise Restaurant (Midtown East)
151 E. 49th St.
Manhattan, NY
212-319-6876
Japanese

Menchanko-Tei 55
   (Midtown West)
43 W. 55th St.
Manhattan, NY
212-247-1585
Japanese

Menchanko-Tei Restaurant
   (Grand Central)
131 E. 45th St. 1st Fl.
Manhattan, NY
212-986-6805
Japanese

Sapporo (Midtown West)
152 W. 49th St.
Manhattan, NY
212-869-8972
Japanese

Zen Restaurant (East Village)
31 St. Marks Pl.
Manhattan, NY
212-533-6855
Japanese

Niboshi ramen (noodles in dried anchovy broth) is a hot trend in Japan right now, and *astoria* says the Forty-ninth Street branch of **Ise** is the only place serving it in New York City. It's not on the menu, so you have to ask your waiter. We don't know if the other Ise location, or their downtown sister Eisay, has this dish.

A jazz musician who's also a ramen fanatic allegedly makes **Zen Restaurant's** *tonkotsu* (pig bone) *ramen*. *astoria* says the guy traveled all over Japan to find his own recipe for the ultimate ramen. It used to be an after-midnight, fifty-bowls-per-night limited item, but became an all-day menu item this year.

Menchanko-Tei, long a favorite of hounds, now makes *kurobuta tonkotsu* (black pig bone) ramen, and no-frills **Sapporo** gets high marks for consistency, fast service, and great prices.

For more noodle soups, see also Downtown *Noodle* Slurp-Off.

○ **Menchanko Tei 55:** *see also* p. 233.
○ **Menchanko-Tei Restaurant:** *see also* p. 141.
○ **Sapporo:** *see also* pp. 234, 339.

The Royal (**JAPANESE**) Treatment

Inagiku Restaurant (Midtown East)
111 E. 49th St., at the Waldorf Astoria Hotel
Manhattan, NY
212-355-0440
Japanese

From the minute you walk into **Inagiku** you receive the royal treatment from your hosts and the crew of kimono-clad wait-resses, who don't let your glass go empty or your soy sauce bowl run dry. Tempura is light, puffy, and perfect, says *Daniel*. Uni came on a wafer that added crispness to the texture of the urchin. Sushi and sashimi are fresh and very good, though not on the same rung as the highest level places. Coconut cake is amazing. The menu also has a lot of hot foods like shabu-shabu and stone-cooked steak.

Student-Friendly **JAPANESE** for a Large Group

Donburi-Ya (Midtown East)
137 E. 47th St.
Manhattan, NY
212-980-7909
Japanese

Go Restaurant (East Village)
30 St. Marks Pl.
Manhattan, NY
212-254-5510
Japanese

Izakaya Riki (Grand Central)
141 E. 45th St.
Manhattan, NY
212-986-5604
Japanese

Typhoon Lounge (East Village)
79 St. Marks Pl.
Manhattan, NY
212-979-2680
Japanese

Village Yokocho (East Village)
8 Stuyvesant St.
Manhattan, NY
212-598-3041
Japanese

Yakitori East (Grand Central)
210 E. 44th St.
Manhattan, NY
212-687-5075
Japanese

Yakitori Taisho (East Village)
5 St. Marks Pl.
Manhattan, NY
212-228-5086
Japanese

It never fails; the more specific the question, the more plentiful the advice. Here, then, are student-friendly Japanese places suitable for large groups.

Yakitori East is great for large groups, and **Izakaya Riki** has a private karaoke room that can handle a good-sized party. **Donburi-Ya** caters mostly to Japanese businessmen but has room for a group.

Village Yokocho and **Yakitori Taisho** accept no reservations, so if you have a large group, get there early to avoid lines. **Go Restaurant** and **Typhoon Lounge** are great for yakiniku, yakitori, or other Izakaya fare, says *CkOne*. The latter can accommodate larger parties in its tatami rooms. Cooked food is preferable to raw here, so try yakitori-ish brochettes made with chicken skin, fried oysters, saikoro steak, kalbi beef, and octopus fried rice.

- ○ **Donburi-Ya:** *see also* **p. 235.**
- ○ **Izakaya Riki:** *see also* **p. 153.**
- ○ **Village Yokocho:** *see also* **p. 234.**

Queens **JAPANESE** Tips

Mickey's Place (Queens)
10116 Queens Blvd.
Rego Park, Queens, NY
718-897-9898
Japanese

Natural Fruit & Vegetable
  (Queens)
7256 Austin St.
Forest Hills, Queens, NY
718-268-4477
Japanese Store

Oishi's (Queens)
109-09 71st Rd., right behind
  the huge Keyfood
Forest Hills, Queens, NY
718-544-8877
Japanese Store

Sato Japanese Cuisine (Queens)
9812 Queens Blvd.
Rego Park, Queens, NY
718-897-1788
Japanese

Wasabi Japanese Cuisine
  (Queens)
39-11 Queens Blvd.
Sunnyside, Queens, NY
718-482-8777
Korean

Sato is a Japanese restaurant that dumbs down its menu to appeal to local tastes. If you want the kitchen to cook to a Japanese palate, you might have to ask for the "real stuff."

To experience the absolutely best sushi that **Mickey's** has to offer, sit at the sushi bar and order omakase, which always includes new and surprising items. The sushi chefs here remember your preferences. The catch is the price, which starts at $60 per person. The rest of the menu is much more Westernized.

Wasabi Sushi offers a large and varied menu including oysters on the half shell, baked oysters, baked clams, and many other cooked items. Large clams are so lightly baked that they remain tender and briny, delicious when mixed with the special Japanese mayo and spice sauce, says *HLing*. Tempuras arrive piping hot with light and crispy batter. Both eel sushi and a special eel-inside-eel roll get raves, as does crisped salmon skin and cucumber sushi.

Oishi's is a small store with a large inventory of Japanese products covering just about any cooking need. If you can't find the Japanese items you seek, nearby **Natural** is a good backup.

JAPANESE in Northern Suburbs

Azuma Sushi
  (Westchester County)
219 E. Hartsdale Ave.
Hartsdale, NY
914-725-0660
Japanese

Gyosai Seafood
  (Westchester County)
30 Garth Rd.
Scarsdale, NY
914-725-3730
Japanese

Hana-Sushi (Dutchess County)
7270 South Broadway, in
  Hardscrable Plaza
Red Hook, NY
845-758-4333
Japanese

Masuki Japanese Deli
  (Westchester County)
109 Halstead Ave.
Harrison, NY
914-777-0775
Japanese

Sakana (Rockland County)
25 Rockland Plaza
Nanuet, NY
845-623-2882
Japanese

Tenbo Cuisine
  (Westchester County)
16 Cedar St.
Dobbs Ferry, NY
914-674-2138
Japanese

A husband (chef) and wife (counterwoman) team operate **Masuki** in Harrison, which they claim is the first Japanese deli in New York. There are bento box lunch specials with choice of roll, vegetable, and chicken teriyaki for timid tastes. Be more adventurous and ask for what Japanese people order; when *LisaM* did, she received a lovely plate with several items: a largish absolutely greaseless potato croquet (fried to order, and crisp on the outside, creamy inside), a small mound of lovely cooked daikon, a bit of chilled bok choy (cooked with Japanese spices and a smoky hint of tamari), potato salad with egg, red pepper, and onion; and a bowl of white rice dotted with black sesame seeds and strewn with tart Japanese pickles. All that, plus a tiny lettuce and tomato salad with addictive ginger dressing, for $7.50. Lots of interesting things in the deli case.

Hana Sushi, in Red Hook, serves impeccably fresh fish. This is a sushi and sashimi haven, plus one udon dish and the usual appetizers. Good shumai and fairly large but delicious cuts of sushi, reports *lucia*. Mackerel is meltingly tender and tasty, and the specials are particularly good, especially a sensational lobster maki special with a touch of tobigo. Broiled yellowtail collar/cheek ($6) is excellent. Other rotating specials have included natto roll and unagi. Caveat: Be specific when ordering as the language barrier can be a problem. Service slows when the place is busy.

Nanuet's **Sakana** is a popular Rockland County sushi destination. In a recent small omakase, two items stood out: four small slices of hugely rich and velvetty Kobe beef sushi-style (on rice and bound with seaweed, topped a tiny dab of sauce), which *Michele Cindy* deemed scrumptious. Also terrific: sliced live scallops on a shell with mirin and a couple pieces of ikura sushi (blended with more of the scallop prepared in a spicy sauce), all topped with quail eggs. All for only $16.00.

Lunch specials are dinner sized at **Tenbo**, a Dobbs Ferry Chinese-Japanese crossover, and entrées come with cabbage appetizer, soup, and expertly done vegetable fried rice, reports *Budinado*. Hot and sour soup is sometimes too sweet.

At Scarsdale's **Gyosai** go omakase (i.e. let the chef decide). **Azuma** in Hartsdale is a popular choice.

Chowhound Nametag: JH Jill

○◯○

Location:
Jackson Heights, New York City.

Occupation:
I'm a linguist and cultural geographer.

Cholesterol Level:
Normal.

Farthest Out of the Way Traveled Just for Chow: About eighty miles one way to a fabled desert Italian place when I was growing up in Southern California. We went once without a reservation, only to find they were closed by a fire, so we returned (sometime later, after calling ahead) and had a wonderful many-course dinner that left us stuffed and satisfied.

Nabe Most Full of Explorable Unknown Chow:
Any place in Flushing, Queens.

Top Chinatown Pick: The Vietnamese one on Mulberry near the park that looks like a village courtyard. Some kind of Pho name.

Underrated by Chowhounds: John's Italian in the East Village.

Favorite Comfort Chow: Jackson House (Thirty-seventh Avenue and Eighty-third Street in Jackson Heights, Queens) for a Reuben sandwich close to home, perhaps, or a bowl of hot borscht at Lomnzynianka in Williamsburg or Veselka in the East Village.
    Outside New York, anything at Taquería Tlaquepaque on Santa Fe in Placentia, California (Orange County), and boiled crawfish made at the seafood market attached to the Frog's Breath Saloon on the Tickfaw River in Livingston, Louisiana.

Guilty Pleasure:
Spareribs in all guises.

Favorite Gelato Flavor: Actually it's a granita called *gelsi* (mulberry). Haven't been able to get it in this country.

Weird **JELLIES**

Blue Apron Foods (Brooklyn)
814 Union St.
Park Slope, Brooklyn, NY
718-230-3180
Store

Blue Apron sells weird jellies designed to accent cheese and crackers, such as an apricot cumin jelly intended to match soft ripened cheeses like camembert. Each jelly comes with cheese pairing suggestions. New trend?

○ **Blue Apron Foods:** *see also* **p. 54.**

Great **JERK** in Brooklyn, Bronx, and Long Island

Ali's T & T Roti Deli Grocery
   (Brooklyn)
1267 Fulton St.
Bedford-Stuyvestant,
   Brooklyn, NY
718-783-0316
Trinidadian

Chicken Center (Brooklyn)
Utica Ave., near Carroll St.
Crown Heights, Brooklyn, NY
Jamaican

Sugarcane's (Brooklyn)
238 Flatbush Ave.
Park Slope, Brooklyn, NY
718-230-3954
Trinidadian

Vernon's New Jerk House
   (Bronx)
987 E. 233rd St.
Bronx, NY
718-655-8348
Jamaican

Village Deli (Suffolk County)
1513 Straight Path
Wyandanch, NY
631-491-9053
Jamaican

The jerk chicken at **Sugarcane**—available as a chicken wing appetizer or a half-chicken entree—is *really* good. It brings on the heat, but also has layers of subtle, complex, spectacular flavors! The chicken isn't as smoky as at some jerkeries, and it's definitely pricier (the half bird plus two sides runs $15), but it's worth it, raves jerk aficionado *Paul Lukas*. But other hounds argue that the price is ridiculous when there's very good jerk around for half as much. On the other hand, it's one of the few "nice" sit-down places serving real jerk.

The jerk chicken at **Chicken Center** is delicious enough to have changed *astoria*'s entire perception of the genre. Barbecued via traditional methods in a metal oil drum, it's a heavenly mixture of spices, tenderness of the chicken, and smoky flavor of charcoal.

Although not served as screamingly hot as some might like, jerk chicken at **Vernon's Jerk House** has a nice kick to it. Still, it might pale in comparison to side dishes like rice and peas, fried plantains, and stewed vegetables.

There's a Brooklyn branch of the reliable North Bronx chain of **Ali's**.

The best jerk chicken *Jim Leff* has ever had is made by a guy named Phil in Wyandanch, Long Island, owner of the anonymous-seeming **Village Deli**. Great jerk pork, too, when he has it. Seek him out, he's a genius. His other dishes, especially his ackee, are also excellent, and don't miss the Scotch bonnet-spiked mac and cheese.)

Also see cuisine index for more Jamaican choices, many of which make good jerk.

Chinatown Beef **JERKY**

Jung's Dried Beef (Chinatown)
58 Mulberry St.
Manhattan, NY
212-732-0850
Chinese

Malaysian Beef Jerky (Chinatown)
95A Elizabeth St.
Manhattan, NY
212-965-0796
Malaysian

New Beef King (Chinatown)
89 Bayard St.
Manhattan, NY
212-233-6612
Chinese (Hong Kong)

A report on Chinatown beef jerky, courtesy of *ultbil*:

At **Jung's Dried Beef** (on Mulberry), sweet beef and sweet pork jerky are moist and quite tasty. Spicy beef and pork jerkies are mild, and not as tasty as the sweet varieties. **Malaysian Beef Jerky** on Elizabeth serves beef jerky in squares about the size of two credit cards, which they grill and keep warm—and that can make the jerky greasy. They serve more varieties (including chicken jerky) than other places. Spicy jerkies here are real spicy, but the pork still retains some sweetness. **New Beef King** is not a favorite of *ultbil*, who says all jerkies have an unidentifiable unpleasant flavor, but other hounds love the place.

○ **New Beef King:** *see also* p. 74.

On the Way to **JFK AIRPORT**

Annie's Roti Shop (Queens)
123-28 Rockaway Blvd.
South Ozone Park, Queens, NY
718-323-9444
Trinidadian

Furci Food Products (Queens)
103-09 101st Ave.
Richmond Hill, Queens, NY
718-849-6661
Italian

Daleo's Pizza (Queens)
9010 Jamaica Ave.
Jamaica, Queens, NY
718-849-9300
Italian/Pizza

La Tavernetta (Queens)
75-01 88th St.
Glendale, Queens, NY
718-896-3538
Italian

Maurya (Queens)
63-108 Woodhaven Blvd.
Rego Park, Queens, NY
718-416-4007
Indian

Trini Delight (Queens)
110-02 Liberty Ave.
Jamaica, Queens, NY
718-322-1203
Trinidadian

Pio Pio (Queens)
62-30 Woodhaven Blvd.
Woodhaven, Queens, NY
718-458-0606
Peruvian

As thousands head daily toward the southeastern corner of Queens for their flights, they're passing great Italian, Caribbean, and Indian food. Sadly, they have no idea. We won't stand for this. You must stop and eat something great on your way— and on your way back. Some of these places are more out of your way than others; if you're in a big hurry, take the Liberty Avenue exit off the Van Wyck, turn right off the ramp, and enter Trinidadian/Guyanese takeout heaven.

Among the sea of roti shops in Ozone Park, *Chicago Mike* prefers **Annie's Roti Shop**. *Ivan Stoller* recommends the Indian/Caribbean specialties at **Trini Delight**, which has shaped up as a chowhound fave.

La Tavernetta makes amazing gnocchi, says *knoedel*, with a rich and fragrant gorgonzola sauce and topped with a generous amount of truffle oil, which works wonders. The gnocchi themselves are perfect: not too dense, yet also not overcooked and watery. Also, calamari are perfectly fried, and come with a fresh and garlicky marinara sauce.

Furci's is a great takeout spot for Italian food. **Daleo's** makes superior pizza.

Maurya is a good choice for Indian, but you must order everything "very spicy" if you want any heat at all.

Pio Pio makes outstanding Peruvian rotisserie chicken.

JOEY THAI, the Alter Ego of the Blimpie's Sub Shop on Thirty-first Street

Blimpie Subs & Salads (Murray Hill)
17 E. 31st St.
Manhattan, NY
212-213-3773
Thai

Joey Thai is a Thai restaurant operating subversively inside a **Blimpie's** sandwich shop. The wisdom on this place is to avoid steam-table stuff and order only menu items, which are cooked to order. Aside from the trippiness of the entire enterprise, the food is, in some ways, terrific. Owner Joey sincerely wants to offer a real Thai food experience, rather than the usual pandering gringo stuff, and this franchise was the best way he could get a foothold. But he's walking where no restaurateur has tread before, and it's sort of a work in progress. But the food's sincere and authentic.

Joey's *pad kee mow* impressed *ahab*, who exults: "What a dish! Seriously outstanding. One of the best Thai dishes I've had in recent memory. Flat rice noodles, onions, beef, a good amount of fresh basil and lots of spicy brown sauce. The key is to convince whoever takes your order to make it spicy. My meal was taken to a level of heat I've never experienced at Joey before." But he reports that business is very slow and the owner is thinking about cutting back to Thai food at lunch only.

Brooklyn **JURY DUTY** Lunch

Brooklyn Ice Cream Factory
   (Brooklyn)
1 Water St.
Dumbo, Brooklyn, NY
718-246-3963
Ice Cream or Gelato

Lassen & Hennig (Brooklyn)
114 Montague St.
Brooklyn Heights, Brooklyn, NY
718-875-6272
Sandwich Shop

Teresa's Restaurant (Brooklyn)
80 Montague St.
Brooklyn Heights, Brooklyn, NY
718-797-3996
Polish

Jury duty is less of a drag if you can do some serious chowing on lunch break. In Brooklyn there's no reason you can't eat well while doing your civic duty. **Lassen & Hennig** serves tasty sandwiches and has a helpful, friendly staff. **Teresa's** Luncheonette is an inexpensive Polish restaurant with terrific soups, says *Penelope*. Service is pretty efficient, so you might actually have a few minutes after lunch to walk the Promenade. The only bright point of *Gvalenti*'s two weeks of recent grand jury duty hell was a daily visit to the **Brooklyn Ice Cream Factory** (and the fifteen-minute walk burns off all the calories).

See also Atlantic Avenue Arabic.

KABAB CAFE AND MOMBAR:
Magical Personal Food and Trippy Café in Astoria

Kabab Cafe (Queens)
25-12 Steinway St.
Astoria, Queens, NY
718-728-9858
Egyptian

Mombar (Queens)
25-22 Steinway St.
Astoria, Queens, NY
718-726-2356
Egyptian

Ali's a magician when he wants to be, and often the best way to order at **Kabab Cafe** is to just let Ali cook whatever he wants. A couple of his newer concoctions hounds love: phyllo pastry stuffed with spiced beef (cinnamon predominating), topped with roasted veggies; and roast chicken topped with tart apricot sauce. *Aaron S.* really got worked up over the latter: "You can't believe how amazing the flavor of this dish was! Our forks were practically dueling as we devoured the entire plate in about two minutes flat!" Ali's lamb shank with apricot is excellent, too, as is his stuffed chicken, and salads of warm artichokes and beets.

One reason for Ali's inconsistency is that while he's equally adept with meat items, the meat he buys is often low quality and not commensurate with his cooking skills. Avoid roast meats (kebabs are good, though) in favor of fish preparations or a mixed appetizer plate containing falafel, hummus, foul, smoky baba ghanoush and some crisped green (often Swiss chard). Kofta is also good, and, if they're available as a special, be sure to order humitas done as crêpes with homemade farmer's cheese, corn, onions, garlic, and fresh tomato sauce. Desserts are very good when fresh. While much of his cooking is "Ali Fusion", he can also make authentic traditional Egyptian foods upon request.

Down the block, Ali's brother Mustafa has built **Mombar**, a jaw-dropping café, after years of painstaking labor piecing together found objects. (Imagine if Gaudí had been born in Alexandria and cooked really well, explains *Jim Leff*.) The problem is that while Mustafa is as extraordinary a chef as he is an artisan, his attempts at ambitious fusion cooking can sometimes fall short, disappointing at the relatively high prices he charges. However, rumor has it Mustafa may be switching his menu to simpler cooking at better prices, and, in any case, ambience alone makes it well worth a visit.

○ **Kabab Cafe:** *see also* p. 16.

KINGS COUNTY HOSPITAL
Chow

Crown Fried Chicken (Brooklyn)
504 Clarkson Ave.
Flatbush, Brooklyn, NY
718-778-7721
American

No, we're not recommending hospital food, but around the corner from Kings County Hospital (home of the second-busiest

.emergency room in the country), Mediterranean Grill/**Crown Chicken** serves what *perry* calls amazing chicken off a gyro spit. Look for the big red awning.

And check out the roti truck, usually parked on either Clarkson between New York Avenue and about Thirty-fifth, or else on New York Avenue between Clarkson and Lenox. *Allie* notes this Roti Lady is usually there around lunchtime on weekdays. The excellent vegetarian roti comes with spinach, potatoes, chickpeas, and cauliflower, and meat roti are excellent, too. And the Roti Woman is extremely kind. You *must* ask for the spicy sauce!

Subway **KOREAN**

Fulton Station (Lower Manhattan)
150 Fulton St.
Manhattan, NY
Korean

Fulton Station is a Korean restaurant right in the arcade of the sprawling Fulton Street subway station (1, 2, 3, 4, 5, and A, J, Z, and M lines). The food's top-notch, says *elvisjr*, who favors their bibimbap and also dotes on their kim bap sushi rolls, which have a nice balance between sweet (egg omelet), crunchy (carrots, cucumbers), and mellow (spinach with sesame oil). Everything comes with lots of fresh veggies.

Newish Flushing **KOREAN** Choices

Nam O Jung (Queens)
16013 Northern Blvd.
Flushing, Queens, NY
718-539-5674
Korean

Tong Tong & Gibum (Queens)
15809 Northern Blvd.
Flushing, Queens, NY
718-762-7656
Korean

24 hour B.B.Q. Place (Queens)
154th & Northern Blvd.
Flushing, Queens, NY
Korean

Tong Tong & Gibum is an extremely casual Korean joint. Order at the front counter, and someone will bring your order to one of four folding tables. *Lisa* reports excellent kim bap, and kimchi *bokkumbap* is nice and spicy, and not oily. Koreans order pork cutlet plates with salad and big bowls of *dokkbokki*.

They make serious *kalbi jim* (beef short ribs cooked for ages with a sweet sauce of chestnuts and carrots, among other things) at **Nam O Jung**; *john farago*, whose taste favors marinades heavy on sugar and garlic, calls this the best BBQ in the city.

Panchan at the newish **24 hour BBQ** place are tasty and the meat quality's very high.

Bargain **KOREAN** Lunch

Won Jo (Herald Sq/Garment District)
23 W. 32nd St.
Manhattan, NY
212-695-5815
Korean

The extensive lunch menu at **Won Jo** spans two pages of classic Korean dishes, most for under $10. A full assortment of panchan is included. A dish listed simply as "baby octopus with vegetables over rice" surprised *charliebaltimore* when it arrived as a large sizzling stone pot chock full of rice, vegetables, baby octopus, and hot sauce on the side. *Deena* loves Won Jo's beef soup for its deep, delicious rich broth (but beware the beef innards lurking inside).

KOREAN-STYLE CHINESE

Hyo Dong Gak (Herald
   Sq/Garment District)
51 W. 35th St.
Manhattan, NY
212-695-7167
Korean/Chinese

Te Min Quan (Bergen County)
270 Broad Ave.
Palisades Park, NJ
201-592-8993
Chinese/Korean

Sang Choon
   (Herald Sq/Garment District)
30 W. 32nd St.
Manhattan, NY
212-629-6450
Korean/Chinese

Typical Korean-style Chinese food dishes (made by ethnic Koreans from China . . . or is it vice versa?) include ja-jang myun (noodles with black bean sauce), jjam ppong (noodles in spicy seafood broth), and na jo gi (sweet/sour chicken wings).

Go to **Hyo Dong Gak** at lunchtime and you'll find it packed with Koreans. Jjam ppong is their signature dish but the jjajang myun and tang soo yook (deep-fried pork in sweet/sour sauce) are very good too, says *halo*. Portions are large, but Europeans get a Chinese-American menu and fried wontons with orange sauce when they sit down, while Asians get the "Korean-Chinese" menu and a variety of Panchan, so be sure to do the right thing.

At **Sang Choon** jjajang myun and tang soo yeok are popular.

halo says yuni jja jang myun at **Te Min Quan** is far superior to anything you can get in the city.

Chic **KOSHER** with Serious Cuisine

Orchidea (Brooklyn)
4815 12th Ave.
Borough Park, Brooklyn, NY
718-686-7500
Kosher New American

Orchidea is a kosher place combining chic ambience with delicious food, says *AmyT*, who reports enjoying the best tasting, most beautifully presented kosher meal she's had in years. Chilean sea bass and ultrafresh spinach ravioli in a delicious herbed cream sauce with a hint of walnut oil are knockouts. It's important to note that Amy was a veteran Chowhound.com participant before turning kosher. She's eaten around a lot, so when she says this ambitious New American kitchen blew her away, it really means something!

Lunch at **LA CARAVELLE**

La Caravelle Restaurant (Midtown West)
33 W. 55th St.
Manhattan, NY
212-586-4252
French

The basic prix fixe lunch at **La Caravelle** is $38. There are plenty of opportunities to boost the check higher, but the meal's well worth the expense, says *Susan Marme*, who reports that tuna sashimi and gravlax are sumptuous and incredibly appetizing—so much so that she could taste it on the inside of her cheeks (which we're assuming is a good thing). She also raves about wonderful rare lamb tenderloin slices, cut about a quarter inch thick, very thin slices of rare leg, and a piece of breast of lamb, all perfectly cooked—the breast a sticky, sumptuous, savory counterpoint to the leaner meat. It's served on a bed of sautéed baby greens, surrounded by perfectly cooked baby Shanghai cabbages and a foamy curry sauce, which beautifully complements the flavor of the lamb. Buckwheat—roasted and sprinkled on top—offers a crunchy counterpoint. The menu is divided between modern and classical dishes. The wine list is large and very expensive (cheapest bottle: $42).

Cosmic **LAMB CHOPS**

Simchick Meats (Midtown East)
944 1st Ave.
Manhattan, NY
212-888-2299
Store

Simchick is one of the few places carrying prime lamb, and *erica* says an order of un-Frenched (i.e., fat left on the bone) American lamb chops changed her life. Very pricey, about $5 a chop. This is a great old-fashioned butcher shop offering much personal attention.

Park Slope's **LATIN AMERICAN CAFE** for Soulful Pan-Hispanic

Latin American Cafe (Brooklyn)
661 Sackett St.
Park Slope, Brooklyn, NY
718-857-7720
Eclectic Latin American

Latin American Cafe is a homey, unpretentious (yet elegant) café with both common and uncommon pan-Hispanic foods. *Barry Strugatz* reports that food is prepared with care and soul. Chicken stew (from the lunch special menu) is superior, made with saffron. Toasted bread is served with olive paste/oil dip, and rice and red beans are excellent, while *ann marie* recommends loin of pork with mustard, pine nuts, and pears, though the rendition can vary. One time it was a very artful presentation of little fanned-out food bits dabbled with sauce, while another time it was a more manly-man plate with big pork chunks, fruit and nuts on the side, sauce aplenty. Each was delicious, with mild, creamy, mustard-spiked sauce, perfect with the moist and tender pork. Prices are very moderate ($14.95 is as high as it goes). Lots of Argentinian choices on the wine list.

East End **LATINO**

Chiquita Latina (Suffolk County)
480 Montauk Hwy., beside the
   Dutch Motel on Pantigo Rd.
East Hampton, NY
631-329-6624
Latin American

Embassy Market (Suffolk County)
S. Embassy Rd. and Euclid
Montauk, NY
631-668-2323
Latin American

Continental Market
   (Suffolk County)
34 Eton Rd.
Montauk, NY
631-668-6060
Latin American

Montauk and the Hamptons seem to offer only overpriced tourist chow venues with lousy food. Spice it up by going Latino. The Latin places are serving some of the most delicious, good-value food on the East End. Tourists may not want rice and beans if they're on holiday for a few days, but locals find them a godsend, says *Blondie*, who recommends *pernil asado* and *papas relleñas* at **Embassy**, and roast chicken at **Continental**. **Chiquita Latina** is very good, with no standouts.

Elegant, Relaxing **LE MADRI**

Le Madri (Chelsea)
168 W. 18th St.
Manhattan, NY
212-727-8022
Italian

Le Madri is an elegant, relaxing restaurant with excellent service and outstanding food that leaves you satisfied without feeling stuffed, reports *Sethy*. Risotto with slivers of asparagus and lemon zest, topped with two succulent seared diver sea scallops, is perfectly seasoned. Bucatini (hollow spaghetti) comes topped with mounds of lobster meat in a sauce resembling fra diavolo only more subtle and flavorful. Espresso is excellent. One complaint: fruit compote accompanying light and delicate panna cotta is overwhelmed by the flavor of cloves.

Yonkers **LEBANESE**

Ya Hala (Westchester County)
326 S. Broadway
Yonkers, NY
914-476-4200
Lebanese/Middle Eastern/North African

Ya Hala must do most of its business at night because at lunchtime *Deven Black* has found himself the only customer for their very inexpensive and tasty Lebanese food. The Middle East platter ($4.99) is a generous serving of baba ghanoush, hummus, falafel and tabbouleh, served with pita, pickles, and olives. Baba ghanoush is wonderfully smoky and had a great, thick but not chunky texture. Two falafel balls were freshly fried, not at all oily, with a crisply crunchy exterior. Hummus is very smooth and delicately flavored. Lebanese tabbouleh is very heavy on freshly chopped parsley. Turkish coffee ($.99) is freshly hand roasted and flavored with cardamom.

Two Hours of Professionals at **L'ECOLE**

L'Ecole (Soho)
462 Broadway
Manhattan, NY
212-219-3300
New American/French

L'Ecole is, of course, the dining room at the French Culinary Institute, where students prepare and serve all meals (with inherently inconsistent results). We've received a fabulous piece of insider info: while lunches and five-course dinners after 8:00 p.m. are student productions, L'Ecole quietly serves an earlier four-course dinner from 6:00 p.m. to 8:00 p.m. prepared by professionals—really *good* professionals. *Helen Rennie* calls it the best French meal $30 can buy in New York. She had an outstanding duck with berry sauce; the medium-rare breast was deliciously tender under the crisp skin, the leg confit fell apart at the touch of a fork, and a sauce of fresh seasonal blueberries added the perfect touch. Rare and juicy grilled tuna came with red pepper stew and garlicky roasted potatoes, and appetizers and desserts, especially passionfruit cheesecake, garnered high praise as well.

○ **L'Ecole:** *see also* **p. 69**.

LINGERING Welcome

Ceci-Cela (Soho)
55 Spring St.
Manhattan, NY
212-274-9179
French Café

Stella del Mare (Murray Hill)
346 Lexington Ave.
Manhattan, NY
212-687-4425
Italian

Lil' Frankies Pizza (East Village)
19 First Ave.
Manhattan, NY
212-420-4900
Pizza/Italian

Trio (Murray Hill)
167 E. 33rd St.
Manhattan, NY
212-685-1001
Croatian/Italian

Some restaurants are like hot-sheet motels: they'd charge you by the minute if they could. Other places don't mind if you linger for a while. The following are some of the latter. (Remember to tip a little extra if you've lingered at a table!):

Croatian specialties stand out at **Trio**, where long stays are encouraged and the staff is doting and generous. (The staff always offers *Sean* a digestif with dessert.) Croatian-owned **Stella del Mare** specializes in northern-Italian seafood in a very friendly atmosphere, especially at the piano bar downstairs, where lingering is encouraged; *jjm* says the upstairs dining room has excellent service and a fine wine list to accompany very good food. **Lil' Frankies** is actually *looking* for lingerers. Their takeout menu offers a specific invitation to relax over coffee or a glass of wine with a book, chess game, or friend. To **Lil' Frankies**, it harkens back to the way neighborhood pizzerias function in Italy. They've even got a garden area in back for outdoor relaxation. **Ceci-Cela** gets crowded at lunch, but in off hours it's relaxed and you can linger over their tasty coffees and wondrous pastries (don't miss the financiers!).

○ **Ceci-Cela:** *see also* **pp. 67, 96.**
○ **Lil' Frankies Pizza:** *see also* **p. 244.**

LITTLE PIE COMPANY Discovery

Little Pie Co. (Chelsea)
407 W. 14th St.
Manhattan, NY
212-414-2324
Bakery

Little Pie Co. (Clinton)
424 W. 43rd St.
Manhattan NY
212-736-4780
Bakery

Little Pie Co. (Grand Central)
E. 42nd St. and Lexington Ave.,
   Grand Central Dining
   Concourse
Manhattan, NY
212-983-3538
Bakery

Fans say Little Pie Company is nothing if not consistent, with many items tasting exactly as they did at the first location twenty years ago. It is hard to pass by favorites to try something new, but *Dave Feldman* did and discovered a chocolate chunk cookie and an orange roll that looked like a cinnamon roll but had a slight orange aroma. Their chocolate chunk cookie has the richness and chocolate quality of David's Cookies back during its prime. It isn't huge, and costs a buck, but one is a perfect snack or lunch dessert. The orange roll suffered from having stood around, but Feldman thinks it'd be "killericious" when fresh.

Everything isn't equally great here, but we'd like to remind you to run out and try their sour cream walnut apple pie (recommended in Perfect *Pie,* held in such chowhound awe that we're fully prepared to keep repeating the tip throughout the book.

○ **Little Pie Co:** *see also* **p. 240.**

LIVERWURST Sandwiches

Eisenberg's Sandwich Shop
(Gramercy)
174 5th Ave.
Manhattan, NY
212-675-5096
Dinner or Coffee Shop

Second Avenue Deli (East Village)
390 2nd Ave.
Manhattan, NY
212-777-2808
Kosher Eastern European Jewish

McSorley's Old Ale House
(East Village)
15 E. 7th St.
Manhattan, NY
212-473-9148
American Pub

The perfect liverwurst sandwich is homely but satisfying, and it's awfully hard to fit a bill like that in a cosmopolitan city like this. The following are the holdouts:

Second Avenue Deli makes their own liverwurst, and *bryanj* says a sandwich made from it is amazing. Liverwurst is a popular choice among diners at **Eisenberg's Sandwich Shop**. And while **McSorley's** is a sloppy, rollicking, fratty beer bar by night, in the afternoon it's quiet and when the light comes through the front windows you're transported back a century—the best possible setting to enjoy liverwurst sandwiches or a liverwurst, onion, and cheese platter.

Large LOBSTER

Francisco's Centro Vasco (Chelsea)
159 W. 23rd St.
Manhattan, NY
212-989-9109
Spanish

You can get any size lobster you want at **Francisco's Centro Vasco**— even monsters well over five pounds. Other items worth ordering include garlic soup, baked clams, and fried shrimp (ask for extra tartar sauce). Sangria is also reportedly very good. Very reasonable prices.

LOBSTER TAILS

La Bella Ferrara Pasticceria (Little Italy)
108 Mulberry St.
Manhattan, NY
212-966-7867
Italian

No, not the shellfish . . . the Italian pastry! These are large cones of very crispy pastry filled with whipped custard. **La Bella Ferrara Pasticceria** (which we don't particularly recommend for most things) only makes them on Fridays, though sometimes you can still get them over the weekend—obviously not as fresh. They're impeccably brown, crispy, and delicate on the outside, with a filling that's whipped and light yet very rich and custardy tasting, with a truly grandmotherly flavor, reports *elvislives*, who says this item been consistently great here for fifteen years. A mini version is also available if you're, like, dieting.

LOW-Budget UWS

Alibaba (Upper West Side)
515 Amsterdam Ave.
Manhattan, NY
212-787-6008
Kosher Sephardic/Israeli

Flor de Mayo (Upper West Side)
484 Amsterdam Ave.
Manhattan, NY
212-787-3388
Peruvian/Latin American/Chinese

Sal's & Carmine Pizza (Upper West Side)
2671 Broadway
Manhattan, NY
212-663-7651
Pizza

Bargains on the Upper West Side are few and far between, but longtime UWS resident *Dave Feldman* offers his best affordable picks:

Alibaba's makes great turkey shwarma on homemade laffa (bread), excellent soups (especially chicken), and offers an unlimited salad bar (check out the spicy carrots!). **Flor de Mayo** is a solid pick for rotisserie chicken, as well as great daily specials. On Sundays, they make a wonderful parihuela, and pork adobo on Thursdays is always a good choice. And a slice of pizza at perpetual Chowhound favorite **Sal and Carmine**'s always hits the spot.

Inexpensive **LUNCH** in the Heart of Capitalism

Ho Yip Restaurant
   (Lower Manhattan)
189 Broadway
Manhattan, NY
212-267-2521
Chinese

Kitchenette (Tribeca)
80 W. Broadway
Manhattan, NY
212-267-6740
American/Diner or Coffee Shop

Kitchenette Uptown (Harlem)
1272 Amsterdam Ave.
Manhattan, NY
212-531-7600
American/Diner or Coffee Shop

Mangez Avec Moi
   (Lower Manhattan)
71 Broadway
Manhattan, NY
212-385-0008
Thai/Laotian

Pakistan Tea House (Tribeca)
176 Church St.
Manhattan, NY
212-240-9800
Pakistani

ROC (Tribeca)
190 Duane St., A
Manhattan, NY
212-625-3333
Italian

Salaam Bombay (Tribeca)
317 Greenwich St.
Manhattan, NY
212-226-9400
Indian

Sheezaan Indian Restaurant
(Lower Manhattan)
183 Church St.
Manhattan, NY
212-964-6259
Pakistani

Seh Jeh Meh (Lower Manhattan)
26 John St.
Manhattan NY
212-766-5825
Korean

Downtown lunch options tend to divide between really inexpensive and inflated expense-account places. Good picks among the former:

- Sturdy, spicy South Asian fare (with plenty of vegetarian options) at **Sheezaan and at Pakistani Tea House** (see *South Asian* Cabbie Haunts).
- Despite its French name, **Mangez Avec Moi** serves inexpensive Thai and Laotian food.
- **Seh Jeh Meh** specializes in bibimbap (Korean rice stew), but also has very good *dol sot* and lunchbox specials.
- **Kitchenette** has well-prepared American diner-type food: blue plate specials, a highly praised turkey club sandwich, and good homey desserts.
- **ROC's** carryout Italian lunch menu is a steal compared to their sitdown lunch prices, but the $20 prix fixe lunch is still a good deal.
- **Salaam Bombay** has a well-regarded all-you-can-eat buffet at lunch.
- **Ho Yip** is a hole-in-the-wall Chinese restaurant with lots of seating and very good pork dishes.

○ Kitchenette: *see also* **pp. 42, 130, 151, 240, 280.**
○ Kitchenette Uptown: *see also* **pp. 42, 104, 151, 240.**
○ Pakistan Tea House: *see also* **p. 282.**
○ Sheezaan Indian Restaurant: *see also* **p. 283.**

The Ever-Craveable **MAC AND CHEESE**

Artisanal (Murray Hill)
2 Park Ave. (enter on 32nd St)
Manhattan, NY
212-725-8585
French

Blue Smoke (Gramercy)
116 E. 27th St.
Manhattan, NY
212-447-7733
Barbecue/American

Canteen (Soho)
142 Mercer St.
Manhattan, NY
212-431-7676
American

Chat 'n' Chew (Union Square)
10 E. 16th St.
Manhattan, NY
212-243-1616
Diner or Coffee Shop

City Bakery (Gramercy)
3 W. 18th St.
Manhattan, NY
212-366-1414
Café

Duke's (Gramercy)
99 E. 19th St.
Manhattan, NY
212-260-2922
Southern

Eatery (Clinton)
798 9th Ave.
Manhattan, NY
212-765-7080
Eclectic New American

Fred's (Upper West Side)
476 Amsterdam Ave.
Manhattan, NY
212-579-3076
American

Mama's Food Shop (East Village)
200 E. 3rd St.
Manhattan, NY
212-777-4425
Southern

Mayrose (Gramercy)
920 Broadway
Manhattan, NY
212-533-3663
American

Tea & Sympathy
   (Greenwich Village)
108 Greenwich Ave.
Manhattan, NY
212-807-8329
British

The Tomato (Chelsea)
676 Ave. of the Americas
Manhattan, NY
212-645-6525
American

Mac and Cheese is always a rousing topic. Lots of great tips:

- **The Tomato:** Sauce is always perfectly creamy, and pasta consistency is always just right, says *David*.
- Asiago cheese gives the Canteen version some extra bite.
- **Eatery:** Very rich—almost too rich to eat as an entrée— and comes with some sort of lightly frizzled onions on top, says *Alexandra Halsey*.
- Mac and cheese at **Blue Smoke** consistently earns high marks.
- **Artisanal** makes mac and cheese in a very shallow dish so that the ratio of crunchy top to soft middle is high.
- **Tea & Sympathy**'s version is extra rich and full of cheddar.
- **Duke**'s version has a particularly crispy top.
- The exceptional mac and cheese at **Mayrose** arrives at your table absolutely molten, as it's in a shallow dish and finished under the broiler, says *ThorNYC*, and they do an even better version with chunks of ham. But another chowhound dissents, saying it tastes like Kraft's in the blue box.
- You can customize the version at **Fred**'s (not sure exactly what that means . . . but it sounds good!).
- Other versions drawing attention: **City Bakery, Mama's Food Shop,** and **Chat 'n Chew**.

○ Artisanal: *see also* pp. 32, 66, 132, 266.
○ Blue Smoke: *see also* p. 85.
○ City Bakery: *see also* pp. 96, 161.
○ Mama's Food Shop: *see also* p. 64.
○ Tea & Sympathy: *see also* p. 43.

MALAGUETA: Hidden Brazilian Treasure

Malagueta (Queens)
25-35 36th Ave.
Long Island City, Queens, NY
718-937-4821
Brazilian

Malagueta is hidden on a residential block of Long Island City, and makes excellent Brazilian food. (Caring owners make the difference.) Opt for Bahian fare like *corvina com vatapa*, which goes best with an appetizer of *acarajé*. Linguica ("so tasty, almost bacon-y, I could eat that forever . . . nicely grilled and crisp," drools *alithang*) comes with cucumber sauce and yucca. Tomato sauce accompanying crisp fried calamari is especially tasty, and sides of mellow red beans and garlicky, almost crunchy collard greens satisfy nicely. *Carne guisada* can be too salty, but desserts are a high point. Coconut mousse is light and creamy, not too sweet, very refreshing. But the extraordinarily dense flan is pure silky perfection.

○ **Malagueta:** *see also* **p. 16.**

MALAYSIAN Roundup

Chrystie Village (Lower East Side)
95 Chrystie St.
Manhattan, NY
212-966-3663
Malaysian

Franklin Station Cafe (Chinatown)
222 W. Broadway
Manhattan, NY
212-274-8525
French/Malaysian

Ipoh (Chinatown)
25 Canal St.
Manhattan, NY
212-388-0264
Malaysian/Chinese

New Malaysia Restaurant
 (Chinatown)
48 Bowery, in the Elizabeth St.
 alley
Manhattan, NY
212-964-0284
Malaysian

Nyonya (Chinatown)
194 Grand St.
Manhattan, NY
212-334-3669
Malaysian

Overseas Asian Restaurant
 (Chinatown)
49 Canal St.
Manhattan, NY
212-925-3233
Malaysian

Penang (Soho)
109 Spring St.
Manhattan, NY
212-274-8883
Malaysian

Proton Saga (Chinatown)
11 Allen St.
Manhattan, NY
212-625-1163
Malaysian

Penang Chinatown (Chinatown)
41 Elizabeth St.
Manhattan, NY
212-431-8722
Malaysian

Taste Good (Queens)
82-18 45th Ave.
Elmhurst, Queens, NY
718-898-8001
Malaysian

Penang Malaysian (Queens)
82-84 Broadway
Elmhurst, Queens, NY
718-672-1185
Malaysian

Taste Good II (Chinatown)
53 Bayard St.
Manhattan, NY
212-513-0818
Malaysian

As more Malaysians relocate to New York, home-style Malaysian places are starting to pop up downtown, many of them satellites of frontline places in Queens. Pay close attention to the ordering tips below; each place has its specialties.

Proton Saga (the name of the first car model manufactured in Malaysia) makes excellent sting ray, okra, and kangkong with dried/fermented shrimp paste, reports *FML*. Other hounds are very positive about the place as well.

Chrystie Village can be hard to find (it's a few steps down from street level), but the food makes it worth seeking out even if ambience is lacking, says *Aaron*.

New Malaysia has good home-style foods served in large portions at low prices. Best are curries, Hainanese chicken rice, laksa, *achat, ipoh* bean sprouts, curry vegetable noodle soup, and shaved ice desserts. Their *belachan* (fermented shrimp) is superior to the competition's, and don't miss roti canai (homemade ultrathin roti with curried chicken to dip into). *Mirepoix* highly recommends New Malaysia's $4.95 lunch special combining beef curry and Hainanese chicken rice.

Ipoh is more Chinese Malaysian, with house-made achat, curry fish-ball noodle soup, *nasi lemak*, and skate curry with okra. *Matt* raves that tofu dishes are insanely good if you get the homemade tofu, which is eggy and creamy and luscious.

Nyonya is the name of both a regional style of cooking and of a restaurant featuring that style. This place is extremely variable, probably an issue of one great chef who's not always there, exacerbated by folks not ordering well. Two tips: (1) get noodles and (2) stick with Malay dishes, ignoring the Thai and Chinese ones (always smart advice in Malaysian restaurants!). When it's good, it's truly great, so we deem it worth taking the chance. Nyonya excels at curries and roti canai, but their belachan sauce is a bit too dry, so avoid dishes that include it, says *Isabelle*.

Franklin Station Cafe is a tiny French/Malay hybrid with good food and tremendous coffee, says *mitchh*.

Oversea Asian makes uniformly good noodles, like fantastic chicken noodle soup, and great roti canai. Another bonus is they're open later than the rest of the local competition.

Taste Good is a reliable pick for *roti telur, nasi padang, assam laksa, char kway teow*, and fish cooked in mustard sauce. Also noodle soups and seafood.

Prices are awfully high at Manhattan's **Penangs**, and the branch in Chinatown is considered a no-go. But the front room at the Spring Street Penang is nice. Best bet: Hit the Elmhurst branch for best food, value, and menu choices.

○ **Nyonya:** *see also* p. 74.

MATSURI's Magical Chef/Owner

Matsuri (Chelsea)
369 W. 16th St., in Maritime Hotel
Manhattan, NY
212-243-6400
Japanese

Tadashi Ono was the chef at much lamented Sono and is known for his delicate hand, especially with cold dishes. Now Ono has his own place, a beautiful space in the Maritime Hotel. *HLing* reports that his tuna is magical, and Kobe beef is velvety and beefy, enhanced by the seared thin outer ring. The star of the seafood rice pot is the dark orange gooey goodies in the giant prawn's head, with an intense flavor of the sea (don't discard!)

plus the burnt rice at the bottom of the pot (use the clam shell to scrape off and into the mix). There's no tasting menu; the set-up is like a Japanese tapas bar. Four sushi chefs are on hand. Lobster seems to be a popular and beautifully prepared item.

Mmm, Mmm, **MEATBALLS**

Mai Xiang Tan (Queens)
40-09B Prince St.
Flushing, Queens, NY
718-353-8703
Chinese (Sichuan)

Along with a fabulous selection of tenderly steamed buns, Ms. Tan, the bun maestro at **Mai Xiang Tan** (translation: "the skies full of fragrance"), is crafting heavenly meatballs as well. It seems there's nothing besides meat, finely chopped meat, and air . . . and somehow they're just held together by some invisible but tasty aroma, gushes *Hling*. Their famous bun offerings have changed a bit, too. They now offer large plain steamed bread (manto) for 60 cents a bun and the vegetarian buns have grown larger and are two for $1. A tempting bowl of Slchuan beef noo-dle soup costs $3.

MERMAID INN, Casually Inviting Oyster Bar and Seafood Restaurant

Mermaid Inn (East Village)
96 2nd Ave.
Manhattan, NY
212-674-5870
Seafood

Mermaid Inn is an inviting restaurant boasting a wide choice of fresh and very tasty oysters. The rest of the menu is short and all seafood. Grilled whole dorade comes stuffed with garlic and fresh thyme and perched on a fragrant tangle of stewed red cabbage, reports *LBG*. Cod is done in a blood orange reduction, while salmon filet is served on home fries with asparagus, leeks, and grainy mustard. Dessert's free, but limited to espresso cups filled with a just-decadent-enough helping of chocolate pudding. Most entrées are in the midteens.

Good Little **MEX-TEX** Joint

Taco Taco (Upper East Side)
1726 2nd Ave.
Manhattan, NY
212-289-8226
Mexican

Taco Taco Mex-Tex instead of Tex-Mex, seeing as how preparations tilt toward the south side of the border. Good *huitlacoche* (the mushroomish smut that grows on corn: black, silky, delicate, and usually served in quesadillas). Even though it is quite a small joint, the food's fabulous, says *Jrock*.

Encyclopedic Roosevelt Ave. Area **MEXICAN** Roundup

Deli El Mexicano Corp (Queens)
64-13 Roosevelt Ave.
Woodside, Queens NY
718-396-3605
Mexican

El Poblano (Queens)
75-13 Roosevelt Ave.
Jackson Heights, Queens, NY
718-205-2996
Mexican

Grano de Oro 2000 (Queens)
95-50 Roosevelt Ave.
Jackson Heights, Queens, NY
718-205-8177
Mexican

Las Cazuelas Restaurant (Queens)
86-22 Roosevelt Ave.
Jackson Heights, Queens, NY
718-396-2206
Mexican

Las Cazuelas II (Queens)
4008 Hampton St.
Jackson Heights, Queens, NY
718-507-2901
Mexican

Maria Bonita Cafe (Queens)
41-07 National St.
Corona, Queens, NY
718-335-5955
Mexican

Tacos al Suadero (Queens)
37-57 90th St.
Jackson Heights, Queens, NY
718-507-7100
Mexican

Tacos al Suadero (Queens)
87-21 Roosevelt Ave.
Jackson Heights, Queens, NY
Mexican

Taqueria Coatzingo (Queens)
76-05 Roosevelt Ave.
Jackson Heights, Queens, NY
718-424-1977
Mexican

Tenampa Restaurant (Queens)
96-14 Roosevelt Ave.
Jackson Heights, Queens, NY
718-335-7359
Mexican

Tierras Mexicana (Queens)
65-18 Roosevelt Ave.
Woodside, Queens, NY
718-651-4052
Mexican

Tulcingo Deli 3 (Queens)
40-10 Junction Blvd.
Jackson Heights, Queens, NY
718-424-0404
Mexican

Vallecita Bakery (Queens)
40-06 Benham St., near 91st St.
Jackson Heights, Queens, NY
Mexican Bakery

Jackson Heights specialist *Eric Eto* offers his personal annotated taco encyclopedia, covering the length of Roosevelt Avenue (plus some side streets).

- **Grano de Oro 2000** is one of my favorite taquerias in all of New York City.

- **Taqueria Coatzingo** has very good al pastor, lengua, birria. Excellent chalupas.
- **Deli El Mexicano Corp** makes the best beans. Whole pintos—smoky and not mushy—tortas to go, or breakfast (huevos rancheros with those good beans).
- **El Poblano:** Inquire about special items in the steam trays. They have some unusual items, and good pipián pork chops. Go-to place for tortas.
- **Tacos al Suadero:** I find both al Suaderos to be pretty reliable. Nothing extremely outstanding, but good quality for the most part.
- **Las Cazuelas Restaurant:** A handwritten sign in front window says tortillas are handmade, a pretty good indication (if true). There's a newer branch near 83rd Street.
- **Vallecita Bakery** seems to offer fresh baked stuff like pan dulce around the clock.
- **Tulcingo Deli 3** is one of the twenty-four-hour places on/just off Roosevelt. They have a good al pastor spit going here. Everything else pretty standard.
- **Tierras Mexicana:** The standard menu provides no real standouts; opt for more promising daily specials.
- **Maria Bonita Cafe:** This place, along with Marcia's in the Sixties, really has that homey feel. This place looks very new, with no signage except for a board outside with specials. I need to check this place out.
- **Tenampa** (untried by Eric) is an old respected Mexican landmark.

See also *Jackson Heights* Taste Treats.

○ Taqueria Coatzingo: *see also* **p. 39.**

MEXICAN Wonderland in Sunset Park

La Flor Bakery (Brooklyn)
4021 5th Ave.
Sunset Park, Brooklyn, NY
718-633-1254
Mexican

La Flor de Piaxtla (Brooklyn)
4202 5th Ave.
Sunset Park, Brooklyn, NY
718-437-7356
Mexican

Paleteria La Michoacana
  (Brooklyn)
4118 5th Ave.
Sunset Park, Brooklyn, NY
718-431-9312
Mexican

Ricos Tacos (Brooklyn)
505 51st St.
Sunset Park, Brooklyn, NY
718-633-4816
Mexican

Rico's Tamales Oaxaquenos
  (Brooklyn)
46th St and 5th Ave.
Sunset Park, Brooklyn, NY
Mexican

Speedy's (Brooklyn)
4th Ave. at 59th St.
Sunset Park, Brooklyn, NY
Mexican

Tacos Nuevo Mexico III
  (Brooklyn)
4410 5th Ave.
Sunset Park, Brooklyn, NY
718-686-8151
Mexican

By far the most exciting Mexican chow nabe in the five boroughs. This is just a taste:

Speedy makes whatever he feels like cooking that day, so don't expect menus of any sort. The only strategy is to ask Speedy or his wife what's available. If they say tamales, pounce. The owner seems extraordinarily committed to his vision of serving magically good tamales, and they are, indeed, killer reports *Clams247*. But if Speedy sizes you up and thinks you'd be better off with something other than a tamale, he'll tell you he's out of them and suggest something else. Just go with the flow (or return under disguise and try again). Don't worry; Speedy has other good things, too. The chile relleño is exciting: mildly spicy, stuffed with a meaty-textured cheese akin to a savory ricotta, dipped in batter and pan fried. Nothing remarkable about rice, beans, or salad except their freshness. Everything's very fresh.

La Flor de Piaxtla is an *antojitos* (snacks) joint with weekend specials. The menu is a handwritten card, and other items are listed on signs over the back counter and kitchen area. Lengua (tongue) is one of the best versions *Eric Eto* has found in New York City, but gorditas, while quite good, are fairly standard compared with some Jackson Heights places.

At **Tacos Nuevo** Mexico III, al pastor is cut off a freshly cooked spit. The charring and the slicing of the marinated meat are essential, and the bits of pineapple round out the flavor of the meat, says *Eric Eto*, who considers their al pastor much better than at Tacos Nuevo I.

At **La Flor Bakery**, the torta de chorizo with egg, perked up with jalapeños, is delicious and very messy to eat. The *cemita*, in addition to chicken, had roasted chiles, avocado, cheese, and onion and lettuce. Both came on incredibly fresh rolls, lightly roasted right before serving. Totally amazing and filling, concludes *scrittrice*.

Ricos Tamales is in the shack at Forty-sixth Street and Fifth Avenue. (See The Search for Perfect *Tamales* [Plus Digressions]). **Ricos Tacos** (no relation; it's named for a value judgment, not a dude named Rico) on Fifty-first has good-looking al pastor, but we've heard no reports yet.

Neon signs at **Palateria La Michoacana** advertise burritos and ice cream, but be sure to check out the freezer full of delicious, colorful, irregularly shaped fruit ice pops (*paletas de fruta*). Flavors range from traditional Mexican (tamarind, mamey, guava, and chile-infused cucumber) to mainstream Americano (strawberry and cantaloupe).

○ **Rico's Tamales Oaxaquenos:** *see also* p. 299.

Chowhound Nametag: elvislives

○○○

Location:
Lower East Side.

Occupation: Manager/Producer of music news and features publication. Recently bought a small restaurant/building in Upstate New York, working toward our dream of opening an old-fashioned ice-cream/hotdog stand in the Catskills.

Cholesterol Level:
Around 140, thanks for asking.

Number of Visits to McDonald's in Past Decade: Pleadin' the fifth (I like their salads for a fast bite).

Farthest Out of the Way Traveled Just for Chow: My favorite eatin' trip was when we drove to Austin and back (instead of flying) to explore different regions of the United States. For a born and raised New Yorker this was an amazing experience. I loved everything—boiled peanuts from a gas station outside of Charleston, South Carolina; buckets of crabs we smashed apart with mallets at a local hall in Lafayette, Louisiana; BBQ shacks; county fairs; one regional specialty after another—this country is chow heaven!

Top Chinatown Pick:
Saigon Banh Mi—Under the Manhattan Bridge on Forsythe, a stall on the outside of the East Broadway Mall. The most amazing Vietnamese sandwiches—fresh baked bread, lots of crunchy vegetables, tasty meat, crispy pork, spicy sauce, and their heavenly garlic mayo. They are so good, I try and make 'em last but end up inhaling. The super nice people who work there plus out-of-the-way location add to the reward.

Underrated by Chowhounds:
Natural Restaurant—Chinese restaurant on Allen Street and Broome. Looks a bit seedy but amazing casserole dishes and fresh seafood.
NYC Icy—Avenue B and 2nd Street. Better than any gelato spot in the city.

Castillo De Jagua—Rivington and Essex. Excellent Cuban sandwiches, fresh roast pork (pernil), chicharrones (fried chicken chunks), rice and beans, stews, massive plates of great homey food for $6.

Favorite Comfort Chow: Behold the power of cheese. Fondue at Artisanal, French onion soup at Blue Ribbon, mac and cheese from Le Zoccele.

Guilty Pleasure:
Popeyes fried chicken (spicy, with a side of onion rings).

Favorite Mail Order Chow:
- **Turkey Jerky** from www.nbsmokehouse.com.
- **California Brittle** from www.sees.com
- **Twiglets and Hobnobs** from www.expatshopping.com

Favorite Big Bucks Restaurants—Gramercy Tavern (warm space, heavenly homey food), Jean George (inventive and unusual dishes, so tasty), Le Bernardin (impeccable service, seafood nirvana). One of the great pleasures in life is eating at places like these, where every bite of food blows you away.

Great **MEXICAN** in Long Island City

Tierras Mexicanas (Queens)
31-01 36th Ave.
Long Island City, Queens, NY
718-777-6603
Mexican

Tierras Mexicanas is a comfortable restaurant with delicious food—everything fresh and flavorful, right down to the homemade chips. Tequila-loaded margaritas are made from scratch with lime juice; chunky guacamole is flecked with jalapeños; and amazing tacos de camaron (shrimp) use warm and soft tortillas. Great enchiladas filled with flavorful steak, and also lemony rice and beans. Mole poblano and *arrachera* (flank steak) are superb, guacamole awesome. Papas rellenas with seafood are a basket of shredded fried potato loaded with baby squid and shrimp and cheese sauce. Also touted: queso fundido with chorizo and very tasty tacos al pastor. There's also an intriguing Spanish menu, notes *dpw206*, which includes a fantastic steak dish.

Amazing Jersey **MEXICAN**

Charritos (Hudson County)
4900 Bergenline Ave.
Union City, NJ
201-863-0345
Mexican

Charritos (Hudson County)
121 Washington St.
Hoboken, NJ
201-418-8600
Diner or Coffee Shop

Mi Pueblo Grocery
  (Bergen County)
71 S. Washington Ave.,
  just south of movie theater
Bergenfield, NJ
201-385-0266
Mexican

Amazing, amazing food, especially the ridiculously good guacamole made at your table. Expensive, but worth it, raves *robin edgarton* about the Union City branch of Charritos. If they have tamales when you visit, order them. Otherwise opt for one of the tasty moles. The Hoboken branch is solid, too, we've heard.

Don't tell the other gringos, but tucked back in the rear of Mi Pueblo Grocery there's a counter with about seven stools where you can get great tacos and tortas, says *sixela!*, who claims to be the only non-Mexican she's ever seen in the joint. That's the whole menu: tacos and tortas, which come in tripe, lengua (tongue), chorizo, beef, and chicken.

The **MINIBURGERS** Craze

Bubby's (Tribeca)
120 Hudson St.
Manhattan, NY
212-219-0666
American

Bubby's Brooklyn (Brooklyn)
1 Main St.
Dumbo, Brooklyn, NY
718-222-0666
American

Patriot Saloon
(Lower Manhattan)
110 Chambers St.
Manhattan, NY
212-748-1162
American Pub

POP Burger (Chelsea)
58-60 9th Ave.
Manhattan NY
212-414-8686
American

Rare Bar & Grill (Murray Hill)
303 Lexington Ave., in the
Shelburne Hotel
Manhattan, NY
212-481-1999
American

Shag (Greenwich Village)
11 Abingdon Sq.
Manhattan, NY
212-242-0220
American

Miniburgers are maxipopular.

The **Patriot** serves wondrous miniburgers (minicheeseburgers are better) and sensational fries and onion rings, and an order of each costs only a buck (friendly staff and a good jukebox of classic country hits, too). **POP Burger** serves miniburgers (two for

$5) on supersoft mini brioche rolls with cheese, shredded lettuce, a slice of nice plum tomato, and a special sauce containing what seems to be a mixture of ketchup, mayo, and diced-up cornichon pickles. Flame-broiled to perfection, says *brianj*. French fries are better than onion rings.

Highly addictive miniburgers can be found at **Bubby's**. Miniburgers compensate for otherwise forgettable food at **Shag**.

Rare is a high-end burger joint in the Shelburne Hotel that serves a trio of miniburgers: an interesting seafood burger, a very good guacamole/black bean/chipotle Mexican burger, and a lackluster pesto mozzarella burger. Go for the traditional fries rather than waffle or sweet potato fries.

○ **Bubby's Brooklyn:** *see also* **p. 130.**

Curing Hunger Emergencies
Near **MOUNT SINAI HOSPITAL**

El Paso Deli (Upper East Side)
64 E. 97th St.
Manhattan, NY
212-996-1739
Mexican

El Paso Taqueria
   (Upper East Side)
1642 Lexington Ave.
Manhattan, NY
212-831-9831
Mexican

Falafel Express (Upper East Side)
1406 Madison Ave.
Manhattan, NY
212-987-6185
Middle Eastern/North African

Soft tacos are fresh drop-dead gorgeous at **El Paso Taqueria**, says *Porthos*, who recommends al pastor (roast pork with pineapple), tongue, or *cecina* (salted beef) varieties. Huge burritos and tamales are tasty, and guacamole is always made fresh to order. *Horchata* (a rice drink) is on tap. The branch a few blocks uptown is just as good.

Falafel Express stays open late and delivers to the hospital.

Good falafel, hummus, and rice-based *mujadara* are all available as moderately priced platters.

Master of **MOUSSE**

Something Sweet Inc. (East Village)
177 1st Ave.
Manhattan, NY
212-533-9986
Bakery

Long praised for its mango **mousse** (among other things), Something Sweet also makes really good pear and raspberry-banana mousse, with dots of bitter espresso balancing the sweetness. Both are very rich and creamy, raves *Aki* ("Whoever makes these mousses must be a mousse master!"). Other recommendations: apricot sandwich cookies and $1 minicupcakes with vanilla or chocolate icing on top.

Asian **MOUSSES**

Ennju (Union Square)
20 E. 17th St.
Manhattan, NY
646-336-7004
Japanese

Panya Bakery (East Village)
10 Stuyvesant St.
Manhattan, NY
212-777-1930
Japanese

The Japanese bakery Panya has a special autumnal menu, including a sweet potato mousse that's not to be missed. *Aki* says the semisweet mousse has a very light, delicate, silky consistency, with chestnut puree and sweet azuki beans on the top. He also recommends Panya's sweet potato tarts and green tea almond cookies. Mousse lovers might also check out the green tea mousse at **Ennju**.

MOZZARELLA That Can Weaken Your Knees

A&S Pork Store (Brooklyn)
274 5th Ave.
Park Slope, Brooklyn, NY
718-768-2728
Italian Deli

A&S Pork Store in Park Slope is renowned for its meats, but also makes particularly good mozzarella. When they reopened after a renovation, *Mara* stopped taking the place for granted: "I don't know how I ever lived without this: I was making do with Russo's mozzarella, and I guess I just forgot what A&S's tasted, or more importantly, felt like. Chewy, salty milk. So pure and such an incredible foil for the farmers' market sun gold cherry tomatoes, with a little balsamic and some salt . . . my eyes literally rolled back in my head and my knees weakened with that first taste. I feel like I've come home again."

MUFFIN Love

Buttercup Bake Shop (Midtown East)
973 2nd Ave.
Manhattan, NY
212-350-4144
Bakery

"I'm no expert on this, but I think I've just bitten into one of the best blueberry muffins I've ever had in this city. Soft, chewy, ungreasy, and chock-a-block with blueberries. I could take or leave the sugar frosting on the top, but against the overall taste, that's nothing," raves *Tim H.* about **Buttercup Bake Shop**.

○ **Buttercup Bake Shop:** *see also* **p. 9.**

MUSSELS in (and Near) the Slope

Bar Tabac (Brooklyn)
128 Smith St.
Cobble Hill, Brooklyn, NY
718-923-0918
French Bistro

Belleville (Brooklyn)
330 Fifth St.
Park Slope, Brooklyn, NY
718-832-9777
French Bistro

Chez Oskar (Brooklyn)
211 De Kalb Ave.
Fort Greene, Brooklyn, NY
718-852-6250
French Bistro

Cocotte (Brooklyn)
337 Fifth Ave.
Park Slope, Brooklyn, NY
718-832-6848
French Bistro

LouLou (Brooklyn)
222 De Kalb Ave.
Fort Greene, Brooklyn, NY
718-246-0633
French Bistro

Bar Tabac on Smith Street has good moules frites (**mussels and fries!**). **Belleville** serves a nice-sized portion of them for $13.95— and tasty frites, too. (*Woog23* loves the latter with aioli.) Every Tuesday night **Chez Oskar** in Fort Greene does all-you-can-eat mussels and a single bowl of frites for $10. **Cocotte** and **LouLou** are owned by the same people, and both serve very good moules frites, say *Charlotte* and *DeeDee*.

NASSAU COUNTY Gems

Big Papa's Soul Food
    (Nassau County)
338 Nassau Rd.
Roosevelt, NY
516-867-3274
Southern

Cafe Le Monique (Nassau County)
2014 Wantagh Ave.
Wantagh, NY
516-781-8822
French

C.P. Michael's Cafe & Grill
(Nassau County)
41 Covert Ave.
Floral Park, NY
516-775-9004
American

Kabul Grill Kabob & Tea House
(Nassau County)
129 N. Broadway
Hicksville, NY
516-933-8999
Afghan

Persian Grill (Nassau County)
210 Mineola Ave.
Roslyn Heights, NY
516-484-7100
Iranian

Poppa Rick's Fine Food/Real
Texas BBQ (Nassau County)
South side of Jericho Tpk., just
past Woodbury Common and
next door to a wood-carving
place
Woodbury, NY
Barbecue Street Cart/Truck

Sushi Tatsu (Nassau County)
377 Denton Ave., in Spring Rock
PGA Professional
New Hyde Park, NY
516-739-5095
Japanese

Taste of Portugal (Nassau County)
503 Newbridge Rd.
East Meadow, NY
516-409-1965
Portuguese

At **Big Papa's Soul Food**, chicken and ribs are slow-cooked in a barrel outside the storefront, and *lisa sz* says everything's quite good (but don't miss collard greens and yams).

Tasty savory crêpes at **Cafe Le Monique** have a slightly greenish hue because they're made the traditional way, with buckwheat flour. The lunch menu lists twenty different varieties, including sweet crêpes made without buckwheat. Pretty good chocolate soufflé, too (must order at meal's start), says *Paul Trapani*. Dinner menu is seasonal and features French cuisine. Reservations required for dinner.

They take both grilling and tea seriously at **Kabul Grill Kabob & Tea House**, an Afghan sit-down with quick, efficient service, fourteen different teas on the menu, and a host of kebabs. But the menu goes deeper. *Khoresht ghimeh badenjan* is a beef stew with eggplant, tomato, and yellow split peas. *Paul Trapani* says there wasn't that much beef in it, but all ingredients worked in harmony. "I did find a small rock in my stew, which apparently someone missed while picking over the peas, but such minor inconveniences are easy to overlook when you follow them with bite of perfectly cooked eggplant. I'd gladly order this dish again and again, even if I knew it would have a small rock in it every time." *Barg* kebab a marinated beef kebab, and lamb tikka kebab, are expertly seasoned and grilled, and come with enough meat to satisfy two hearty eaters. Lunch specials are a bargain at $7.50 to $9.50, especially considering portion size.

Persian Grill is bright and clean, like a diner, but they don't serve diner food. *Uncle Dave* says fried eggplant with tomato sauce and yogurt and lamb kebab are very tasty. Rice is piping hot and fresh, not rewarmed and rehydrated. After you order, you're brought warm pita with butter, raw quartered red onion, and fresh mint sprigs. Service is prompt, casual, and friendly. Most patrons are Iranians. Appetizers $3–$6, entrées $8–$15, with most kebabs under $10.

The chef at **C.P. Michael's Cafe & Grill** previously worked at several Manhattan places and it shows, says *mel tobias*, who praises the place's good, honest food. Recommended: cassoulet; flat iron steak; hamburger platter.

Churrasquiera-**Taste of Portugal** is a mom-and-pop operation with bare-bones decor. It sounds like a real find. Whole barbecued chicken ($10.95) is a smallish bird that comes crisp and juicy with fresh french fries, fresh hot potato chips, and grilled carrots and green beans, says, *mel tobias*, who also recommends grilled pork chops or salmon, mussels, and clams.

Sushi Tatso is part of a driving range, so you can hit a bucket of balls before eating. *Uncledave* notes very good quality and selection, and outstanding value.

Changes have occurred at **Poppa Rick's** Fine Food/Real Texas BBQ. No more pork loin, but they've added ribs, pulled pork, and BBQ meat loaf. They've also spruced the place up a bit. But the food still gets mixed reviews. Beef ribs and pulled pork are tender and tasty, says *dermot*, but brisket is precut and reheated with sauce. Gumbo is reported outstanding by *michael*.

Reveling in **NATTO!**

Soba-ya (East Village)
229 E. 9th St.
Manhattan NY
212-533-6966
Japanese

Natto is somewhat gelatinous fermented soybeans, which tend to form sticky, slimy strings when you try to lift a bite. Both taste and texture make natto a challenge for some eaters, but others revel in it, like *Eric Eto*, who enjoyed it at **Soba-ya**. He reports that a set there comes with a large bowl of cold soba with chiffonade of shiso leaf, another smaller bowl filled with natto and grated yam, garnishes of wasabi, grated daikon radish and green onions, and a container of a cold soy/dashi broth. Take the broth and mix it into the natto/grated-yam mixture with the garnishes to your liking and mix thoroughly and pour it on top of the soba. The only element lacking: a raw egg to mix into the natto mixture.

○ **Soba-ya:** *see also* p. 234.

NEW GREEN BO, Chowhound Chinatown Fave

New Green Bo (Chinatown)
66 Bayard St.
Manhattan, NY
212-625-2359
Chinese (Shanghai)

New Green Bo is perhaps the single most raved over Chinatown spot among chowhounds. This humble boxy place always has an energetic buzz, and is very well run (make friends with the manager lady at the cash register). They make delicious Shanghai cuisine in large servings at low prices. Here are some ordering tips. First, anything with yellow fish is good, as is anything in brown sauce. And only order Shanghai dishes, no middle-of-road items. (Exception: delicious General Tso's chicken, which you can order in a whisper, as the waiters are discreet.) These are the best-loved dishes:

Appetizers:

- scallion pancakes
- soup dumplings with crab and pork

- crispy eel
- aromatic beef
- ham/winter melon soup

Vegetables:

- foo yee bok choy (you've got to lobby for the foo yee, which isn't on the menu)
- soybeans with bean curd sheets
- mushroom with tofu puff

Noodles / Rice:

- rice cakes with shredded pork and preserved cabbage
- spicy beef noodles
- an off-menu dish that's sort of a block of fried rice (literally "fried rice," as opposed to "Fried Rice")

Main Courses:

- braised beef
- braised pork
- braised pork meatballs (aka lions head)
- kaufu
- another off-menu dish: stuffed bean curd skin and puff with minced pork with bean noodle casserole
- crab with egg and kingfish potage
- yellowfish with dried seaweed (like fish sticks that went postdoctorate)

○ **New Green Bo:** *see also* **pp. 74, 83.**

Chowhound Nametag: mrnyc

○◯○

Location: West Village/Meatpacking/Chelsea border.

Occupation: School psychologist.

Cholesterol Level: That reminds me: I have not been to Peter Luger's, Wallse, or The Doughnut Plant in a while.

Number of Visits to McDonald's in Past Decade: One . . . It was a dark and stormy night, the wolves were howling . . .

Farthest Out of the Way Traveled Just for Chow: As a teenager, more than two hundred miles from Cleveland to Columbus to go Garcia's Mexican Restaurant. How was it? Terrible, but I had a jones.

Nabe Most Full of Explorable Unknown Chow: The Ironbound in Newark. It's really changing quickly around there.

Top Chinatown Pick: Sweet-N-Tart because it's user friendly and there is a lot of unusual stuff going on in that fun menu. In Flushing Chinatown, hands down, the Food Court on Main Street.

Underrated by Chowhounds: Miniburgers at The Patriot bar on Chambers could use some more hype. I don't know if it's because of the beer combo that goes with them, but they sure are tasty good.

Weight Management Tip: Eat and keep moving. Celery has negative calories.

Favorite Comfort Chow: Café Bruxelles on Tuesday, their hangar steak special night.

Guilty Pleasure: Crack my knuckles, sister, but I like the bland Chinese-American food at Mama Buddha even though I only seem to go after I'm a barleywine or two down from the Blind Tiger bar.

Favorite Gelato Flavor: Otto's olive oil

Favorite Mail Order Chow: Pierogi Palace rules! www.piepal.com

Chowhounding Rule of Thumb: In Texas I find the Joe Bob Briggs rule works out real well: seek out the "BBQ" spots and avoid the "barbecue" or "b-b-q," and so on, places.

NEW ROCHELLE Tour

The Bread Factory
  (Westchester County)
30 Grove Ave.
New Rochelle, NY
914-637-9514
Bakery

Helen's Promises Restaurant
  (Westchester County)
580 North Ave.
New Rochelle, NY
914-235-5310
Southern

Little Mexican Cafe
  (Westchester County)
581 Main St.
New Rochelle, NY
914-636-3926
Mexican

Mexican Corner Kitchen
  (Westchester County)
497 Main St.
New Rochelle, NY
914-633-9696
Mexican/Diner or Coffee Shop

All breads baked at **The Bread Factory** look beautiful, and *Pat Hammond* says an onion baguette is particularly good—crusty outside and nicely chewy within and tasting of sourdough. Pumpernickel dinner rolls are tasty but not dense enough. Lots more to explore here.

Helen's Promises for Southern. *Rob S.* reports excellent fried catfish, wonderful collards, potato salad, and string beans, and good ham and turkey dishes. Mac and cheese is inconsistent, and mashed potatoes are rich to a fault. Open only Thursday through Sunday and only from 11:30 a.m. to 8:30 p.m. And Helen does *not* promise to always answer the phone even when she's there.

Little Mexican Cafe makes fabulous posole in your choice of red or white. *Pat Hammond* says the red is deeply flavorful and spicy, with lots of hominy, and large chunks of pork. They top it with shredded raw lettuce, avocado slices, cilantro, maybe scallions, too. Squeeze lime over all. They also serve excellent chicken enchiladas, spicy chorizo tostadas, and chiles rellleños. You can eat at the bar or in the main dining room. Either way the strolling musicians will find you.

The Mexican Corner Kitchen is a bit two-faced, seemingly a mild American coffee shop but quietly serving some of the best homemade sopes north or south of the border.

Scoring a Res at **NOBU**

Next Door Nobu (Tribeca)
105 Hudson St.
Manhattan, NY
212-334-4445
Japanese

Nobu (Tribeca)
105 Hudson St.
Manhattan, NY
212-219-0500
Japanese

Scoring a reservation at Nobu can seem like an impossible feat. Here are tips.

- If you're a Sprint PCS customer, *Faren* advises calling their operator and getting connected to their concierge service. For a $5 fee they can make the reservation for you.
- Try calling first thing in the morning. If that fails, there's always **Next Door Nobu,** which never requires reservations (*Jon S.*).
- Stopping by in person to make a reservation sidesteps the frustrating calling process.
- One wag (we're not sure he was serious) suggested: "Go there during the lunch time. After lunch, on the way out, give the reservationist a $100 bill and make a reservation."
- If you do manage to get in the vaunted doorway, don't order sushi. Instead, dig deeply into the Japanese-Peruvian fusion dishes, prix fixe dinners ($80/$100/$120), and the huge sake selection. Toro tartare, spicy creamy crab, and black cod with miso are amazing, says *Caitlin Wheeler*

○ **Next Door Nobu:** see also **p. 234.**

What to Order at **NOHO STAR**

Noho Star (Greenwich Village)
330 Lafayette St.
Manhattan, NY
212-925-0070
New American/Chinese

Noho Star has two menus. One offers simple Sichuan/Hunan
specialities (e.g. good crunch orange beef), while the other's eclectic, ranging from burgers to fried chicken salad with endive and
stilton. All sandwiches come with excellent fries. They're much
respected for their world-class homemade ginger ale. Other
hounds' favorites include ginger spinach (a honking plate that
must have started out as five pounds of spinach, notes *lala*),
Aztec corn soup, crab cakes and potato pancakes with tuna
sashimi and wasabi crème fraîche. Fridays only they make a
chocolate pudding that completely flips out says *Jim Leff*, who
also says it tastes strange (considering its luxurious texture), like
the essence of great freshly baked brownies. If you don't like hus-
tle and bustle and noise and jostling, this isn't the place for you.

○ **Noho Star:** *see also* **pp. 43, 105.**

Downtown **NOODLE** Slurp-Off

Chikubu Japanese Restaurant
   (Midtown East)
12 E. 44th St.
Manhattan, NY
212-818-0715
Japanese

Ebisu (East Village)
414 E. 9th St.
Manhattan, NY
212-979-9899
Japanese

Men Kui Tei (Midtown West)
60 W. 56th St.
Manhattan, NY
212-757-1642
Japanese

Menchanko-Tei 55 (Midtown West)
43 W. 55th St.
Manhattan, NY
212-247-1585
Japanese

Next Door Nobu (Tribeca)
105 Hudson St.
Manhattan, NY
212-334-4445
Japanese

Omen Restaurant
   (Greenwich Village)
113 Thompson St.
Manhattan, NY
212-925-8923
Japanese

ONY (Greenwich Village)
357 6th Ave.
Manhattan, NY
212-414-8429
Japanese

Rai Rai Ken (East Village)
214 E. 10th St.
Manhattan, NY
212-477-7030
Japanese

Sapporo (Midtown West)
152 W. 49th St.
Manhattan, NY
212-869-8972
Japanese

Sapporo East (East Village)
245 E. 10th St.
Manhattan, NY
212-260-1330
Japanese

Shiki Sushi (East Village)
135 1st Ave.
Manhattan, NY
212-614-1605
Japanese

Soba-ya (East Village)
229 E. 9th St.
Manhattan, NY
212-533-6966
Japanese

Village Yokocho (East Village)
8 Stuyvesant St.
Manhattan, NY
212-598-3041
Japanese

- **Rai Rai Ken**'s specialty is ramen, in flavorful stock, with a nice selection of items to mix in.
- **Chikubu** prepares ramen only Fridays, as a lunch special. "If you eat the noodles and everything and leave the pork slices in the bowl until the end, they just taste like buttah, it's incredible," says *mmyc*.
- **Shiki**'s kitchen makes particularly good ramen.
- **Menchanko-Tei** has two branches in Midtown, plus **Ony** Downtown, but *Peter Cuce* prefers the Fifty-fifth Street location. Nearby **Men Kui Tei** only rates OK for ramen.

- Also check out ramen at **Sapporo** in Midtown and **Sapporo East** in the East Village.
- **Village Yokocho** makes decent ramen, by chowhound (i.e. high) standards.
- **Omen**, whose name is dialect for "udon," is a good place to start trying its namesake dish.
- Don't forget the wonderful Inaniwa udon at **Ebisu.**
- **Next Door Nobu** serves soba and udon dishes at surprisingly reasonable prices.
- **Soba-Ya** excels at soba noodles (udon is rumored to be house made as well).

See also *Japanese* Noodle Soups.

○ Ebisu: *see also* p. 236.
○ Menchanko Tei 55: *see also* p. 179.
○ Next Door Nobu: *see also* p. 232.
○ ONY: *see also* p. 338.
○ Rai Rai Ken: *see also* p. 339.
○ Sapporo: *see also* pp. 179, 339.
○ Sapporo East: *see also* p. 269.
○ Soba-ya: *see also* p. 227.
○ Village Yokocho: *see also* p. 181.

OCHAZUKE, the Ultimate Japanese Comfort Food

Donburi-Ya (Midtown East)
137 E. 47th St.
Manhattan, NY
212-980-7909
Japanese

Ochazuke, or tea rice, is broth-infused tea that's poured over a bowl of rice. It may not sound like much, but it's comfort food to many Japanese, and **Donburi-Ya**'s version—with mackerel sashimi—is fantastic, says *Eric Eto*. Finding it on the confusing set of four menus they hand you may be difficult, but you can refer to the photo of the dish in the front window. Cost: $6.50, or $5.75 for the sashimi only.

An inside tip: Any time baseball star Hideki Matsui hits a home run, Donburi-Ya offers a special deal the next day. The San-kan-oh donburi is a ten-don, katsudon, and tamago don combo for half price ($5.50).

○ **Donburi-Ya:** *see also* **p. 181.**

Monkfish Liver and Other Noteworthy **OFFAL**

Prune (East Village)
54 E. 1st St.
Manhattan, NY
212-677-6221
New American

Monkfish have large, slippery livers, and **Prune** serves 'em whole with a soy-based sauce. Many hounds rave. Mammalian offal dishes also garner praise. Other recommendations: suckling pig, duck pastrami, lamb sausages, and marinated sardines. Friendly, competent service, but the dining room can feel small and cramped.

○ **Prune:** *see also* **p. 250.**

Value **OMAKASE** . . . and Ultra-Rare Inaniwa Udon

Ebisu (East Village)
414 E. 9th St.
Manhattan, NY
212-979-9899
Japanese

Omakase **means** letting the sushi chef indulge his whim . . . and, often, his prerogative to charge you unmercifully.

Omakase at **Ebisu** is nearly the quality of the top places in the city but at a fraction of the cost. The chef serves two different but complementary pieces at a time, and the selection's impressive, reports *halo*, who paid $50 for omakase. Nonsushi menu items are good, too, including lots of options for vegetarians, e.g., very good natto. Don't miss the Inaniwa udon, an artisanal product made from a secret recipe from the Akita prefecture of Japan. Warning: food comes out very fast, so plates can pile up and crowd the table.

○ **Ebisu:** *see also* **p. 233.**

Completely **ORGANIC** at Ivo and Lulu

Ivo and Lulu (Soho)
558 Broome St.
Manhattan, NY
212-226-4399
French/Caribbean

Hounds rave about food and prices at **Ivo and Lulu,** where the all-organic cooking is boldly flavored French/Caribbean, and it's hard to spend $25 (especially since it's BYOB). Particular highlights from their limited menu: smoked mussels, pheasant pâté, avocado stuffed with spinach mousse, pear with gorgonzola cheese and garlic oil, chicken with goat cheese-papaya sauce, mushroom cassoulet. We've also heard glowing reports of pheasant terrine served warm with a layer of brie baked on top, and rich, gingery rabbit sausages with couscous. Appetizers are $8, entrées $10. BYOB, but bring your own wine glasses . . . or else put up with tumblers.

Secrets of the **OYSTER BAR**

Grand Central Oyster Bar (Grand Central)
89 E. 42nd St.
Manhattan, NY
212-490-6650
Seafood

Aki has sniffed out a dessert that's offered sometimes in fall at **Grand Central's Oyster Bar**. It's old-fashioned pumpkin pie with a "very beautiful orangeish brown color, it's so fresh, and very, very delicate and silky texture. The crust is super thin, yet it's crispy. This beautiful slice comes with, of course, fresh made semisweet whipped cream—*not* from a can. It's just so good!" Cakes are also good here, but aside from that, stick with New England clam chowder, stews, pan roasts, and a hidden lunch-only sandwich menu (bouillabaisse sandwich, oyster po' boys, and tuna burgers) that you have to ask for and is only available until 3:00 p.m. Oh, and, of course, the superb oysters.

PAIN AU CHOCOLAT

Amy's Bread (Chelsea)
75 9th Ave., in the
   Chelsea Market
Manhattan, NY
212-462-4338
Bakery

Amy's Bread
   (Upper East Side)
972 Lexington Ave.
Manhattan, NY
212-537-0270
Bakery

Amy's Bread (Clinton)
672 9th Ave.
Manhattan, NY
212-977-2670
Bakery

Balthazar (Soho)
80 Spring St.
Manhattan, NY
212-965-1414
French Bistro

Corrado's Bakery (Grand Central)
109 E. 42nd St., Grand Central
    Terminal
Manhattan, NY
212-599-4321
Bakery

Petrossian Boutique & Cafe
    (Midtown West)
911 7th Ave.
Manhattan, NY
212-245-2217
French Café

Corrado's Bakery (Upper East Side)
960 Lexington Ave.
Manhattan, NY
212-774-1904
Bakery

Royal Crown Pastry Shop
    (Brooklyn)
6512 14th Ave.
Borough Park, Brooklyn, NY
718-234-1002
Bakery

Pain au chocolat (chocolate bread) is one of life's pleasures. **Amy's Bread** offers two kinds: a chocolate-cherry roll and a sourdough twist with chocolate bits. Pain au chocolat is baked with Valrhona chocolate at **Balthazar**. *Jim Leff* swears by the pain au chocolat (and other fancy pastries) at **Petrossian Boutique**. Avoid the trip to Brooklyn by buying great stuff (like pain au chocolat) from **Royal Crown Pastry Shop** in Manhattan at **Corrado's Bakery**.

- ○ **Amy's Bread:** *see also* pp. 21, 85.
- ○ **Balthazar:** *see also* pp. 35, 41, 96, 104.
- ○ **Corrado's Bakery:** *see also* p. 35.
- ○ **Royal Crown Pastry Shop:** *see also* pp. 36, 252.

Skipping the Beef at
PETER LUGER

Peter Luger (Brooklyn)
178 Broadway
Williamsburg, Brooklyn, NY
718-387-7400
Steak House

Peter Luger (Nassau County)
255 Northern Blvd.
Great Neck, NY
516-487-8800
Steak House

Steaks at **Peter Luger** satisfy a lot of hounds, but even those who
don't eat beef can be happy here. Both locations offer a huge
slab of salmon fillet (broiled to perfection, says *Lambretta76*),
and both serve creamed spinach and a salad of slabs of tomato
and onion in a special sauce. The Great Neck location's menu is
larger and more varied, with daily fish specials, lobster, salads,
and roast chicken. Don't understimate the desserts, which are
worth saving room for; *Wendy L* says you can't go wrong with
the cheesecakes, but *erika* was blown away by their pecan pie.
The apple streudel is another top contender. "Holy Cow" sundaes and chocolate mousse pie are, too. Desserts come with
huge helpings of *schlag* (vanilla-enhanced whipped cream).

○ **Peter Luger:** *see also* **pp. 51, 69.**

Perfect PIE

Cupcake Cafe (Clinton)
522 9th Ave.
Manhattan, NY
212-465-1530
American Café

Grand Traverse Pie Company N/A
www.gtpie.com
231-922-7437
Mail Order Source

Kitchenette (Tribeca)
80 W. Broadway
Manhattan, NY
212-267-6740
American/Diner or Coffee Shop

Kitchenette Uptown (Harlem)
1272 Amsterdam Ave.
Manhattan, NY
212-531-7600
American/Diner or Coffee Shop

Little Pie Co. (Chelsea)
407 W. 14th St.
Manhattan, NY
212-414-2324
Bakery

Little Pie Co. (Clinton)
424 W. 43rd St.
Manhattan, NY
212-736-4780
Bakery

Little Pie Co. (Grand Central)
East 42nd St. and Lexington Ave.
   Grand Central Station,
   downstairs
Manhattan, NY
212-983-3538
Bakery

Tompkins Square Bakery (East Village)
341 E. 10th St.
Manhattan, NY
212-460-9878
Korean Bakery

Pie nirvana can be attained via sour cream walnut apple pie
from the **Little Pie Company**; *tigerwoman* says it's unlike any other
she's tried, and it's impressive to boot. They do a beautiful crust
and fill it with machine-thin slices of apple stacked densely
with the sour cream layered in between and topped with a wonderful thick brown sugar walnut crust (like a streusel). It's delicious and decadent, and yet not overly sweet. *Susan J* sums it
up more concisely: crispy, sugary-buttery rich crust around
firm, ungloppy apples.

Some other good choices include consistently good and
homemade-looking apple and pumpkin pies at the **Tompkins
Square Bakery,** cranberry walnut pie at **Cupcake Cafe,** and **Kitchenette**'s much-loved cherry pie (and also chocolate pecan, double-
crust apple, pumpkin and sour cream blueberry).

If you're looking to mail order a pie, *BK* deems the cherry,
peach, and strawberry-rhubarb pies from **Grand Traverse Pie Co.** the
best ever.

○ **Cupcake Cafe:** *see also* p. 110.
○ **Kitchenette:** *see also* pp. 42, 103, 151, 205, 280.
○ **Little Pie Co:** *see also* p. 202.

Pop's **PIEROGI**

Pop's Pierogi (Greenwich Village)
190 Bleecker St.
Manhattan, NY
212-505-0055
Central/Eastern European

Pop's is an Eastern European snack shop (eat in or take out)
selling a number of doughy delights such as pierogi, *pelmeny,*

kutabi, and *pirozhki.* The list of interesting beverages includes *kvas* (a ciderish, funky, slightly alcoholic brew made from fermented bread), tarragon cola, and kompote. Chowhound *aaron* recommends all except messy khinkali (Georgian soup dumplings), which aren't worth the required twenty-minute wait.

The **PING'S** Saga

Ping's (Queens)
83-02 Queens Blvd.
Elmhurst, Queens, NY
718-396-1238
Chinese (Hong Kong)/Chinese (Dim Sum)

Ping's was great once, when the great Chef Ping was in residence. Then Ping split to run a high-profile location on Mott Street, and quality sank drastically, though dim sum, prepared by a different chef, has remained top-notch always (perhaps New York City's best). Specialties include a $5.95 dumpling, which comes in a small clay pot holding one large dumpling and broth. The dumpling (about the size of a small fist) is an explosion of seafood—lobster, crab, shark fin, and perhaps some other white fish—and the soup is as robust as the dumpling, reports *Eric Eto*, who says while Ping's dim sum may lack the extensive variety of other places, everything they make is spot on, especially fried taro, which he says they've perfected. Other meals have returned to form, too. The rich, salty, and tangy treat of enormous, three-mouthful oysters topped with rice vermicelli and XO sauce haunts the dreams of *galley girl*. Also good: Chinese pork chops (in a red sauce) and any seafood dishes. A suggestion from *josh L*: order from the specials menu. Ping's is also an excellent spot for banquets.

Thin and Really Really Thin Crust **PIZZA**

Eddie's Thin Crust Pizza
   (Nassau County)
2048 Hillside Ave.
New Hyde Park, NY
516-354-9780
Pizza/Pub

Pizza Gruppo (East Village)
186 Avenue B
Manhattan, NY
212-995-2100
Italian/Pizza

"GREAT CRUST!" at **Pizza Gruppo**, raves *Pamlet*, who reports that this place pulls off a near miracle, keeping the crust "thin and crisp, despite having lots of yummy toppings (don't miss caramelized onion). And the crust is flavorful. I usually don't bother eating the bit that doesn't have topping on it, but here I do." Also recommended: antipasto.

There's thin and then there's *thin*. Eddie's doesn't serve normal pizza. They take the idea of thin crust to the extreme. Paper thin. Razor thin. You have to eat this pizza almost as soon as it comes out of the oven, says *stuart*, who offers further advice: get the full size (not the bar pie), eschew toppings, and avoid the rest of the menu (with the possible exception of antipasto salad, a very large bowl of lettuce with cold Italian salami, provolone, cukes, and tomatoes with Italian dressing). Good potato/egg heros, too.

Raves for Leonardo's **PIZZA**

Leonardo's Brick Oven Pizza (Brooklyn)
383 Court St.
Carroll Gardens, Brooklyn, NY
718-624-9620
Italian/Pizza

Hounds are raving about regular full-sized pies and individual-sized creations at **Leonardo's Pizza**. Garden seating in the rear, but irregular (capricious?) hours.

Note: There are great pizza tips scattered throughout this guide. Check the cuisine index.

PIZZA, Hold the Cheese

Lil' Frankies Pizza (East Village)
19 First Ave.
Manhattan, NY
212-420-4900
Pizza/Italian

Quartino (Lower Manhattan)
21 Peck Slip
Manhattan, NY
212-349-4433
Italian

Sullivan Street Bakery (Clinton)
533 W. 47th St.
Manhattan, NY
212-586-1626
Italian Bakery

Sullivan Street Bakery (Soho)
73 Sullivan St.
Manhattan, NY
212-334-9435
Italian Bakery

A pizza without cheese needs flavorful and well-baked crust. **Quartino's** does a great job with cheeseless pizzas, and their sausage and arugula-based pies have satisfied *djk*'s dairyphobic friends. **Lil' Frankie's** makes delicious pies with a minimum of cheese. You could probably ask them to leave off all cheese on any given pie, but the one totally cheeseless option always on-menu is an anchovy, tomato sauce, and capers pie. And while it's not classic New York-style, **Sullivan St. Bakery** makes delicious cheeseless "pizza." Unfortunately, they're not currently making their much-loved radicchio pizza (but if enough of us ask . . .).

○ **Lil' Frankies Pizza:** *see also* **p. 201.**
○ **Sullivan Street Bakery:** *see also* **pp. 22, 36, 67.**

PIZZA from the Kitchen of Hell

Don Giovianni (Theater District)
358 W. 44th St., #1
Manhattan, NY
212-581-4939
Italian

Little Italy Pizza (Midtown West)
72 W. 45th St.
Manhattan, NY
212-730-7575
Italian/Pizza

L'Allegria Italian Restaurant
  (Clinton)
623 9th Ave. (enter nook
  on 44th St.)
Manhattan, NY
212-265-6777
Italian

Sacco Pizza (Clinton)
819 9th Ave.
Manhattan, NY
212-582-7765
Pizza

Hell's Kitchen, that is. Where the pizza can actually be kind of hellish. Here are the best options (because chowhounding is all about maximizing one's deliciousness regardless of one's condition, location, or hankering).

Tucked away in the back of **L'Allegria** is a (gas-driven) brick-oven pizza nook with a small counter and a couple of tables. *Mark Sinclair* says their slices have nice thin crusts, fresh cheese, and pretty good sauce. According to *Liana*, the quality once rivaled that of New Haven and Italy's best, but a fire led them to alter their formerly whole pie-only menu to a more standard arrangement and quality has suffered . . . but only a bit.

Sacco's Pizza is one of the best in the nabe, says *Ric Zoon*, who's tried them all.

Don Giovanni's bakes in a brick oven. *Dan Geist* says quality is consistent; the vegetables are always fresh and the white clam pizza is world-class. Many other hounds, however, deem the place terrible, so caveat eater!

If you venture a bit east to **Little Italy Pizza,** you'll be treated to what *Westsider* describes as a textbook New York slice.

Long Island **PIZZA** Tips

Amore Pizzeria (Queens)
3027 Stratton St.
Flushing, Queens, NY
718-445-0579
Italian

Centre Pizza (Little Neck)
25425 Horace Harding Expy.
    (LIE south service road), just
    east of Little Neck Pkwy.
Little Neck, Queens, NY
718-229-9879
Italian/Pizza

Genovese Pizza
    (Nassau County)
20 Central Ct.
Valley Stream, NY
516-825-6605
Italian/Pizza

Ginos Pizza (Nassau County)
1615 Dutch Broadway
Elmont, NY
516-561-6664
Italian/Pizza

King Umberto (Nassau County)
1343 Hempstead Tpk.
Elmont, NY
516-483-5464
Italian/Pizza Bakery/
    Cheese Shop/Pizzeria

New Park Pizzeria (Queens)
15671 Crossbay Blvd.
Howard Beach, Queens, NY
718-641-3082
Italian

The Pie (Suffolk County)
216 Main St.
Port Jefferson, NY
631-331-4646
Italian

After a sampling of pies in western Long Island *wishuwerhere* says the best regular slice is at **New Park Pizza** (just over the Queens border), while **Genovese Pizza** has the best Sicilian slice, and **King Umberto's** takes the prize for best grandma slice.

Ginos is good for anything from white pizza to grilled chicken with broccoli rabe panin.

Centre Pizza has been in the same family for forty-five years, and *Steve Drucker* says the pies are still made the same way: nothing fancy or coal fired, just a damn good slice.

Amore is a tiny hole in the wall in a very run down strip mall, and *stuartlafonda* says they serve a very good, no frills slice. It's right alongside the Whitestone Expressway just past Shea and before the exit for the Whitestone Bridge.

Chowhound Nametag: Deven Black

○○○

Location:
Rockland County.

Occupation: Former reporter, former radio talk show host, former restaurant manager, former freelance writer and editor, currently a graduate student aiming to become a special education teacher. (Yes, I'm going for the big bucks!)

Your Cholesterol Level: Artificially controlled.

Farthest Out of the Way Traveled Just for Chow: NYC to Montreal, involuntarily (I was kidnapped), by train, just to have dinner at a place called Chez Bardet. It was spectacular. The quality of the food was surpassed only by the level of service. I would gladly have made the trip again, but Monsieur Bardet got into some trouble with the tax authorities, and the restaurant was shuttered.

Nabe Most Full of Explorable Unknown Chow: There are so many. I've suggested to my wife that we take a motel room almost anywhere in Queens for a weekend and just eat stuff we've never heard of.

Underrated by Chowhounds: I love the food and vibe at San Juan Cafe, a lunch-only place in Nyack—especially Mondays, when they serve ropa vieja.

Guilty Pleasure: Trader Joe's crunchy natural peanut butter on really good crusty rye bread with lots of caraway seeds.

Favorite Gelato Flavor: Pistachio from Il Laboratorio del Gelato.

Chowhounding Rules of Thumb: So far the best I've done is listen to a Korean cab driver in Chicago when he told me—after I'd asked where to get good Korean food—where to get the best corned beef in town.

The Pie in Port Jefferson makes a top-notch pizza in the New Haven/Pepe's style (try the white clam). Great meatball heroes, too.

PLUM DUMPLING Bliss

Thomas Beisl (Brooklyn)
25 Lafayette Ave.
Fort Greene Brooklyn NY
718-222-5800
Austrian

Meat is the main attraction at **Thomas Beisl**, and *Kitchop* heaps praise on tender and tasty beef goulash with spaetzle and ultra-tender pork cheeks with sauerkraut and dumplings, before working into a froth about the plum dumplings, a dessert special. "Words cannot describe how yummy that plum dumpling is— a whole plum surrounded by a melt-in-your mouth dumpling, covered with a delicious plum sauce with chunks of more fresh plums. It's plum-dumpling bliss."

Two Boots' Surprisingly Tasty PO' BOYS

Two Boots (East Village)
37 Avenue A
Manhattan, NY
212-505-2276
Pizza/Cajun/Creole

Two Boots is more famous for its family-friendly ambiance than for the quality of its pizza. But *xavier* puts forth an unlikely rave for their chicken po' boy sandwich, nicely spiced with Cajun seasonings, and served on wonderfully soft, fluffy bread.

Outstanding **POLISH** Actually Good for Vegetarians

Lomzynianka (Brooklyn)
646 Manhattan Ave.
Greenpoint, Brooklyn, NY
718-389-9439
Polish

Lomzynianka is a very inexpensive Polish restaurant run by a sister and brother team (Lomzynianka means "girl from Lomzy," the siblings' hometown and inspiration for the celebrated Antonio Carlos Jobimski bossa nova). Incredibly great cold red borscht costs something like a dollar a bowl, and is loaded with sour cream and fresh dill; *Adam Neaman* would have a bowl every day if he lived anywhere near them. Avoid complex dishes in favor of Polish staples like kielbasa (crisscross sliced and crunchy on the tips from grilling . . . excellent) or fantastic white borscht, or *bigos* (sauerkraut with shredded pork and kielbasa, kicked up with fresh ground pepper and seasoning— almost like a hash). Also good: stuffed cabbage and pierogies (fried, not boiled). Potato pancakes here can be great, but skip them if the place is busy because they go rapidly downhill if not served right out of the pan. One variant, Hungarian pie, sounds irresistible: a superlight, deliciously crispy potato pancake stuffed with wonderfully rich, meaty goulash. Friendly mom-and-pop (bro-and-sis?) atmosphere. Skip overly sweet Polish sodas in favor of kompote, the sweet/tart fruit-infused water, or BYOB. Prices are very cheap, but go early, as they close around 9:00 p.m.

○ **Lomzynianka:** *see also* p. 281.

PORCINE Manhattan

Dominic (Tribeca)
349 Greenwich St.
Manhattan, NY
212-343-0700
Italian

Gramercy Tavern (Gramercy)
42 E. 20th St.
Manhattan, NY
212-477-0777
New American

Maloney & Porcelli
    (Lower Manhattan)
225 Broadway
Manhattan, NY
212-227-8600
Steak House

Maloney & Porcelli
    (Midtown East)
37 E. 50th St.
Manhattan, NY
212-750-2233
Steak House

New Big Wong Restaurant
    (Chinatown)
72 Bayard St.
Manhattan, NY
212-964-0540
Chinese (Cantonese)

NY Noodle Town (Chinatown)
28½ Bowery
Manhattan NY
212-349-0923
Chinese (Cantonese)

Peasant (Little Italy)
194 Elizabeth St.
Manhattan, NY
212-965-9511
Italian

Prune (East Village)
54 E. 1st St.
Manhattan, NY
212-677-6221
New American

South Ocean (Chinatown)
14-18 Elizabeth St., in
    Chinatown Arcade
Manhattan, NY
212-285-0020
Chinese (Taiwanese)

Trattoria Paolina (East Village)
175 Avenue B
Manhattan, NY
212-253-2221
Italian

Vittorio Cucina Regionale Italiana
    (Greenwich Village)
308 Bleecker St.
Manhattan, NY
212-463-0730
Italian

Yeah Shanghai Deluxe (Chinatown)
65 Bayard St.
Manhattan, NY
212-566-4884
Chinese (Shanghai)

The array of porcine goodness in Manhattan restaurants is staggering. Here are places where swine become pearls:

Hounds rave about rich roast pork at **Prune**, which comes with a hunk of skin, black-eyed pea salad, and tiny sour pickles. *Abbylovi* says the sharp vinegary dressing on the black-eyed peas and the sour pickles perfectly cut through the richness of the pork.

At **South Ocean**, Taiwanese-style braised pork is dark chocolate brown in color and tastes like it's been cooked for hours. The outside can be a bit dry, but the inside is moist and tender. When you bite into the whole thing, everything melts in your mouth, says *Aki*. Three well-seasoned and herbed pieces and a boiled egg are $4.50, but you can save a quarter by getting the dish as part of a lunch special with rice, soup, nuts, and pickled vegetable.

Miscellaneous quick pig tips: **Yeah Shanghai Deluxe** (honeyed pork), **Maloney Porcelli** (crackling pork shank with firecracker apple sauce), **Dominic** (roast suckling pig), **Peasant** (more roast suckling pig), **NY Noodletown** (yet more roast suckling pig—call ahead to make sure it's available), **Trattoria Paolina** (milk-cooked pork stuffed with spinach), **New Big Wong** (roast pork, aka *char sieu*), **Gramercy Tavern** (braised bacon), and **Vittorio Cucina** (wild boar with blueberries),

○ **Dominic:** *see also* p. 170.
○ **Gramercy Tavern:** *see also* pp. 104, 139.
○ **NY Noodle Town:** *see also* p. 74.
○ **Peasant:** *see also* p. 139.
○ **Prune:** *see also* p. 236.

PORCINE Brooklyn (Pork Slope and Beyond)

B & B Meat Market (Brooklyn)
168 Bedford Ave.
Williamsburg, Brooklyn, NY
718-388-2811
Store

El Viejo Yayo (Brooklyn)
36 5th Ave.
Park Slope, Brooklyn, NY
718-622-8922
Dominican

El Viejo Yayo Restaurant
  (Brooklyn)
317 9th St.
Park Slope, Brooklyn, NY
718-965-7299
Cuban

Emily's Pork Store (Brooklyn)
426 Graham Ave.
Williamsburg, Brooklyn, NY
718-383-7216
Italian

La Parada (Brooklyn)
341 Broadway
Williamsburg, Brooklyn, NY
718-963-1944
Puerto Rican/Dominican

Royal Crown Pastry Shop
  (Brooklyn)
6512 14th Ave.
Borough Park, Brooklyn, NY
718-234-1002
Bakery

Sur (Brooklyn)
232 Smith St.
Cobble Hill, Brooklyn, NY
718-875-1716
Argentinian

W-Nassau Meat Market
  (Brooklyn)
915 Manhattan Ave.
Greenpoint, Brooklyn, NY
718-389-6149
Polish, Store

Argentineans sure love meat. Perhaps that's why the standard side order of bacon at **Sur**'s brunch is fourteen slices. Yes, fourteen thickly cut slices for about $3, the going price for a normal-sized (three to six slices) bacon order in the neighborhood.

La Parada/Chicken Q seems to offer the same menu as the late, lamented Alex Bar B Q, a rigorously authentic and flabbergastingly great Puerto Rican barbecue place across the street from this location. La Parada makes excellent barbecued pernil (roast pork) as platters or sandwiches. Homemade morcilla (blood sausage) is awesome, and rolled pernil and *cuajito* are real fine, too, says *Mark DiBlasi*. Bacalaitos (fried crab pancakes) and other fried stuff are real good. *Lechon* (roast suckling pig) on weekends. Mostly takeout.

W-Nassau Meat Market is just one of several butchers along its stretch of Manhattan Avenue. *Eric Eto* reports myriad interesting-looking pork products to choose from and everyone speaking Polish. Customers seemed to be buying one- to three-pound slabs off a semifatty hunk of meat the size of a whole loin from the "hot meats" section of the counter, so, in best chowhound fashion, *Eric Eto* followed suit. "I took slices off the bacon-y slab and we were astounded with how good it was. It wasn't quite bacon, perhaps closer to a fatty ham, but regardless,

it was damn good." Other meats recommended include *boczek pieczony* (baked bacon from the side of the pig), *boczek wedzony* (smoked bacon), and *mysliwska* (a mixed pork and beef sausage).

El Viejo Yayo makes some amazingly rich pernil (roast pork) with great porky flavor. It's perfectly moist and served with little bits of cracklings on top. *Penelope* likes the pernil best in a sandwich, spread with garlic sauce. She also loves Viejo Yayo's beans.

Royal Crown (mostly a bakery—and a good one) only sells its pancetta by the full piece (about a pound). It comes in a flat strip spiced with red pepper and herbs.

B&B is *Adam*'s top pork pick.

Emily's is Williamsburg's only dedicated salumeria. Naturally, they make their own sausages.

Also see Italian deli/pork stores in cuisine index.

○ **La Parada:** *see also* p. 101.
○ **Royal Crown Pastry Shop:** *see also* pp. 36, 239.

PORTUGUESE Seafood Palace in Newark

Seabra's Marisqueira (Essex County)
87 Madison St.
Newark, NJ
973-465-1250
Portuguese

Considering Portugal's geography, the phrase "Portuguese seafood restaurant" is somewhat redundant. Still, rumor has it the owner of **Seabra's Marisqueira** has some deal where the Portuguese airline flies in seafood daily from Lisbon. *Susan* reports that the mariscada is amazing, as is the cod, plus octopus that puts prime rib to shame. Extra bonus in the bar area: Portuguese satellite TV, complete with Portuguese versions of *Weakest Link* and *Who Wants to Be a Millionaire*. There's tons more Portuguese (and, increasingly, Brazilian) goodness in the

Ironbound neighborhood of Newark. Watch for coverage in the next edition of this guide.

PRE- OR POSTTHEATER
Suggestions

Arriba Arriba (Clinton)
762 9th Ave.
Manhattan, NY
212-489-0810
Mexican

Basilico (Clinton)
676 9th Ave.
Manhattan, NY
212-489-0051
Italian

El Deportivo (Clinton)
701 9th Ave.
Manhattan, NY
212-757-6869
German

Esca (Theater District)
402 W. 43rd St.
Manhattan, NY
212-564-7272
Italian

Grand Sichuan International
   (Clinton)
745 9th Ave.
Manhattan, NY
212-582-2288
Chinese (Sichuan)

Hallo Berlin (Clinton)
402 W. 51st St.
Manhattan, NY
212-541-6248
German

Hallo Berlin (Clinton)
626 10th Ave.
Manhattan, NY
212-977-1944
German

Lattanzi (Theater District)
361 W. 46th St.
Manhattan, NY
212-315-0980
Italian

Pam Real Thai (Clinton)
404 W. 49th St.
Manhattan, NY
212-333-7500
Thai

Queen of Sheba (Clinton)
650 10th Ave.
Manhattan, NY
212-397-0610
Ethiopian or Eritrean

Rinconcito Peruano (Clinton)
803 9th Ave.
Manhattan, NY
212-333-5685
Peruvian

Zuni (Clinton)
598 9th Ave.
Manhattan, NY
212-765-7626
New American

Wondee Siam (Clinton)
792 9th Ave.
Manhattan, NY
212-459-9057
Thai

Chowhounds have different priorities. Tell them about pretheater specials, and they'll wonder what great stuff they're missing when the curtain goes up. **Lattanzi** makes general upscale Italian restaurant food for the pretheater hordes, but after 8:00 p.m. they unveil special dishes from Rome's Jewish community (you must ask for the special menu) and fast-paced food service segues into relaxed dining. The signature Roman Jewish dish is artichokes fried in olive oil and garlic, but *Deb Van D* reports pastas are varied, well conceived, and well executed. Swordfish, lamb, and a mixed grill also have been successful.

Esca, too, is transformed after pretheater. Before curtain, the place is crowded and rushed, but it's a completely different, more relaxed experience after 8:00 p.m. Come here posttheater (they're open till 11:30 p.m. Monday–Saturday) for the best experience of their excellent fish and interesting preparations. *eljo* loves the crudo course of raw fish (actually a delicious ceviche of giant geoduck clams with mint) and tuna-stuffed grape leaves and buckwheat pasta spirals with prawns and wild nettle pesto. Esca is very expensive, and they'll try to raise the bill by pushing additional items, but many hounds deem it worth the cost. There's patio dining, but you must make same-day reservations (call after 10:00 a.m.) because of weather considerations.

At **Zuni**, *Deb Van D* recommends roast chicken with black pepper polenta, crispy corn fritters, and penne with shrimp.

When two people order the $21 pretheater (until 6:45 p.m.) special at **Basilico**, the deal includes a bottle of wine. Desserts are homemade and delicious at this Italian spot, says *Brian W*.

Grand Sichuan International for terrific Sichuan and **Rinconcito Peruano** for Manhattan's best (though inconsistent) Peruvian.

Pam Real Thai is another chowhound favorite for spicy and inexpensive Thai food, and **Wondee Siam** (see Unlocking Wondee Siam *Thai*) is also within range.

Arriba Arriba has a good lunch menu with a free minimargarita.

The two **Hallo Berlin** locations serve reasonably priced sausages and beer. Bratwurst on a roll is under $5.00, and a liter of German beer is about $5.50.

El Deportivo's daily specials, usually meat stews, as well as rice and beans, are recommended by *ultbil*.

Queen of Sheba serves Ethiopians dinners for under $13 (their lunch specials are "enormous" for less than $11, says *Ken*).

○ **Grand Sichuan International:** *see also* p. 142.
○ **Queen of Sheba:** *see also* p. 117.
○ **Wondee Siam:** *see also* p. 303.

Tasty **PUERTO RICAN ROAST PIG**

El Bohio Lechonera (Bronx)
791 E. Tremont Ave.
Bronx, NY
718-299-4218
Puerto Rican

The former El Gran Bohio has had a change of ownership and is now called El Nuevo Bohio. If you are a fan of lechon (roast suckling pig or roast pig), you won't notice the change. The window is full of succulent hunks of lechon, which come with *cuerito* (crispy skin) and a little bowl of mojo (garlic in oil) to dip it in. "The pork was truly yummy and juicy (no highfalutin adjectives for this kind of down-home place). The garlic was just the thing. If it isn't the best lechon around, it's got to be close," says *JH Jill*. Other interesting menu items: *chivito* (a goat stew) with a really tantalizing aroma, and marinated octopus.

QUESADILLAS de Pompano
at Pampano

Pampano (Midtown East)
209 E. 49th St.
Manhattan, NY
212-751-4545
Mexican

The (nearly) eponymous quesadilla de pompano at **Pampano** is actually made with swordfish . . . and it works! The combination of swordfish, Oaxaca cheese, crema, salsa verde, salsa roja and black bean puree with a sprinkling of cotija cheese hits the bull's eye for *Mark*. Chayote, served with salmon in piloncillo glaze, is very tasty. Both dishes are part of the $20.03 lunch. Tuna ceviche, an extra lunch offering, was too heavy with cilantro on one visit.

RED CAT:
Convivial Chelsea Oasis

The Red Cat (Chelsea)
227 10th Ave.
Manhattan, NY
212-242-1122
New American

Convivial and warm, **Red Cat** draws fine reviews for both food and service. Tempura green beans are popular (though greasy at the bottom of the order), and *scrittrice* reports that trout with mustard crust is served with very good mashed potatoes and a dense and plate-licking delicious cherry tomato/preserved lemon sauce that perfectly cuts the strong flavor of the trout.

Central American Whirlwind Chow Tour . . . All at the
RED HOOK SOCCER FIELD!

Red Hook Soccer Field (Brooklyn)
Between Clinton and Court, and Halleck and Bay Streets
Red Hook, Brooklyn, NY
Latin American

On Sundays (maybe Saturdays too, we're not sure), a small colony of food tents and stands are set up on the street just outside the park in Red Hook to feed crowds going to the pool or watching the (often very good) soccer games. *Steve R.* nabbed a great soft beef taco with green sauce, sour cream, radishes, hot carrots, and more; a freshly griddled meat and cheese pupusa; and a deep-fried chicken flauta with red sauce. Different things were at other stands. *Mike R.* recommends mango on a stick: usually a perfectly ripe and refreshing specimen, peeled and cross-hatch sliced for your convenience. Particularly noteworthy are the pupusas sold from a tent by vendors from El Salvador and Guatemala; *at203* was mystically drawn to the heavenly pork and cheese pupusas, hot off the griddle, and reports that shredded pork and mild cheese come together in hot gooey goodness. Other vendors not to miss: the mango-on-a-stick people (who spike the fruit with lemon juice, chili pepper, and salt) and the people making quesadillas (especially chorizo) from fresh masa.

Hours vary based on when soccer games are being played, and vendors close whenever their supply runs outs. One vendor *bosshog* noticed had run out of atole around 6:00 p.m.

RICE PUDDING Specialist

Rice To Riches (Soho)
37 Spring St.
Manhattan, NY
212-274-0008
Store

Rice to Riches specializes in rice pudding in unusual flavors, and is converting hounds who say they never liked rice pudding before. Special vanilla pudding is made with three vanillas. The texture is thick and creamy, with rice grains fully swelled and slightly chewy, but pleasantly so, and the perfume from the three vanillas is pretty heavenly, describes *AnnChantal*. Other favorite flavors include mascarpone-cherry, coconut-banana, and maple. The friendly staff is generous with samples.

RICEBALLS on the Run

OMS/B (Grand Central)
156 E. 45th St.
Manhattan, NY
212-922-9788
Japanese/Pan-Asian Fusion

Omusubi are Japanese rice balls and **OMS/B**, the first all-omusubi cafe in New York (OMS/B . . . get it?), is serving them near Grand Central Station. They offer a large assortment of freshly made nouveau rice balls along with whole-leaf teas, beverages, and soft-serve green tea ice cream. *Aki* has sleuthed out word that Matsuri's Tadashi Ono has created many of the restaurant's new-school creative rice balls aimed at Western tastes. Ono's creations include the prosciutto/pastrami wrapped rice, the popcorn shrimp with hot sauce on rice wrapped in lettuce, and the BBQ beef (Kalbi) on rice wrapped with lettuce.

RIDGEWOOD Shopping Rundown

Forest Pork Store (Queens)
66-39 Forest Ave.
Ridgewood, Queens, NY
718-497-2853
German, Store

Karl Ehmer Quality Meats
    (Queens)
63-35 Fresh Pond Rd.
Ridgewood, Queens, NY
718-456-8100
German, Store

Tony Mule Meat Market (Queens)
66-26 Fresh Pond Rd.
Ridgewood, Queens, NY
718-821-4774
Italian Deli

Valentino's (Queens)
66-64 Fresh Pond Rd.
Ridgewood, Queens, NY
718-386-2907
Store

Wawel Meats Deli (Queens)
68-33 Fresh Pond Rd.
Ridgewood, Queens, NY
718-821-2730
Polish, Store

Valentino's looks like an ordinary produce store, but inside you'll hear Italian ladies chat about whose daughter got married to whose son. You'll find olives, sun-dried tomatoes, fresh mozzarella, cheeses, Italian imports, dried sausages, and more at the deli counter. And in the back there's a butcher with great fresh sausages, veal, lamb cuts, and more, reports *knoedel*, who says if you see the braided semolina bread, get as many loaves as you can carry.

An Italian bakery nearby (a few block from Valentino's, on same side) stocks a full line of pastries and breads; *knoedel* thinks it's called Grimaldi's Bakery, but Grimaldi's (2101 Menahan Street, Ridgewood, Queens, 718-497-1425) doesn't quite fit that bill. Happy hunting!

Wawel is a Polish deli and import store with homemade salads, sausages, ham, smoked fish, and an excellent bread and roll selection. They stock everything from candy and cookies to jam, butter, great pierogi, *palacsinta*, coffee, and mustards (the same ones sold at Dean & Deluca, here one-third the price). Owner Peter is a sweetheart.

Karl Ehmer Quality Meats is a neighborhood institution with a full line of German sausages and breads, chocolate, cheese, butter, quark, spices, pickled items, and German canned goods. *Kassler rippchen* (smoked pork chop) is a favorite of *knoedel*.

Tony's Meat Market is Italian, and there's a big shelf of sauces, oils, and the like.

Go for the bratwurst at **Forest Pork Store**.

○ **Forest Pork Store:** *see also* p. 136
○ **Karl Ehmer Quality Meats:** *see also* p. 137

Tribeca **ROTI** Special

Hudson Square Cafe (Tribeca)
480 Canal St., #1
Manhattan, NY
212-334-7935
Eclectic

Delicious and huge roti are sold at the otherwise mediocre **Hudson Square Cafe.** Goat or chicken are $5.95, and shrimp are $6.95. Just to torture us, they're made Fridays only!

RUSSIAN Coronaries

Arenichnaya-Pelmini Varenichky
(Brooklyn)
3086 Brighton 2nd St.
Brighton Beach, Brooklyn, NY
718-332-9797
Russian

Cafe Sarmish (Brooklyn)
1162 Coney Island Ave.
Midwood, Brooklyn, NY
718-421-4119
Russian

As the name suggests, vareniky (Russian stuffed dumplings) are the specialty at **Arenichnaya-Pelmini Varenichky**. They come in a bowl (fifteen to twenty per order), topped with a variety of condiments. Potato is the most common stuffing, but you can get anything from fried cabbage to sweet cottage cheese. Warning: They come swimming in an inch-deep pool of butter and topped with an ice-cream scoop dollop of fresh sour cream.

Don't ignore the rest of the menu. Stew in a pot is "veerrry thick stew comprised mainly of what felt like entire potatoes and maybe whole cows. A very nice, cool tomato essence runs through all of it. Good meat and potatoes are never *this* good," says *TastyLlama*. Lamb soup has plenty of freshly cooked lamb chunks, and fantastic broth, great for bread dipping. Skewers of lamb ribs are bits of bone barely clinging to glistening heaps of immensely fatty lamb meat.

Wrap one hand around a bottle of Stolichnaya and use the other to chow on Russian delights at **Cafe Sarmish**. Eggplant salad is exceptionally herbed and spiced, liver kebabs are tender and rich, and skewers of lamb and chicken are very satisfying, reports *Mike R.*. He also recommends golden, greasy *samsa* pastry filled with lamb and onions, fresh garden salad, and french fries. Mashed potatoes aren't buttery enough.

Rare **RUSSIAN BREAD**

Brach's Glatt Kosher Meat Mkt
   (Queens)
7251 Main St.
Kew Gardens, Queens, NY
718-544-7448
Kosher

Russian Bread (Brooklyn)
1631 E. 18th St.
Gravesend, Brooklyn, NY
718-336-3956
Russian

Top-notch Russian bread called Borodinskiy (from Handmade Products) is sold at **Brach's Glatt Kosher Meat**. *Ivan Stoller* describes it as tan in color, with mostly rye flour plus some wheat. The bread is loaded with whole coriander seeds. Sensational.

Tamara offers a vague but intriguing report about wonderful Borodinsky-style bread available at the small Russian bakery called, simply, Russian bread.

You can probably also find this sort of bread around Brighton Beach.

RUSSIAN SAMOVAR

Russian Samovar Restaurant (Clinton)
256 W. 52nd St.
Manhattan, NY
212-757-0168
Russian

Vodka is the fuel that drives Russian Samovar, but they have lots of hot and cold appetizers to help pace you. Make sure you find a Russian to teach you "the system," which involves shots of flavored vodka at timed intervals interspersed with lots of water and food. Cold appetizers particularly shine, says *elvislives*, who recommends cucumber salad and *satsivi* (cold chicken breast chunks in delicious coriander sauce).

Reliable Orders at SABOR

Sabor (Upper West Side)
462 Amsterdam Ave.
Manhattan, NY
212-579-2929
Cuban

Order carefully at Sabor and you'll enjoy some delicious food in a very high-energy atmosphere. While not everything is good, *Brian Crist* suggests sticking with first-rate chorizo, goat cheese empanadas, and lobster quesadillas. He also recommends their mojitos.

Beautifully Craft-Ed **SALADS**

Craftbar (Gramercy)
43 E. 19th St.
Manhattan, NY
212-780-0880
New American

Consensus is developing that entrées are unnecessary and may even detract from your experience at **Craftbar**. Salads, however, are not to be missed. "Frisée salad with gorgonzola and lardons was extraordinary. Impeccable ingredients dressed perfectly—this might be the only restaurant I've ever visited where the dressing is always perfect. The beets with horse-radish crème fraîche was the dish of the night, a spectacular combination. The crème fraîche tasted like a soft, seasoned goat cheese—lush and delicate at the same time," reports *Dave Feldman*. Sandwiches, vegetables, appetizers, and risotto also stand out. Entrées can suffer from overly high expectations, agrees *wurtle*, who nonetheless insists that, dollar for dining, the place rocks.

○ **Craftbar** *see also* **pp. 51, 266.**

Tarrytown **SANDWICH SHOP/DOMINICAN CAFE**

Mi Bohio (Westchester County)
12 Main St.
Tarrytown, NY
914-332-7272
Dominican

Mi Bohio is a restaurant with a split personality. Not only does it sell very tasty Dominican food, but it bills itself as the best sandwich maker in town. Unlike some ethnic restaurants where you feel like the good stuff is hidden on the native-language only

Chowhound Nametag: Tom Meg

∘◯∘

Location:
Sunnyside, Queens.

Occupation:
Classical singer.

Number of Visits to McDonald's in Past Decade: Maybe ten. I only need to go once a year because the smell of their burgers lingers in my burps for months.

Top Chinatown Pick:
Mai Xiang Tan in Flushing.

Underrated by Chowhounds: Natural Tofu in Sunnyside. La Lupe in Sunnyside. OMS/B (rice ball cafe) on Forty-fifth and Third Avenue in Manhattan.

Weight Management Tips: Run a lot. Don't eat after 9:00 p.m. Avoid soft drinks. Only eat delicious food.

Favorite Comfort Chow: Menchanko-Tei (any location) where I order *buta kaku-ni* (braised pork belly) and hakata ramen.

Guilty Pleasure:
Reese's Peanut Butter Cups.

Favorite Gelato Flavor:
Pistachio.

Favorite Mail-Order Chow:
Kay and Ray's DARK potato chips (1-800-THE-CHIP).

menu, all the Dominican dishes here are in both English and Spanish, while sandwiches and salads are listed only in English. Yours truly, *Deven Black*, reports flavorful but slightly chewy goat stew, nicely spiced chicken stew, and tasty whole red snapper that could have been cleaned better. Very refreshing *batidos* (fruit milk shakes in papaya, guineo, pina, melon, fresa, mango, naranja, or mamey flavor). Very large servings.

High-end **SANDWICHES**

AKA Cafe (Lower East Side)
49 Clinton St.
Manhattan, NY
212-979-6096
New American

Artisanal (Murray Hill)
2 Park Ave. enter on 32nd St.
Manhattan, NY
212-725-8585
French

Blue Ribbon Bakery
   (Greenwich Village)
33 Downing St.
Manhattan, NY
212-337-0404
American

Blue Ribbon Brasserie (Soho)
97 Sullivan St.
Manhattan, NY
212-274-0404
French Brasserie

Britti Caffe (Soho)
110 Thompson St.
Manhattan, NY
212-334-6604
Italian Sandwich Shop

Craftbar (Gramercy)
43 E. 19th St.
Manhattan, NY
212-780-0880
New American

DB Bistro Moderne
   (Midtown West)
55 W. 44th St.
Manhattan, NY
212-391-2400
French

Four Seasons (Midtown East)
99 E. 52nd St.
Manhattan, NY
212-754-9494
French/New American

'ino (Greenwich Village)
21 Bedford St.
Manhattan, NY
212-989-5769
Italian

'inoteca (Lower East Side)
98 Rivington St.
Manhattan, NY
212-614-0473
Italian

La Goulue Restaurant
(Upper East Side)
746 Madison Ave.
Manhattan, NY
212-988-8169
French

Mercer Kitchen (Soho)
99 Prince St.
Manhattan, NY
212-966-5454
New American/French

Metropolitan Museum of Art
Trustees' Dining Room
(Upper East Side)
1000 5th Ave.
Manhattan, NY
212-570-3975
French/New American

Mix (Midtown West)
68 W. 58th St.
Manhattan, NY
212-583-0300
American/French

Molyvos (Midtown West)
871 7th Ave.
Manhattan, NY
212-582-7500
Greek

Morrell Wine
(Midtown West)
1 Rockefeller Plaza
Manhattan, NY
212-688-9370
Wine Store

Payard Patisserie & Bistro
(Upper East Side)
1032 Lexington Ave.
Manhattan, NY
212-717-5252
French Bistro/French

Rue 57 (Midtown West)
60 W. 57th St.
Manhattan, NY
212-307-5656
French Brasserie/Japanese

Tabla (Gramercy)
11 Madison Ave.
Manhattan, NY
212-889-0667
Eclectic South Asian

'Wichcraft (Gramercy)
49 E. 19th St.
Manhattan, NY
212-780-0577
New American

Brown bag lunch items served on white linen tablecloths? More and more high-end restaurants are going for mass-market appeal by adding upscaled sandwiches to their menus:

- **The Four Seasons:** an interesting trio of burgers: duck, bison, and tuna.
- **DB Bistro Moderne:** signature foie gras and short rib–filled DB burger.
- **Mercer Kitchen:** luxurious lamb sandwiches.

- **Artisanal:** interesting takes on traditional sandwiches like cheese steak and ham and cheese at lunchtime.
- **AKA Cafe:** menu consists primarily of upscale sandwiches.
- **Tabla:** fusiony pulled lamb and mashed potato "nanini" (God help us all . . .).
- **Blue Ribbon Bakery** has replaced their muffaletta, blue reuben, and shrimp salad sandwiches with a duck club (also available at **Blue Ribbon Brasserie**).
- **Molyvos** makes an out-of-this-world lamb sandwich.
- **Morrel Wine Bar** serves a foie gras club sandwich.
- **Rue 57** offers a seared tuna sandwich with a layer of black sesame mayo and scallion tempura.
- Celebrity chef turned high-end sandwich entrepeneur, Tom Colicchio offers a nice selection of sandwiches at both **'Wichcraft** and the more upscale **Craftbar**.
- **'ino** is a shrine to great Italian wine, panini, and antipasti . . . and fantastic truffle egg toast. The panini selection is extensive, and both bread and fillings are excellent.
- 'ino offshoot **'inoteca** offers a large selection of Italian-inspired sandwiches, panini, and tramezzini. Also extensive and very reasonably priced wine list and terrific small dishes, best of which are truffled egg toast, grilled calamari salad, panini, meatballs, triple cream goat cheese, parmesan aged two years, and panna cotta with roasted peaches.)
- The owners of **Britti Caffe** came to New York from Italy seven years ago, and now spend their time creating tasty panini available on focaccia or ciabatta. Chowhound *mg* thinks the fillings are just as tasty as 'ino's . . . at a lower price.
- **Mix** makes good BLTs.
- **La Gouloue** and the Trustees' Dining Room at the Met both offer worthy sandwiches, and Payard has a separate menu devoted to sandwiches

Secret Orders at **SAPPORO EAST**

Sapporo East (East Village)
245 E. 10th St.
Manhattan, NY
212-260-1330
Japanese

Thanks to *Aki*'s judicious research, we've been tracking an upswing on the overall quality of food at **Sapporo East**. The latest triumph is their miso katsu, a famous regional dish from Nagoya, listed anonymously as "Japanese style beef cutlet." You can also choose (more traditional) pork or (a lesser choice) chicken, with either tonkatsu sauce or homemade special miso sauce. (Aki recommends the latter.) Unlike in Japan, here the sauce is served on the side—a concession to American habits. No matter what ingredients you choose, though, Aki insists you "pour the sauce all over the katsu—this is pretty fun!—*immediately*."

Another Aki discovery at Sapporo East: maguro nakaochi, a traditional Japanese delicacy of medium-fatty tuna, scraped off from bones, finely chopped, and then served over rice. Sapporo East offers this dish only when they have good quality tuna on hand, when it's listed on the specials menu. For $8.75 they make quite a presentation, carefully and precisely distributing sauce over tuna and vinegared rice. Call ahead to ensure they've got it. The strategic tip is to ensure that Mr. Hide is making the maguro nakaochi. Mr. Hide is off on Mondays and Thursdays, and the other chef's version, though respectable, is not as mind shattering. Other items to get: medium-fatty tuna sushi, a steal at $15 for seven pieces, and white fish tempura, one of New York City's finest. Note that

Mr. Shige, the tempura master, is off Tuesdays and sometimes Thursdays.

○ **Sapporo East:** *see also* p. 234.

The Great Pasta Dish at **SAVOIA**

Savoia Pizzeria (Brooklyn)
277 Smith St.
Cobble Hill, Brooklyn, NY
718-797-2727
Italian

One dish at Savoia caught *Cathy Elton*'s attention: a penne with sausage/green pepper ragu has no visible evidence of green peppers in the meaty sauce, yet brims with the most incredible deep green pepper flavor. They must cook down a ton of green peppers for a long time, and the result is delicious. They also make very good gnocchi with wild mushrooms (not as rich and creamy as a lot of wild mushroom sauces).

○ **Savoia Pizzeria:** *see also* p. 140.

SCANDINAVIAN SANDWICHES
and Swedish Tapas

Good World Bar & Grill
   (Chinatown)
3 Orchard St.
Manhattan, NY
212-925-9975
Swedish

Smorgas Chef (Lower Manhattan)
53 Stone St.
Manhattan, NY
212-422-3500
Scandinavian

Smorgas Chef specializes in Scandinavian sandwiches (though they offer a full menu), and while we've had only a preliminary report, the place sounds interesting for the nabe. Their signature item is an open cold-water shrimp (canned and imported from the North Sea) sandwich with mixed greens and a dash of caviar on sourdough bread. *Aki* wasn't impressed $9.95 worth, but he thinks the Swedish meatballs, foie gras and apple, and Fjord salmon sandwiches may merit checking out.

   Good World Bar is an odd but cozy place serving what seem to be Swedish-style tapas, as well as other items. Tasty gravlax and delicious grilled salmon, reports *eeee*, as well as a huge bowl of sweet smoked shrimp, and an extremely thin and crispy potato pancake with lumpfish caviar (that can make your teeth turn green!), among other small appetizerlike servings. Service is fast and efficient despite crowds.

SHANGHAI HOT POT
All-You-Can-Eat

Shanghai Tang (Queens)
135-20 40th Rd.
Flushing, Queens, NY
718-661-0900
Chinese (Shanghai)

Shanghai Tang offers an all-you-can-eat hot pot deal for $21 per person, including many appetizers (like scallion pancakes, sesame pancakes, and pork soup dumplings—but not the ones with crab), desserts (like hot, sweet bean soup, sweet red-bean rice cakes) and drinks, including all the Budweiser you can down in two hours. It's a typical Sichuan hot pot . . . only in a Shanghai restaurant. The ingredients are too numerous to mention, but *Eric Eto* urges you to make sure you get clams, blue crab, and lots of meat dishes as they give the broth a great flavor (especially the clams). They also have a dipping sauce bar from which you can create your own sauces. The leek sauce is a real standout.

SHAVED ICE: Two Toppings for $2

Fortune Gourmet (Queens)
135-02 Roosevelt Ave.
Flushing, Queens, NY
718-321-9070
Chinese (Taiwanese)

Fortune Gourmet started as a shaved ice parlor and expanded into a restaurant with some merely OK food choices. But the shaved ice is still tops, and a great value. Two dollars gets you two toppings, and additional ones are twenty-five cents each. The display menu is in Chinese, but toppings are listed in English on table menus, and *bigjeff* recommends red beans with crunchy peanuts, hard jelly, condensed milk, and minitapioca combo. You can also ask for it without simple syrup, since it's too sweet . . . but really . . . nothing beats this stuff.

Jumbo Guatemalan **SHRIMP**

Blue Ribbon Bakery (Greenwich Village)
33 Downing St.
Manhattan, NY
212-337-0404
American

Having their heads and shells intact isn't the only thing that separates **Blue Ribbon Bakery**'s jumbo Guatemalan shrimp from more plebeian decapods that get all their flavor from the dipping sauce. These shrimp have that wonderful slightly funky/shrimpy aroma like good Mediterranean shrimp. *YSChow* sucked the juices from their heads to enjoy a virtual reality plunge into the Guatemalan sea—and ordered an extra dish.

○ **Blue Ribbon Bakery:** *see also* **pp. 42, 104, 266.**

Iraqi/Israeli **SHWARMA** Made by Mexicans (Plus Greek Alternatives)

Karavas Place (Greenwich Village)
162 W. 4th St.
Manhattan, NY
212-243-8007
Greek

Village Shawarma
  (Greenwich Village)
321 6th Ave,
Manhattan, NY
212-924-8007
Sephardic/Israeli

Village Shawarma makes *Jim Leff*'s favorite shwarma in Manhattan. An additional attraction is the mango hot sauce served with it, an Iraqi/Jewish tradition. Nice staff, too, of entrepreneurial Mexican-Americans. Eggs with tomato and pepper sauce with hummus in a pita is a bargain at $3, and comes with a side salad you compile from the Israeli salad bar. All sandwiches are served on pillowy bread. A nice selection of Israeli drinks (such as fruit nectars) is available. Falafel is large and crunchy but machine made, a turnoff to some, but others might appreciate the uniformity. *David Lerner* recommends heading up the block to **Karavas** for much better Greek-style falafel, albeit with slightly more formal table service.

Surprisingly **SICHUAN** Neighborhood Takeout

Master Wok East (Midtown East)
1003 2nd Ave.
Manhattan, NY
212-753-3680
Chinese (Sichuan)/Chinese

Abandon your assumptions that **Master Wok** is just an average neighborhood Chinese takeout joint! *Sir Gawain* reports that both food and decor have been designed with pride. The extensive menu includes a section marked "Popular Szechuan Dishes," including flavorful pork wontons with Sichuan roasted chili oil and equally good double-sautéed fresh bacon with pickled vegetables (with explosively flavored black beans), and intensely—maybe excessively so, depending on your feelings about anise—flavored braised beef and vegetables in roasted chili vinaigrette. Excellent pan-fried pork dumplings and dry fried beef, adds *Richard*, are both unabashedly spicy. Master Wok is busiest at lunchtime and empties out during the dinner hours, and the Sichuan menu (available online at www.masterwok.com/sze-MENU.htm) is available upon request.

Two **SMALL PLATE** Places

AKA Cafe (Lower East Side)
49 Clinton St.
Manhattan, NY
212-979-6096
New American

Tasting Room (East Village)
72 E. 1st St.
Manhattan, NY
212-358-7831
New American

The **Tasting Room** may be a wine geek's paradise, but food doesn't take second place. Chef Colin Alevras (formerly in the kitchen at Daniel) creates an ever-changing menu of small dishes, most of which can be upgraded to full-sized entrées. Typical dishes: squid with chorizo, braised rabbit, asparagus terrine accompanied by savory grapefruit *supremes* and poached cod with spring peas in a cardamom-laced sauce ("so delicious, even though there was still string in the cod from poaching, and the peas were very undercooked. Still, I would eat this one again and again," says *winnie*). The room is small and service is very informal and enthusiastic.

AKA Cafe's menu is designed to encourage sampling lots of small dishes. Manhattan clam chowder comes with whole clams and nuggets of spicy sausage. Slightly spicy shrimp ceviche is a tasty and generous portion for $8. The one salad has nice spicy pecans on it. There are only two entrées on the menu: barbecued trout over mustardy mayo-free potato salad and fish of the day with hard-boiled eggs and olives, both $13. An amazing bargain for quality of food, says *eeee*. AKA Cafe is, we believe, the only restaurant in this book that appears in both high-end and low-end roundups! Just goes to show what can be done with small-portion sizes. . . .

○ **AKA Cafe:** *see also* **pp. 64, 266.**

Soulful SOONDOOBOO

Cho Dang Gol (Midtown West)
55 W. 35th St.
Manhattan, NY
212-695-8222
Korean

Natural Tofu (Bergen County)
520 Bergen Blvd.
Palisades Park, NJ
201-585-9515
Korean

Natural Tofu (Bergen County)
223 Closter Dock Rd.
Closter, NJ
201-750-6400
Korean

Natural Tofu (Queens)
40-06 Queens Blvd.
Sunnyside, Queens, NY
718-706-0899
Korean

Natural Tofu (Queens)
152-22 Northern Blvd.
Flushing, Queens, NY
718-961-2001
Korean

Seoul Garden
   (Herald Sq/Garment District)
34 W. 32nd St., #2
Manhattan, NY
212-736-9002
Korean

Soondooboo **is a crushed** soft tofu stew usually served in clay casserole pots called ddookbaegi, which help maintain the sizzling heat throughout the meal. **Seoul Garden** offers about a half-dozen types of soondooboo, each with an assortment of panchan (the freebie little appetizer plates), for under $10. The combination soon tofu with kimchi, beef, and seafood ($8.95) is the best choice, *cabrales* says. (For a $4 supplement, you can add kalbi, barbecued in the kitchen.) BYOB, too. Also in Little Korea, **Cho Dang Gol** makes a specialty of soondooboo, and the far-flung **Natural Tofu** locations offer soondooboo as well as a variety of other tasty hot and cold soups.

Uptown **SOUL FOOD**

Amy Ruth's (Upper West Side)
113 W. 116th St.
Manhattan, NY
212-280-8779
Southern

Miss Mamie's Spoonbread Too
    (Upper West Side)
366 W. 110th St.
Manhattan, NY
212-865-6744
Southern

United House of Prayer Cafeteria
    (Harlem)
2320 Frederick Douglass Blvd.
Manhattan, NY
212-749-5797
Southern

The cafeteria entrance at **United House of Prayer** isn't marked. Just go in the door on Frederick Douglass between 124th and 125th and up a flight of stairs. They offer about half a dozen main courses from lunch till about 7:00 p.m., including great fried or baked chicken, good turkey wings and meatloaf, and a choice of sides. *Lorna* loves okra, mac and cheese, sweet potatoes, collard greens, and wonderful sweet potato pie, but doesn't recommend the black-eyed peas.

Amy Ruth's is small and wildly popular. Chicken and waffles will please everyone. Very good honey chicken and cornbread.

Miss Mamie's Spoonbread Too is bright and cheerful, and has delicious food in copious servings (particularly sides). Meat loaf can be sweet, but ribs will melt in your mouth. *Jim Leff* disagrees, finding them second-rate and unsoulful (though he hasn't visited recently).

Brooklyn **SOUL FOOD**

Duncan's Fish Market (Brooklyn)
385 Myrtle Ave.
Fort Greene, Brooklyn, NY
718-923-1115
Caribbean

Soul Spot Restaurant (Brooklyn)
302 Atlantic Ave.
Boerum Hill, Brooklyn, NY
718-596-9933
Southern

Mitchell's Fish & Chips (Brooklyn)
617 Vanderbilt Ave.
Prospect Heights, Brooklyn, NY
718-789-3212
Southern

Two lesser-known Brooklyn soul food spots:

Mitchell's is a fine place. *Barry Strugatz* reports an amazing plate of pigs feet, cabbage, and collard greens, and, for dessert, a slice of sublime coconut-pineapple cake. He marvels that a place this tasty mostly gets ignored.

Soul Spot comments are always positive. They do an excellent chicken and fish special with freshly fried whiting and perfectly spiced roasted chicken, says *Brian Cohen*. Noteworthy side dishes include not-over-sweet, slightly spicy yams and not-too-porky, nicely smoky collard greens and corn bread. Fried chicken, ribs, and mashed potatoes are also recommended by *marthaly*.

As a fish market, **Duncan's** has a limited selection. But Duncan's takeout counter offers inexpensive soul food and occasional Caribbean options; *cj* says the standard order is a fish dinner ($7) with fried whiting, two sides and corn bread. Generous whiting sandwiches are $3.50. The folks at Duncan's know how to fry up some fish. The thin coating is crisp, the fish tender. Side orders include very good mac and cheese, as well as candied yams, a couple of greens, and french fries.

Long Island **SOUL FOOD**

Long Island Fish Establishment
(Suffolk County)
1522 Straight Path
Wyandanch, NY
631-254-5433
Southern/Seafood

Roman & Ann Soul Food
(Nassau County)
1005 Prospect Ave.
Westbury, NY
516-997-9001
Southern

Parker's Fish & Chicken
(Nassau County)
213 Front St.
Hempstead, NY
516-565-1147
Southern

Village Deli (Suffolk County)
1513 Straight Path
Wyandanch, NY
631-491-9053
Jamaican

Expertly fried chicken, excellent "taters" (potato wedges coated with fried chicken batter), and densely delectable banana pudding (packed with vanilla wafers and ripe bananas) are just a few of the charms of **Parker's Fish & Chicken**, according to *Paul Trapani*. A friendly and concerned staff completes the package.

The Long Island Fish Establishment is a fried fish and soul food find. The fish is amazingly fresh and spiced creole style with a strong celery flavor. They also make a nicely sweet hot sauce and a pretty solid banana pudding as well.

Across the street from Long Island Fish Establishment is **Village Deli**, where owner Phil barbecues jerk chicken that is quite possibly the most soulful thing there is to eat on Long Island. All other items are sensational as well. (Note: Phil is hoping to open a new location. If you find this address closed, just ask around about where he went!)

Roman & Ann Soul Food is another top soul food pick, with friendly service and terrific cooking. Try their stuffing and their banana pudding.

Spectacular **SOUP** at Woo Chon

Woo Chon (Midtown West)
10 W 36th St.
Manhattan, NY
212-695-0676
Korean

Yang kalbi tang is a soup created by Soo, the owner of **Woo Chon**. "A large heated stone bowl arrives at the table with the lava-red soup still bubbling furiously. The base is a rich-tasting beef broth made red with ground chili. The soup is spicy, definitely a nose-runner, but the heat does not obscure the flavors. It contains all things good: intensely beefy-tasting short ribs (melt-ingly tender and falling off the bone); honeycomb tripe; pieces of small beef intestines; *dang myun,* the long, thin, chewy Korean noodles made from sweet potato starch; and squares of daikon radish and scallion. It is simply delicious," raves *Eddie Bennet*, who says panchan (the small side dishes at every Korean meal) are fantastically fresh, widely varied, and changed frequently. Typical offerings: pieces of monkfish tail cartilage; fried (no batter) and tossed in a sweet and spicy chili-based sauce; cooked chicken gizzards in a spicy chili sauce; raw, quartered blue crab in the same sauce and snails in a similar, spicy chili sauce.

SOUPS On

Brothers Bar-B-Que
  (Greenwich Village)
225 Varick St.
Manhattan, NY
212-727-2775
Southern/Barbecue/American

Financier Patisserie
  (Lower Manhattan)
62 Stone St.
Manhattan, NY
212-344-5600
French

Kitchenette (Tribeca)
80 W. Broadway
Manhattan, NY
212-267-6740
American/Diner or Coffee Shop

Polonia (East Village)
110 1st Ave.
Manhattan, NY
212-254-9699
Polish

The Pink Tea Cup
(Greenwich Village)
42 Grove St.
Manhattan, NY
212-807-6755
Southern

Veselka Restaurant (East Village)
144 2nd Ave.
Manhattan, NY
212-228-9682
Ukranian/Central/Eastern
European

Terse tips for swell soup:

- **Veselka:** hot red borscht.
- **Polonia:** lima bean stew (very thick and full of broad flat limas and slices of smoky porkalicious kielbasa, says *lintsao*).
- **Financier Patisserie** has a different soup every day, and all are great, gushes *Abbylovi*.
- **Pink Tea Cup:** try chicken soup.
- **Brothers Bar-B-Que:** cold yellow gazpacho (note: we're not fans of the rest of the menu, so this tip especially intrigues!).
- The downtown branch of **Kitchenette** serves a very nice gazpacho as a regular summertime special. *Rachel M.* describes the soup as nice and fresh tasting with just the right amount of chiles or something for a little spicy zing.

See also *Japanese* Noodle Soups and *Soups* in the Boroughs.

○ **Kitchenette:** *see also* **pp. 42, 103, 151, 205, 240.**
○ **The Pink Tea Cup:** *see also* **p. 151.**
○ **Veselka Restaurant:** *see also* **p. 32.**

SOUPS in the Boroughs

Fast & Fresh Deli (Brooklyn)
84 Hoyt St.
Cobble Hill, Brooklyn, NY
718-802-1661
Mexican

Kowus African Carribean (Bronx)
3396 3rd Ave.
Bronx, NY
718-401-6232
Ghanaian/Caribbean

La Pequeña Colombia Restaurant
    (Queens)
8327 Roosevelt Ave.
Jackson Heights, Queens, NY
718-478-6528
Colombian

Lomzynianka (Brooklyn)
646 Manhattan Ave.
Greenpoint, Brooklyn, NY
718-389-9439
Polish

Meson Asturias (Queens)
4012 83rd St.
Jackson Heights, Queens, NY
718-446-9154
Spanish

Natural Tofu (Queens)
40-06 Queens Blvd.
Sunnyside, Queens, NY
718-706-0899
Korean

Pho Tay Ho (Brooklyn)
2351 86th St.
Bensonhurst, Brooklyn, NY
718-449-0199
Vietnamese

Registan (Queens)
6537 99th St.
Rego Park, Queens, NY
718-459-1638
Kosher Central Asian

Salut (Queens)
6342 108th St.
Kew Gardens, Queens, NY
718-275-6860
Kosher Central Asian

- **Kowus African Carribean** [sic]: Ghanaian soup with a ball of rice or fufu in the bottom. Add in pieces of goat or fish.
- **Fast and Fresh Deli:** deeply impressive and fiery *pancita* (the Mexico City version of menudo, the tripe soup) . . . and lots of other good things at this place, too.
- **Pho Tay Ho:** pho (Vietnamese beef soup), natch.
- **Lomzynianka:** amazing white borscht.

- **Meson Asturias:** *caldo Gallego* (a cabbage-and-pork specialty of Galicia).
- **La Pequeña Colombia:** *sopa de blanquillos* (white beans).
- *Lagman*, a delicious Uzbek beef broth with noodles, cilantro, and spices is a hit at both **Registan** and **Salut** in Rego Park.

Natural Tofu serves a special cold noodle soup (summertime only) that's not to be missed, according to *HLing*. It's served in a chilled metal bowl with shaved ice (fine as snow) floating in cold broth, with thin slices of pear, beef, light brown translucent noodles, slivers of vegetables, and very smoky spices. Spiced similarly to a pho, the end result has a powerful flavor (too powerful for some). During nonsummer months you can still enjoy their very good LA Galbi and pancakes. Just take a pass on the shockingly bad kimchee and other panchan (freebie appetizers).

○ **Kowus African Carribean:** *see also* p. 138.
○ **La Pequeña Colombia Restaurant:** *see also* p. 38.
○ **Lomzynianka:** *see also* p. 249.
○ **Natural Tofu:** *see also* p. 275.
○ **Salut:** *see also* p. 59.

SOUTH ASIAN Cabbie Haunts

Cuisine of Pakistan (Clinton)
478 9th Ave.
Manhattan, NY
212-714-0657
Pakistani

Kasturi (Gramercy)
83 Lexington Ave.
Manhattan, NY
212-679-7993
Bangladeshi

Lahore Deli (Soho)
132 Crosby St.
Manhattan, NY
212-965-1777
Pakistani

Pakistan Tea House (Tribeca)
176 Church St.
Manhattan, NY
212-240-9800
Pakistani

Shaheen Sweets (Murray Hill)
130 E. 29th St.
Manhattan, NY
212-251-0202
South Asian

Sheezaan Indian Restaurant
 (Lower Manhattan)
183 Church St.
Manhattan, NY
212-964-6259
Pakistani

Kasturi is a homestyle Bangladeshi place popular with taxi drivers. A plate—big order of rice, with either meat and veg or two vegs from a steam table—costs $6.50. Naan and other items are made fresh for you. No menu, just point at the steam table (nothing's heated, so your assembled plate will be microwaved). Chowhound *jen kalb* promises very soul-satisfying spicing, distinct flavors and character to each dish, a real pleasure, and singles out channa dal and fish balls for extra praise. You'll see veg and meat dishes you don't often find in other local South Asian restaurants.

Lahore is a 24/7 Pakistani joint popular with taxi drivers and others looking for tasty but simple dining. One cabbie there told *jake pine* to order whatever's on top of the counter, since that is usually the freshest and fastest-moving item. Chicken curry and fresh-brewed tea are favorites, but he warned that the roti is not made on premises and recommends rice instead. Vegetable and lamb dishes, samosas, and tea are delicious. Don't miss their chai (tea).

The same cabby also recommends **Cuisine of Pakistan** (aka Kashmir 9), where prices are low and portions are large. You choose from the steam table and your food's warmed in a microwave, but everything's nonetheless tasty and wholesome. (This is how many fancier-seeming South-Asian restaurants work; Cuisine of Pakistan is just out of the closet about it.) Hounds report good meatballs and ground beef, turnips, and zucchini in stewy preparations, and *Melanie Wong* praises the fried, chili-laced chicken patty. Chicken and lamb curries and naan are decent, but tandoori chicken is undistinguished, even right out of the tandoor. Roti, however, is a speciality that *jake pine* reports to be fresh, fluffy, and flavorful. Generally, the food is delicious, tasting strongly of cardamom, ginger, cloves, and pepper.

Pakistani Tea House is a venerable taxi haunt known for its goat and lamb curries and chicken makkani, but it's gone downhill, and **Sheezaan**, across the street, is now the place. Sheezaan serves a homey, solid, unexceptional menu of vegetable dishes, along with a working tandoor. *Mike R.* reports that you can load up on veggie choices like *aloo saag* (spinach/potatoes), *bhindi* (okra), and cabbage (could've been a tad spicier) with quality basmati rice. For meat lovers, there's herbaceous chicken sheekh kebab and nice samosas. Maaza Mango is the beverage of choice.

Shaheen is also popular with taxi drivers.

○ **Pakistan Tea House:** *see also* p. 205.
○ **Sheezaan Indian Restaurant:** *see also* p. 206.

Nontouristy **SOUTH STREET SEAPORT** Choices

The falafel cart in Liberty Park
   (Lower Manhattan)
NE corner of Liberty and
   Broadway
Manhattan, NY
Middle Eastern/North
   African/Lebanese

Jeremy's Ale House
   (Lower Manhattan)
254 Front St.
Manhattan, NY
212-964-3537
American

Paris Cafe (Lower Manhattan)
119 South St.
Manhattan, NY
212-240-9797
American

Rosario Bistro (Lower Manhattan)
38 Pearl St.
Manhattan, NY
212-514-5454
Italian

The West Indian lady's van
   (Lower Manhattan)
at Broadway and Bridge St.
Manhattan, NY
Jamaican

The South Street Seaport complex has long been derided as an overpriced, mediocre dining scene geared toward tourists, but the surrounding area has chow of interest.

• To the west, **Rosario's** dispenses cheap, tasty, and thoroughly unsophisticated (in a good way) pasta. The perennial long line is amazingly fast moving.

- The **West Indian lady's van** serves fine, cheap jerk chicken.
- **Jeremy's Ale House** has the look and feel of a frat boy hangout, including draft beer served in thirty-two-ounce styrofoam schooners. But the food's better than you'd expect (though not great), e.g. well-marinated tuna steak with rice and salad for $6.95. Some like the cheap fried clam strips, apparently as a guilty pleasure.
- **Paris Cafe** is a pub in the former Edison Hotel (supposedly where Edison first produced commercial electricity) with good burgers.
- The **Liberty Park falafel cart** does perfectly moist and crunchy falafel sandwiches for $2.50, though it's a bit of a walk from the seaport.

SPICY AND TASTY (and Authentic and Scallion Festooned)

Spicy and Tasty (Queens)
39-07 Prince St.
Flushing, Queens, NY
718-359-1601
Chinese (Sichuan)

Glowing reports roll in about Spicy and Tasty, a Sichuan former hole-in-the-wall that has gone (relatively) posh. *Bob Martinez* raves about hot and sour noodles, sautéed Chinese broccoli that's crisp, spicy, and perfect, and cold noodles with red chili sauce ("the waitress warned, 'Very, *very* hot. OK for you?'" Bob fervidly agreed, and she delivered as promised. The hot and sour soup and dan dan noodles are both good but may be a notch below the versions served at the old spot. A trio of excellent pork dishes includes spicy double-cooked pork, shredded pork with dried bean curd, and the mysteriously titled "enhanced pork," which consists of rectangles of thinly sliced spicy pork that have an almost bacony quality. Bob loves scallions and so does the chef who prepares this; loads of sautéed scallions are a great foil for this perfect dish. *HLing* likes their pickled greens and purple fiddleheads in hot oil, and says cold plate selections (you can see them right at the entrance) all look expertly prepared, with very skilled "knife kung fu."

STATEN ISLAND Picks

La Riveria Restaurant
  (Staten Island)
1976 Forest Ave.
Staten Island, NY
718-816-5294
Italian

Philips Candy (Staten Island)
8 Barrett Ave.
Staten Island, NY
718-981-0062
Chocolate/Candy Shop

Trattoria Romana (Staten Island)
1476 Hylan Blvd.
Staten Island, NY
718-980-3113
Italian

Vida (Staten Island)
381 Van Duzer St.
Staten Island, NY
718-720-1501
New American

Lengthy waits are common at Trattoria Romana, even now that it's expanded into a second room. Pastas shine here, with salads and appetizers not far behind. Portions are enormous, and the price–quantity–quality ratio is very good, says *bosshogg*, who warns that fish dishes have repeatedly disappointed. It also gets very crowded, with little space between tables, and lately they've added cheezy live electric piano music.

La Riveria's prices are about twice those at Trattoria Romana, and portions aren't as big, but *bosshogg* reports outstanding fish, and very good veal and pasta dishes. Spacious and relaxed with superior service, even by high Staten Island standards.

Vida has an interesting menu of salads, sandwiches, and a blue plate special each night. A pâté plate is nicely detailed with homemade mustard, toast rounds, and cornichons. Also excellent: egg salad with capers and aioli on a warm roll, and a blue plate special of slow-roasted pork served over corn cakes with pico de gallo. Pumpkin walnut cheesecake for dessert. Sandwiches are $5–$6, and blue plate is $12.

Vida is in Staten Island's Stapleton nabe, on the island's North Shore. It's easy to get to: take the 78 bus from the ferry terminal, which lets you off right on the corner of Van Duzer and Beach.

Philips Confection, a long-time presence in Coney Island much missed after it closed, has reappeared on Staten Island. We haven't heard yet whether the charlotte russe cupcakes and saltwater taffy are as good as in the old days.

Note: In aiming to make this guide as fresh as possible, we disregarded untold thousands of older tips, and unfortunately most of our Staten Island coverage occurred before our cutoff. There are tons of great eating on Staten Island, and we look forward to covering much more of it in future editions of this guide.

○ **Vida:** *see also* **p. 69.**

Alternative STEAK

Keen's Steakhouse
   (Herald Sq/Garment District)
72 W. 36th St.
Manhattan, NY
212-947-3636
Steak House

Strip House (Union Square)
13 E. 12th St.
Manhattan, NY
212-328-0000
Steak House

La Fusta (Queens)
8032 Baxter Ave.
Jackson Heights, Queens, NY
718-429-8222
Argentinian

Hounds recommend filet mignon, rib eye, and porterhouse steaks at **Strip House,** as well the eponymous strip steak. But no matter the cut, be sure to order a step rarer than your preference. Sides earn high praise from *TK Baltimore,* who says that truffled creamed spinach is to die for, the fries rock, and goose fat potatoes are very good . . . but be cautious with the raw garlic on top. Chocolate fondue dessert is large enough to serve four.

Keen's is best known for mutton chops (hounds are divided on quality), but there's more than aged sheep on the menu. Double- or triple-cut lamb chops have lots of crusty chewy stuff along the bone (amazing great flavor and texture, raves *jesse*), while *billyblancoNYC* says the filet is outstanding (nicely charred outside, buttery on the inside), and the creamed spinach is the best ever (spinach with the taste of wonderful cream, not vice versa). Hash browns are equally great. Also praised: Iowa caramel custard (flan), a nice pool of caramel and perfectly creamy flan. There are about two hundred single malt scotch whiskies to choose from and a knowledgeable staff to help steer your choice. Check out the ninety thousand or so clay pipes on the ceiling (each one with a story) and the upstairs private rooms with secret doors and cubbies.

Vacio (pronounced ba-SEE-o) is a flank steak usually reserved for regular customers, but eager-to-please waiters at **La Fusta** will serve you this special off-menu steak if you're hip enough to ask for it. Otherwise, skirt steak comes almost crusty on the outside and very juicy on the inside. Spinach cannelloni à la Rossini (with red and white sauces) are amazing, says *JH Jill*, who also says they mix ground chicken with the spinach to great effect, and the tomato sauce is a revelation—nothing from the can and perhaps a hint of ginger. It's a must-try dish. La Fusta is right across from Elmhurst Hospital's emergency entrance, should the red meat put you into cardiac arrest.

Chowhound Nametag: Caitlin McGrath

∘◯∘

Your Neighborhood: Chelsea.

Occupation: Editor (of a bit of this and a bit of that).

Cholesterol Level: Ignorance is bliss . . .

Weight Management Tip: Try not to indulge unless it's wholly satisfying.

Favorite Comfort Chow: Yellow curry with chicken and potatoes at Cafe
Asean (Manhattan) or Saysetha (Oakland, California). Warm, honey,
just a little spicy—it's very soothing.

Guilty Pleasure: A chocolate-dipped chocolate cone from the Mr. Softee
truck.

Favorite Gelato Flavor: Hazelnut, or a really strong espresso.

Favorite Mail Order Chow:
Conserves from Frog Hollow Farm. Chunks of perfectly-ripe,
sugared organic peaches, apricots, or nectarines—any time of
year. Just try not to eat them straight from the jar
(www.froghollow.com).
XOX chocolate truffles. Small, simple, intense, and delicious
(www.xoxtruffles.com).

Chowhounding Rules of Thumb:
A restaurant that smells like good food is a good bet.
If every table has a certain dish on it, maybe yours should, too.
When in doubt, choose the simpler dish.

Favorite Places to Shop for Food:
Kalustyan's (Manhattan)—A truly impressive selection of spices,
ingredients, and condiments from several continents, in a very
compact space.
Chelsea Market (Manhattan)—An arcade of multiple temptations
(from locally produced dairy to imported Italian goods) under
one roof, high quality but low-key.
Berkeley Bowl (Berkeley, California)—The best: beautiful produce,
local artisanal breads, huge bulk foods selection, the convenience of a supermarket, and excellent prices.
What They Have in Common: they make food shopping fun, and I
discover something new each time I'm there.

Groundbreaking **STRAWBERRY CREAM CHEESE** Roundup

Bagels on the Square
   (Greenwich Village)
7 Carmine St.
Manhattan, NY
212-691-3041
Bagel Shop

Bagel Shoppe (Upper East Side)
1421 2nd Ave.
Manhattan NY
212-585-0990
Bagel Shop

David's Bagel (East Village)
228 1st Ave.
Manhattan, NY
212-533-8766
Bagel Shop

Di Palo Fine Foods
   (Lower East Side)
206 Grand St.
Manhattan, NY
212-226-1033
Store

The Giant Bagel Shop
   (Greenwich Village)
120 University Pl.
Manhattan, NY
212-243-2775
Bagel Shop

Pick A Bagel (Midtown West)
891 8th Ave.
Manhattan, NY
212-582-0017
Bagel Shop

Pick A Bagel (Upper East Side)
1101 Lexington Ave.
Manhattan, NY
212-517-6590
Bagel Shop

Pick A Bagel (Upper West Side)
130 W. 72nd St.
Manhattan, NY
212-595-1300
Bagel Shop

Pick A Bagel At Battery Park
   (Lower Manhattan)
102 North End Ave.
Manhattan, NY
212-786-9200
Bagel Shop

Pick A Bagel On 57
   (Midtown West)
200 W. 57th St.
Manhattan, NY
212-957-5151
Bagel Shop

Pick A Bagel On Second
   (Upper East Side)
1475 2nd Ave.
Manhattan, NY
212-717-4662
Bagel Shop

Pick A Bagel On Sixth (Chelsea)
601 Ave. of the Americas
Manhattan, NY
212-924-4999
Bagel Shop

Pick A Bagel On Third
   (Gramercy)
297 3rd Ave.
Manhattan, NY
212-686-1414
Bagel Shop

Times Square Bagels
   (Theater District)
200 W. 44th St.
Manhattan, NY
212-997-7300
Bagel Shop

Aki has turned chowhounds on to great finds of Mexican French toast, marsala-flavored gelato, Inaniwa udon, Japanese grilled fish breakfasts, pear mousse, and lobster soufflé. As the only possible next step in this progression, *Aki* has been exploring strawberry cream cheese.

At **David's Bagels** (Stuyvesant Town location only) the strawberry cream cheese is very creamy, very delicate. The sweetness is just right, a perfect balance of cream cheese and strawberry condiment. Nice pale pink color. *Aki* advises having this cream cheese on its own, because putting it on a bagel or in a sandwich ruins the delicate texture.

The pink color looks too artificial at **Times Square Bagel**, but the texture's smooth and delicate—even if the taste is a bit too sweet. Other cream cheeses here are also good.

Bagel Shoppe's strawberry cream cheese is very similar to the spread at Times Square Bagel in look and texture, but in better balance regarding sweetness. **Pick A Bagel** and **Bagels on the Square** put strawberry jam on regular cream cheese, and **Giant Bagel Deli** makes theirs using fresh strawberries. The former look pretty sad and the latter's just not interesting.

There's no strawberry cream cheese at **DiPalo's**, but they do make mango cream cheese as well as pineapple and a couple of savory varieties. Look in the back of the store in the refrigerated cases near the frozen pasta.

○ **Di Palo Fine Foods:** *see also* **pp. 53, 108.**

Supreme **SUSHI** Roundup

Jewel Bako (East Village)
239 E. 5th St.
Manhattan, NY
212-979-1012
Japanese

Kuruma-Zushi (Midtown East)
7 E. 47th St.
Manhattan, NY
212-317-2802
Japanese

Sushi of Gari (Upper East Side)
402 E. 78th St.
Manhattan, NY
212-517-5340
Japanese

Sushi Seki (Upper East Side)
1143 1st Ave.
Manhattan, NY
212-371-0238
Japanese

Sushi Yasuda (Midtown East)
204 E. 43rd St.
Manhattan, NY
212-972-1001
Japanese

Sushiden Madison Ave
   (Midtown East)
19 E. 49th St.
Manhattan, NY
212-758-2700
Japanese

Sushiden Sixth Ave (Midtown
   West)
123 W. 49th St.
Manhattan, NY
212-398-2800
Japanese

Sushisay Restaurant
   (Midtown East)
38 E. 51st St.
Manhattan, NY
212-755-1780
Japanese

For the ultimate in New York City sushi check out these favorites:

- The special chef's sushi platter at **Sushi of Gari** manages to be both inventive and respectful of tradition. And they deliver, too!
- **Sushi Seki** (formerly Sushihatsu) also bridges both worlds. *Eric K* says they excel at the extremes of both very traditional and very modern styles. Opt for omakase.
- **Kuruma Zushi,** say many, represents the pinnacle of traditional sushi in New York. It's priced accordingly, at up to $450 for omakase.
- **Sushi Yasuda** is a consensus winner for quality (sushi better than sashimi) and ambiance. Their eel is

particularly good. Check out their unusual appetizer of small, fresh sea cucumber sliced to reveal cross-sections (very crunchy, like dense fresh abalone, describes *cabrales*) listed only on a special appetizer menu printed on thin, yellow paper.

- **Jewel Bako** prepares excellent sushi, just a notch below the city's best, according to many chowhounds.
- Good sushi at **Sushiden,** but be advised that the east side branch is the better of the two.
- **Sushisay** serves traditional sushi rivaling that of Yasuda. The word is out, though: dinners are extremely busy.

See also Japanese choices in the cuisine index.

The Sensuality of **SUSHI**

Jewel Bako (East Village)
239 E. 5th St.
Manhattan, NY
212-979-1012
Japanese

"**The unrivaled freshness** and uniqueness of the four-hour cavalcade of exquisitely prepared tidbits that **Jewel Bako** served up was everything I ever imagined a chef in Japan would tender in an omakase to a respected guest," gushes *galleygirl* about her multicourse meal at Jewel Bako, a chowhound favorite.

"The Tops of the Pops for me, the morsel that blew my dress up right over my head, was the *anago* (sea eel) poached so low and light that the flesh didn't seize up a bit, didn't need a bit of sauce or grilling, but just melted right away. Sea eel oil must be the King of the Fats!!" While all seafood offerings earned high praise, *yumyum* says graceful pacing is essential, allowing time to ponder and adore each morsel.

But great though the taste sensations are, one chowhound who tried (and loved) the omakase reports leaving hungry.

SUSHI Worth Begging For

Brasserie 360 (Upper East Side)
200 E. 60th St.
Manhattan, NY
212-688-8688
French Brasserie/Japanese

Kozuo Yoshida, the original sushi chef from much-loved Jewel Bako, is now at **Brasserie 360**. One hound warns that you have to sit at the sushi bar and persuade Yoshida-san to give you his very best fish. But you will be rewarded. *Kbee* reports trying a sensational (and uncommonly fresh) piece of bluefin tuna, perfectly seasoned with the right amount of wasabi. While food is traditional, drink service is not. Green tea comes in a French press and sake's served in champagne flutes.

○ **Brasserie 360:** *see also* p. 51.

○ **Brasserie 360:** *see also* p. 51.

Sun-Splashed SUSHI

Aki on West 4th (Greenwich Village)
181 W. 4th St.
Manhattan, NY
212-989-5440
Japanese

The owner of Aki on West Fourth used to cook for the Japanese Ambassador to Jamaica, so many of his otherwise traditional sushi dishes have Caribbean touches of banana, mango, or coconut. *Amanda* praises scallops unilayered in a custard dish with fresh coconut cream—an unusual combination that tastes amazing. There are three tasting menus that include two, three, or four appetizers; chef's choice of sushi/sashimi entrée and dessert ($35, $45, $55, respectively). Everything is fresh and the atmosphere's very casual.

Chow off the **TACONIC PARKWAY**

Del's Dairy Creme
  (Dutchess County)
6780 Rte. 9
Rhinebeck, NY
845-876-4111
Greek

Giovanni's Pizza (Dutchess County)
4246 Albany Post Rd. (Rte. 9)
Hyde Park, NY
845-229-5200
Italian

Grandma's Country Pie
  (Westchester County)
3525 Rte. 202, near the Bear
  Mountain Pkwy. and Taconic
  Pkwy.
Cortlandt Manor, NY
914-739-7770
Diner or Coffee Shop

Green Acres Farm Stand
  (Columbia County)
West of the Taconic Pkwy. on 82,
  about 1 mile east of Rte. 9
Livingston, NY
518-851-7460
Farm or Farm Stand

Hawthorne Valley Farm
  (Columbia County)
327 County Rte. 21c, 1.5 miles
  east of the Philmont exit of
  Taconic Pkwy.
Ghent, NY
518-672-7500
Farm or Farm Stand

La Mexicana Mexican Grocery
  (Dutchess County)
19 W. Market St.
Red Hook, NY
845-758-6356
Mexican

La Terre Garlic Farm
  (Dutchess County)
Field Road
Clinton Corners, NY
914-266-4320
Farm or Farm Stand

Montgomery Place Orchards
  (Dutchess County)
Rte. 9G and 199, 12 miles west
  of Taconic Pkwy.
Red Hook, NY
845-758-6338
Farm or Farm Stand

Our Daily Bread
  (Columbia County)
33 Hudson Ave.
Chatham, NY
518-392-9852
Bakery

Quattro's Game Farm Store
  (Dutchess County)
Rte. 44, about a mile east of
  the Taconic Pkwy.
Pleasant Valley, NY
845-635-2018
Store

Red Hook Curry House
  (Dutchess County)
28 E. Market St.
Red Hook, NY
845-758-2666
Indian

Rhinebeck Farmer's Market
  (Dutchess County)
Municipal Parking Lot
Rhinebeck, NY
845-876-0805
Farmers' Market

Rhinebeck Deli
  (Dutchess County)
112 E. Market St. (Rte. 308)
Rhinebeck, NY
914-876-3614
New American

Spumoni Gardens
  (Dutchess County)
Rte. 199 (W. Church St.)
Pine Plains, NY
518-398-1961
Italian/German

Winding our way up the Taconic Parkway makes chowhounds hungry. On the other hand, everything makes us hungry. The goal, as ever, is to suss out the best options. Starting from the south:

Barely one mile off the Taconic in Cortlandt Manor, **Grandma's Country Pie** bakes pies and other diner fare worthy of a day trip.

In Pleasant Valley, **Quattro's Game Farm** carries loads of meaty, gamey good things like pheasants, quail, house-made sausages, duck, venison, and industrial-sized nonpareil capers, as well as fine olives, imported tomatoes, all kinds of cool pasta, mothballs, and shotguns.

There's not much more than garlic at **La Terre Garlic Farm** in Clinton Corners, but they'll give you lots of recipes for using the stuff.

The unattractive location of **Giovanni's** in Hyde park should not deter you. While it's not technically near the Taconic, *lucia* insists that it's miles better than anything in **Red Hook** or **Rhinebeck** (e.g. Village, Brothers, Boccia, Francesca's) and thus well worth a detour.

Spumoni Gardens is a seasonal outdoor beer garden in Pine Plains with good steamed clams.

Seating's limited at **La Mexicana Mexican Grocery** in Red Hook, but their tortas are worth squeezing in for. Also in Red Hook: the Montgomery Place stand (specializing in corn and tomatoes) and good tarka dal and chicken jalfreze at **Red Hook Curry House**.

In Rhinebeck, **Del's Dairy Creme** is open seasonally; *lucia* recommends Greek-style fresh hot pita with its great, lip-smacking tzatziki dressing, and chocolate ice-cream sodas. And **Rhinebeck Deli** is a good place to grab a quick to-go bacon-and-egg-on-a-roll to sustain you for the trip farther north.

Green Acres Farm Stand in Livingston looks like a run-down barn festooned with big, rough, hand-painted signs. They grow amazing heirloom tomatoes: red, yellow, orange, pink in the craziest shapes and with a huge burst of tomato flavor, says *elvislives*, who also raves over their pumpkin pie, double the height of most and heavenly of flavor and texture.

Vegetables are very good at **Hawthorne Valley Farm** in Ghent, but the real prizes are their cheeses.

Chatham's **Our Daily Bread** sells wonderful French bread (as good as in Montreal, and it freezes well, too), nice fontina bread (the one with onions and mushrooms), and unbelievable chocolate bread, reports *Wanda*. Available at their bakery in Chatham and also at their booth toward the back of the **Rhinebeck Farmers' Market** (Sundays). Their fennel and golden raisin bread pairs well with fresh mozzarella from Popovich Provisions, another vendor at Rhinebeck Farmers' Market, says *Scott Gordon*.

○ **Montgomery Place Orchards:** *see also* p. 10.

TACOS

Matamoros Puebla Grocery
 (Brooklyn)
193 Bedford Ave.
Greenpoint, Brooklyn, NY
718-782-5044
Mexican

Tehuitzingo Deli & Grocery
 (Clinton)
695 10th Ave.
Manhattan, NY
212-397-5956
Mexican

Taqueria de Mexico
 (Greenwich Village)
93 Greenwich Ave.
Manhattan, NY
212-255-5212
Mexican

Mexican immigrants continue to pour into New York, and higher-quality tacos and the like are actually finding their way into Manhattan. At **Taqueria de Mexico** excellent pork tacos are topped with pineapple, onions, and cilantro. The small but complete dinner menu offers a number of tasty items. The taqueria in the rear of **Tehuitzingo** grocery store serves awesome tacos, says *bpearis*, who also enjoys their sopes, quesadillas, tortas, and on weekends, tamales. And Brooklyn's **Matamoros Puebla Grocery** has a counter in back where you can get tacos, sopes, posole, and chicken or pork tamales.

See also *Fish Tacos*.

See also Mexican entries in the cuisine index.

○ **Matamoros Puebla Grocery:** *see also* p. 2.

Killer New Jersey **TAIWANESE**

Soochow Chinese Restaurant (Bergen County)
165 US Hwy. 46 W
Saddle Brook, NJ
201-368-2899
Chinese (Taiwanese)

A reliable source tipped tipped *Jeremy Osner* off to the outstanding Taiwanese food at **Soochow**. Recommended: crispy and tangy salted pork chops with cilantro, "three cup chicken" cooked in basil (very oily, but oh-so-flavorful), fish wrapped in seaweed (an off-menu item costing a pricey $25—and worth every cent!), wonderful *kong xin cai* (literally "empty heart vegetable," but sometimes translated as "water spinach,") stir-fried in garlic and oil, and winter melon soup with ham. Now the big question: do they *also* make Soochow food?

See the cuisine index for lots more Taiwanese tips.

The Search for Perfect **TAMALES** (Plus Digressions)

Arcadia, The Tamale Lady (Soho)
Bowery or Elizabeth between
 Houston and Spring
Manhattan NY
Mexican Street Cart/Truck

Cafe Mexicano (Brooklyn)
671 Union St.
Park Slope, Brooklyn, NY
718-623-6754
Mexican

Choclos woman (Brooklyn)
47th St. and 5th Ave.
Sunset Park, Brooklyn, NY
Mexican Street Cart/Truck

Flowering mango woman
 (Brooklyn)
49th St. and 5th Ave.
Sunset Park, Brooklyn, NY
Mexican Street Cart/Truck

Heated shopping cart vendors
 (Queens)
Roosevelt Ave. near Junction
 Blvd.
Corona, Queens, NY
Mexican/Guatemalan/Salvadoran
 Street Cart/Truck

Hidalgo Grocery (Queens)
30-11 29th St.
Astoria, Queens, NY
718-274-6936
Mexican

Rico's Tamales Oaxaquenos
 (Brooklyn)
46th St. and 5th Ave.
Sunset Park, Brooklyn, NY
Mexican

Street Cart (Chelsea)
23rd St. and 6th Ave.
 in the flea market
Manhattan, NY
Mexican Street Cart/Truck

Sucelt Coffee Shop
 (Greenwich Village)
200 W. 14th St.
Manhattan, NY
212-242-0593
Puerto Rican/Cuban

Tamale vendors outside Pacific
 Market (Queens)
7501 Broadway
Jackson Heights, Queens, NY
Mexican

Tamale woman (Queens)
under the LIRR overpass by
 61st St. on Roosevelt Ave.
Woodside, Queens, NY
Mexican

Taqueria Y Fonda La Mexicana
 (Upper West Side)
968 Amsterdam Ave.
Manhattan, NY
212-531-0383
Mexican

Tortilla Flats
(Greenwich Village)
767 Washington St.
Manhattan, NY
212-243-1053
Mexican

Walking Tamale Woman
(Murray Hill)
around 321 5th Ave., near
33rd St.
Manhattan, NY
Mexican

For a buck, you can purchase a corn tamale from **Arcadia**, a woman who sells legendary tamales on the street. She magically appears at around 9:00 a.m. Wednesdays and Fridays (sometimes other days as well), and her pork tamales with green sauce are her best work. Green-sauce chicken is nearly as good. Go for the green-sauce ones, either way, urges *EV Andrew*.

It is hard to hit a moving target, and the woman who ducks into stores in midtown to sell her tamales to counter workers is definitely a moving target. But if you can manage to track her down, *Jayask* says the chicken tamales are well worth a $1 investment. She also sells pork tamales, cheese with jalapeño tamales, and rice pudding. Look for her early, like 8:30 a.m.

On Saturdays there's a cart outside Chelsea flea market selling incredible pork and chicken tamales. *TommyTamal* raves that the tamales are the best by far he's found in New York City. They're even better than several great ones he's had in the Southwest.

There's a well-known tamale lady in Woodside, Queens. "I thought cheese tamales would be really gooey, melty, and difficult to eat. However, the cheese in these tamales is more of a drier, chewier variety, kind of like paneer in south Asian cooking, or texturally similar to deep fried milk in Chinese (Hong Kong) cooking. The masa and the cheese lend a nice textural harmony with the heat of the chile giving it a good zing," says *Eric Eto* about tamales con queso from the woman under the LIRR overpass by Sixty-first Street on Roosevelt Avenue. He says these cheese tamales are much better than her chicken variety—though *Jim Leff* thinks all are terrific.

Also in Queens, four ladies sell tamales and pork products from carts in Corona. Savory tamales are wrapped in banana leaf and contain eggs, chicken, and peas and carrots. Sweet, creamy ones are wrapped in cornhusks. The pork products are a red pork that seems to be covered in chili, little braised riblets, and some kind of sausage, according to *jason e*, who tried tamales from two carts: both great, but very very different from each other.

Few details, but there are known to be good tamale vendors outside Jackson Height's Pacific Market.

Oaxacan food is a holy grail style of Mexican cooking, says *Jim Leff*, and **Rico's Tamales Oaxacanos**, in Sunset Park, Brooklyn, may be the first real outpost of this cuisine in New York City. Speaking Spanish will definitely help, and there's only room for two people to eat at the counter (there's a park nearby), but *Lambretta76* says what comes out of the insulated vats here is nothing short of perfection. Chicken mole tamales are fantastic—exactly how a mole sauce should be. Pretty hefty, perfectly steamed in a banana leaf, and only $1. There're two more chicken tamales— green and red—which are both tasty and quite spicy. The cheese tamales are also very good. Wash down your meal with horchata (a cinnamony rice drink), agua fresca de limon (homemade lemon/limeade), or a sangrialike fruit drink.

A block south of Rico's, look for the woman selling mayonnaise-slathered corn on the cob ("choclos") sprinkled with cheese and chili powder ($2). And on weekends there's a woman selling flowering mangos—that is, mangos cut open like a flower for eating— for ($2), a couple of blocks farther south on Fifth Avenue.

Some relatively stationary targets:

During lunchtime, a woman makes fresh tasty little moderately priced tamales at **Tortilla Flats** in the West Village, says the poster known as *here today gone tamale*.

Not far away, **Sucelt** sells various tamales and empanadas in a panoply of South American styles. Get them hot there, or take home cold ones for easy warming later. Venezuelan and Colombian tamales are filled with pork, chorizo, whole olives, etc. Fresh batidos (fruit-based sweetened milk shakes) and good *café con leche,* too. Nothing's truly great, but they're more reliably found than cart ladies. (Chowhound truism: Certainty always comes at a price!)

Tacqueria y Fonda is a friendly Tex-Mex taqueria in Astoria, Queens, serving excellent tamales, says *Gabi Bo Babi*. Also in Astoria, **Hidalgo Grocery** makes a variety of great tamales, according to *babar ganesh*.

You probably won't find a better morning snack for a buck or so than chicken mole, salsa, or black beans and cheese tamales from Park Slope's Cafe Mexicano, says *bigskulls*. The black-bean version is really good: not too dry, very warm, and great corn flavor mixed with the beans.

TANGRA MASALA: Whose Menu Actually Marks the UNspicy Dishes!

Tangra Masala (Queens)
87-09 Grand Ave.
Elmhurst, Queens, NY
718-803-2298
Indian/Chinese

Tangra Masala serves an authentic version of the inauthentic Chinese food made in India to please the Indian palate (their equivalent, that is, of egg rolls and General Tso's Chicken), and hounds continue to rave about their cooking. Spice levels tend to be high (the menu marks the dishes that are *not* spicy!), and same for deliciousness levels. Manchurian goat (dry) is spicy and somewhat smoky, and very goaty . . . great if goat's your thing. The meat is almost like goat jerky reconstituted and then cooked in a dry blend of spices, creating a deep, complex, earthy flavor, says *Kenzi*. Tangra masala noodles are full of smoky tangra masala chicken and chili sauce—though you can opt for shrimp or beef instead.

Not Your Typical Cuppa TEA

Wild Lily Tea Room (Chelsea)
511 W. 22nd St.
Manhattan, NY
212-691-2258
Pan-Asian Fusion Café

Wild Lily Tea Market (East Village)
545 E. 12th St.
Manhattan, NY
212-598-9097
East Asian

Wild Lily Tea Room might be what you'd get if you crossed a Japanese teahouse with English afternoon tea and a little aromatherapy. You can approach its extensive menu of black, green, or white teas and tisanes, sandwiches, and scones à la carte, or opt for the $22 Wild Lily Tea Party that comes on a three-tiered lily pad tray. Sandwiches and scones are tasty. Seating ranges from western comfy chairs to floor mats and low stools without backs. Note: Their menu offerings seem to be expanding. Teas can be purchased in bulk at **Wild Lily Tea Market.**

Unlocking Wondee Siam **THAI**

Wondee Siam (Clinton)
792 9th Ave.
Manhattan, NY
212-459-9057
Thai

Wondee Siam II (Clinton)
813 9th Ave.
Manhattan, NY
917-286-1726
Thai

Hounds have had little hesitation recommending the original **Wondee Siam**—the one on the east side of Ninth Avenue at #792. While it is both smaller and dingier than its newer and more comfortable sibling, **Wondee Siam II**, across the street at #813, hounds say the food at the original is tastier and more traditional, and there's wider choice of dishes. Also, the original restaurant is BYOB, with no charge for corkage or glassware.

One problem at the original Wondee is that the best dishes are all listed on a Thai menu—stuff made with supposedly gringo unfriendly ingredients like fish sauce, shrimp paste, and chile peppers. Don't read Thai? When the place isn't busy, ask a waitress to translate. And remember: Almost any dish can be made with beef, pork, chicken, duck, or tofu. Hounds recommend pig offal or any other soup, papaya salad, *nam sod*, and *yum moo yang* (grilled pork salad).

Anyway, that's the canonical view. But there are contrarians, led by *Djpadthai*, who insist that the owner/chef at Wondee Siam II is actually the more skilled but simply lacks confidence in her clientele's spiceworthiness. Ordering authentic items not on the menu such as *gang tai pla*, *pad cha* seafood, *nam kra dook moo*, and steamed chicken ravioli have yielded amazingly delicious results. So next time you go, be sure to be insistent about your love of Thai levels of spice, and you might be blown away by the food there as well. *Jim Leff* didn't stick around to find out, repelled by the awful, sulking, disdainful waiters. He reports an entirely nicer staff at the #792 branch.

○ **Wondee Siam:** *see also* **p. 255.**

THAI Splendor in Queens

Boon Chu (Queens)
83-18 Broadway
Elmhurst, Queens, NY
718-898-6836
Thai

Rice Avenue (Queens)
72-19 Roosevelt Ave.
Jackson Heights, Queens, NY
718-803-9001
Thai

Sripraphai Thai Restaurant
  (Queens)
6413 39th Ave.
Woodside, Queens, NY
718-899-9599
Thai

Thai immigrants pour into Elmhurst and Sunnyside, and chowhounds keep awaiting a great flowering of authentic eateries. Until that day, a few very serious beachheads more than satisfy:

Sripraphai is not only the best Thai in New York City, it's among the best in the country. Here's a cheat sheet of some chowhound favorite items: noodles with chili and basil; BBQ beef appetizer; duck in green curry; "Tom-Zaap" soup with beef offal or seafood; clear soup with lime juice, makrut leaves, galangal and chilis (must be sure to ask for spicy!); pan-fried mussel omelet (hoi-tod . . . order "krob krob", or extra crispy); BBQ chicken/green papaya salad/coconut rice combo (best for solo diners); beef and pork jerky; *kao soi* soup; *kow moo daang* (roast pork on rice with tangy sweet sauce); panang curry with beef (topped with coconut cream and shredded bergamot leaves); any grilled meat dish; bean thread, papaya, tripe, grilled beef salads. There's an especially interesting appetizer of fried watercress (with fried cilantro and mint) dressed with sliced red onions, cashews, shrimp. The most elusive dish: southern curry, which can purportedly raise blisters and is served only to trusted customers.

Sripraphai offers a stunning and deep selection of Thai sweets, most available prepacked to go, none better than the stellar banana stick rice (served hot, wrapped in banana leaf). They run out of this one early, so ask your server to reserve some as you're seated. It seems the extensive menu at Sripraphai is not large enough for some people. That's okay, because the kitchen is willing and able to alter dishes to your specification. A variation of N18 (noodles in soup with meat and vegetables) earned a rave from *plum*. Ask for it dry and with seafood in place of the meat, and get chili sauce on the side to put on the noodles. The result is delicious: glass noodles tossed with shrimp and squid, slightly bitter greens, and a bit of egg. The sesame-chili sauce on the side is smoky and fairly mild.

Sripraphai is closed Wednesdays. But there are good alternatives not too far away:

Rice Avenue bills itself as pan-Asian, but they're as **Thai** as chicken galangal soup. *Jim Leff* says while care and finesse go into preparations (and ambience is tons more relaxing and snazzy than Sripraphai), gringos must be extremely emphatic to demand spice if they want to avoid being served pepper-inert fare. Leff reports *"wonderful"* red curry (though shrimp are semivestigial) and good-but-sweet tom kung gai. Penang curry isn't as elegant as it could be, nor is it as deep as Sripraphai's. But it's definitely delicious and worth getting. Cha-chi fish (or something like that) is crunchy, delicious, a real winner. Basil fried rice is good, though not quite as extravagantly great as it hints that it could be. Other fried rices bear investigation. Generally, rice dishes and curries (and curries over rice) are best here . . . but keep emphasizing to the staff: spicy, spicy, *spicy!*

Boon Chu, an authentic Thai hole-in-the-wall, used to be known as Broadway Kitchen . . . though, confusingly, its awning reads Wing Hing. Oh, and it also used to be a Chinese restaurant run by Thais. But now it's gone fully Thai, and *Eric Eto* says that's a good thing, reporting a pretty killer sausage appetizer, very good squid salad (actually a bit too heavy on the squid), though crispy pork with chili and basil that's merely OK (by Sripraphai standards). The positive news is that these guys aren't afraid to pile up on the spice. Spicy means spicy, reports Eric. But *el jefe* had his spice toned down, so if you want real heat, do be sure to ask for it. Boon Chu is mostly a takeout

Chowhound Nametag: Jim Leff

○◯○

Your Neighborhood: Queens.

Occupation: Writer, jazz musician, Web guy.

Cholesterol Level: That of an eighty-three-year-old deli counterman.

Weight Management Tip: Yoga (specifically, shoulder stand followed by fish position).

Farthest Out of the Way Traveled Just for Chow: I traveled to Spain nineteen times, ostensibly to play jazz but really to stock up on an ordinary brand of Italian supermarket cookie I'm in love with (Pannochie, from Mulino Bianco). They're made with corn.

Favorite Comfort Chow: Arepas from the Sainted *Arepa Lady* (see [11]).

Favorite Gelato Flavor: The best flavor made by the place I'm in (and I'm fully prepared taste through every single one to make this determination).

Nabe Most Full of Explorable Unknown Chow: Ridgewood (near the Queens/Brooklyn border), Staten Island, anywhere in New Jersey, all the burgeoning pockets of immigrants in formerly chowless areas like northern Westchester and southwestern CT.

Top Chinatown Picks:
- *Manhattan Chinatown:* Fulleen's Seafood for old-style Cantonese and New Green Bo for a warm experience with smart, unjaded kibbitzing waiters and soulful Shanghai fare.
- *Flushing Chinatown:* most consistently good: lamb Gou-Bu-Li buns at Gou-Bu-Li (135-28 Fortieth Road), cheap late-night Taiwanese diner fare at Laifood (on Prince), lamb coconut shakes at Sago Tea Cafe (Main Saint and Thirty-ninth), with the elusive semicrunchy bits afloat. Sweet and Tart Cafe (if you learn what to order). Besides that, mostly fleeting treasure.
- *Sunset Park, Brooklyn Chinatown:* Kakala (5302 Eighth Avenue) for weird Hong Kong amalgams like corned beef hash omelet in soup with ramen, malt coffee, and hot lemon ginger cider.
- *Elmhurst, Queens Chinatown:* Ping's, on Queens Boulevard.

Favorite Comfort Chow: Pizza while driving. Having been raised suburban middle class, this is the only culture I have to cling to. The way a Muslim feels upon hearing the early morning call to prayers, or an Inuit ice fishing, or a Frenchman breaking open a steaming croissant—at one with one's own nature and steeped in long ancestral heritage—this is how I feel eating pizza while driving.

Chowhounding NEGATIVE Rules of Thumb:

1. Don't look for people of the restaurant's ethnicity eating there. How many Americans have excellent taste in roast beef or apple pie? Why do we assume Chinese, Afghans, or Peruvians are any hipper to their cuisines? Instead, look for people of mixed ethnicity, eating with passion and exuding electric bliss. That is, look for chowhounds.
2. Don't look for crowds. Crowds are attracted by: (1) low prices, (2) advertising, and (3) crowds.
3. Don't ever order what you feel like eating. Only order what you think the place does best. If you crave something specific, find the specific place that best satsifies that specific craving.
4. Immigrant waiters exultant to guide you through their cuisine are a bad sign. It means the place is aiming for gringo clientele, which means they're pandering and diluting their cuisine. Better are sulky, impatient waiters who view your gringo presence as nothing more than potential aggravation. How many overworked barbecue shack counterworkers would thrill at the prospect of explaining chopped barbecue to a group of Lithuanian tourists? And would you want to eat in a barbecue shack that offered a Lithuanian menu just in case?
5. Don't rely solely on secondhand info . . . even secondhand info as savvy as this book or the Chowhound.com Web site. The search—and thrill of discovery—are half the fun. Do your own chowconnaissance and enjoy the giddy adventure!

joint, but there are a few self-service tables. Prices are low (most items like *pad ka prow* and duck noodle soup are $5.50), but flavors reach new heights. Obviously, this place is not a superestablished spot, so do call ahead.

○ **Rice Avenue:** *see also* **p. 175.**

Rock Solid **THAI**

Secrets of Thai Cooking (East Village)
95 1st Ave.
Manhattan, NY
212-477-4299
Thai

Secrets of Thai Cooking might look like any old Thai place, but *Dan Sonenberg* says the cooking is rock solid. Jade dumplings and papaya salad as starters are as fresh as can be. Spicy eggplant, drunken noodles w/ shrimp, and a vegetarian red curry are all pleasantly (if not overwhelmingly) hot, and a coconut rice side dish is outstandingly delicious. Overall, it's some of the most consistent, fresh, and tasty Thai food in Manhattan.

For more great Manhattan Thai, see the cuisine index (especially important: Wondee Siam *Thai,* which gets its own entry).

Williamsburg **THAI**

Chai Home Kitchen and Sake Bar
   (Brooklyn)
124 N. 6th St.
Williamsburg, Brooklyn, NY
718-599-5889
Thai

Khao Sarn Thai Cuisine
   (Brooklyn)
311 Bedford Ave.
Williamsburg, Brooklyn, NY
718-963-1238
Thai

SEA Thai Bistro (Brooklyn)
114 N. 6th St.
Williamsburg, Brooklyn, NY
718-384-8850
Thai

Thai Cafe (Brooklyn)
925 Manhattan Ave.
Greenpoint, Brooklyn, NY
718-383-3562
Thai

Siam Orchid Thai Restaurant
   (Brooklyn)
378 Metropolitan Ave.
Williamsburg, Brooklyn, NY
718-302-4203
Thai

Siam Orchid might make the best **Thai** food in Williamsburg, but it's mostly for takeout or delivery, as there's not much of a dining room. **Khao Sarn** does well with curries, but their papaya salad's lacking, reports *sarahoc*. **Chai**'s food is spicier and more caringly prepared than that at the other trendy, mod Thai spots in the nabe. Be sure to try their peanut dumplings, papaya salad, green curry, massaman curry, and duck with pineapple. At **SEA**, which seems more like a Thai food factory at times than a restaurant, the Drunk Man's Noodles are the strategic pick on an otherwise lackluster menu, according to *mln43*. Greenpoint's **Thai Cafe** is a bit of a trek from downtown Williamsburg, but it's one of the best Thai restaurants in the area, says *shelz123*.

Generous Brooklyn **THAI**

Thai Sesame (Brooklyn)
160 Smith St.
Cobble Hill, Brooklyn NY
718-935-0101
Thai

New **Thai Sesame** does whopping portions: cups of soup more like bowls, bowls more like quarts. Spicing's also generous. Medium is interpreted spicier than elsewhere, and hot's intense. Appetizers and entrées are mostly fish and seafood oriented, with surprisingly few vegetarian options (though all curries can be made with tofu instead of meat/fish). Penang curry, summer rolls, and curry noodles earn good marks. *Erica Marcus* says tom kha gai is extraordinary. The pieces of chicken have a velvety texture, the creamy coconutty broth is complex—even the straw mushrooms, which can't (?) be fresh—are delicious.

THANKSGIVING TURKEY
Sources

Key Food (Brooklyn)
120 5th Ave.
Park Slope, Brooklyn, NY
718-783-9053
Store

Staubitz Market (Brooklyn)
222 Court St.
Carroll Gardens, Brooklyn, NY
718-624-0014
Store

Los Paisanos (Brooklyn)
162 Smith St.
Cobble Hill, Brooklyn, NY
718-855-2641
Store

Don't settle for jive turkey.

- **Los Paisanos** is a great source for Thanksgiving turkeys, with a friendly staff and a nice variety of organic and higher-end goods.
- **Staubitz** sells organic turkeys that are extremely fresh but commensurately expensive, and the butchers are very knowledgeable.
- *Missmasala* recommends going to **Key Food** on Fifth Avenue, where you can buy a Bell & Evans brand turkey for a lot less than Staubitz charges. They stock Empire Kosher poultry, too.

Premium Panchan and Terrific **TOFU**

Cho Dang Gol (Midtown West)
55 W. 35th St.
Manhattan, NY
212-695-8222
Korean

Cho Dang Gol specializes in tofu made on the premises. Popular dishes making use of it include *ing o bokum* (stir-fried squid in very spicy Korean hot paste sauce with tofu), soondooboo chae gae (bean curd stew with seafood), kim chee bokum or their mixed bean curd dish. Be adventurous and the staff will work with you to make you happy. *mrnyc* recommends kimchi-based dishes, too, as well as the pancakes (pa jeun).

Panchan—the complimentary appetizers served before meals at Korean restaurants—are particularly good.

○ **Cho Dang Gol:** *see also* **p. 275.**

Beautiful **TORTAS** in Williamsburg

Kimberlyn Market (Brooklyn)
785 Grand St. half a block west
of Bushwick Ave.
Williamsburg, Brooklyn, NY
718-599-1208
Mexican

Taqueria Tierra Blanca (Brooklyn)
800 Grand St.
Williamsburg, Brooklyn, NY
718-486-0508
Mexican

Tortas (Mexican sandwiches, sort of like tacos on a hard roll) at **Taqueria Tierra Blanca** contain beautiful layers of ingredients, which offer layers of flavors. Tacos can be uneven; chicken tinga is excellent, goat pretty good, but beef is terrible, says *higgins*.

The middle aisle at **Kimberlyn Market** is loaded with Mexican ingredients. Masarepa is around $1.00 or so a bag. A bag of ancho peppers is $1.29, well under half what you'd pay in Manhattan.

Food-Themed Guided **TOURS**

Big Onion
www.bigonion.com

Myra Alperson's Nosh Walks
www.noshwalks.com

Food Events
www.foodevents.com

Queens Botanical Gardens Tour
718-886-3800

The Institute of Culinary
  Education
www.iceculinary.com

Savory Sojourns by Addei Tome
www.savorysojourns.com

Most chowhounds are intrepid explorers, but sometimes it's fun to go with a crowd. Hounds recommend their favorite food-themed guided tours.

- **Myra Alperson** leads nosh walks, including markets, restaurants and background history in her tours.
- Addei Tome's **Savory Sojourns** has set tours of different nabes and will build custom tours for groups.
- **Big Onion** offers a multiethnic walking and eating tour led by local Ph.D. candidates.
- **The Institute of Culinary Education** (formerly Peter Kump's) has a few tours in its class schedule that sometimes include cooking classes.
- **Food Events** offers a variety of food-oriented walking tours for groups you assemble, including one of the African Diaspora in Harlem.
- The **Queens Botanical Garden** has tours of Flushing that focus on markets and herbs. These popular tours fill weeks in advance.

TOWN for Mind-Blowing Duck Steak with Soba Pilaf

Town Restaurant (Midtown West)
13 W. 56th St. in the Chambers Hotel
Manhattan, NY
212-582-4445
New American

Dinner at Town is delicious from aperitif to petits fours, reports
Caitlin McGrath, who enjoyed the best expensive meal she's had
in a long time there. Drinks, bread, appetizer and *amuse bouche*
are all praiseworthy, but not as lavishly as duck steak with fragrant endive and soba pilaf, which is absolutely stellar. It comes
as two fat slices of duck breast about an inch thick with dark
brown, very crisp skin and almost all the fat rendered out. Inside, it's a thoroughly pink medium rare throughout, and amazingly, exceedingly tender, and more flavorful than any duck
dish she's ever tried. Even so, dessert and petits fours were not
a let down.

Terrific TRINIDADIAN Offshoot

Caribbean Cuisine (Essex County)
74 1st St.
South Orange, NJ
973-313-2877
Trinidadian

Caribbean Cuisine, hidden on a sleepy street right near the inter-
section of South Orange Avenue and Valley Street, is the offshoot of a restaurant in East Orange, and it may be South
Orange's first restaurant worth traveling for, according to *Jeremy Osner*. They have an outstanding pastry chef, so be sure to
order anything involving pastry or bread. The roti is killer and
the various bread appetizers are wonderful, as are desserts

(e.g. currant or coconut rolls). There's a rotating soup menu; callaloo and lentil soups are great, and excellent pumpkin soup is available Thursdays. Spice level is a bit more muted than at other Trinidadian restaurants, so ask for their scotch bonnet sauce (apply cautiously!) if you like it hot.

Multicultural **TURKISH**

Al-Baraka (Midtown East)
154 E. 55th St.
Manhattan, NY
212-546-9007
Turkish Eclectic

Al-Baraka claims to serve Mediterranean and Turkish food, but *Roger Lee* reports that the menu's much broader and reflects Turkey's history as a center for international trade dating back to the Phoenicians. "The food is really tasty. Get yourself a platter of the delicious freshly baked naan, some hummus, baba ghanoush, grilled eggplant, dolma, stuffed cabbage, esme salad, whatever. Go to town. It is all beautifully fresh, perfectly seasoned, and redolent of the spices that made early Europeans think it would be a good idea to take a little jaunt around the Cape of Good Hope. Don't miss the istem kebab either, a braised lamb shank wrapped in a big slice of sautéed eggplant." They also serve an $11 buffet lunch featuring an array of salad items (best of which is the baba ghanoush—smoky as it ought to be, says *Jkos*), beef stew, a grilled chicken dish, and several vegetable dishes. This is a Muslim place, so they don't deal in booze, but the friendly owner doesn't mind if you bring your own, a very Turkish compromise.

TURKISH Treasure

Kebab House (Queens)
255-05 Northern Blvd.
Little Neck, Queens, NY
718-225-5318
Turkish

Mavi Turkish Cuisine (Queens)
42-03 Queens Blvd.
Sunnyside, Queens, NY
718-786-0206
Turkish

Lailla Bar & Restaurant (Queens)
42-24 Bell Blvd.
Bayside, Queens, NY
718-225-2904
Turkish

Kebab House serves amazing tripe soup (with sides of aleppo pepper, garlic, and vinegar), sigara boreks, huge, leafy arugula salad, *aranut ciger* (cubed beef liver), and a particularly good *piyaz* (beans) salad. Also recommended: homemade lamb doner, chicken chops (nicely seasoned inside-out drumsticks), brook trout, and swordfish kebabs, reports *Lo-Lo*.

Other winners: wonderful calamari with a garlic dipping sauce and a sautéed eggplant, tomato, and pepper appetizer, meltingly tender fried calamari with garlic sauce, fried liver cubes with raw red onion, patlican (eggplant) salad, coban salad, grilled swordfish, and lamb kofta kebabs that actually taste like lamb. Everything is done with real attention to flavor and detail, e.g., liver soaked overnight in milk and good grilled pita bread for dipping salads (e.g. excellent baba-esque smoked eggplant salad). There's a parking lot in back, reasonable prices, and friendly, helpful staff.

At **Lailla**, *MeltingMan* reports a fantastic meal from start to finish. Everything fresh as can be, perfect seasoning on the kebabs, top-notch dips, and excellent service.

Mavi is a cozy restaurant with exceptional Turkish food, reports *Tree*. The yogurt-based dipping sauce accompanying fried calamari makes it a particularly killer appetizer, and spicy lamb in the adana kebab is exceptional. *Manti* (tiny tortellini stuffed with lamb and spices and baked in yogurt, butter, and tomato sauce) are melt-in-your-mouth delicious.

Greekish **TURKISH**

Agnandi (Queens)
19-06 Ditmars Blvd.
Astoria, Queens, NY
718-545-4554
Turkish

There's disagreement as to whether **Agnandi** is Greek or Turkish, but everyone concurs that the food's delicious.

Photis explains that it's based on the cuisine of Konstandinoupoli (Istanbul to English speakers), which has a strong Greek influence because of the many Greeks who lived there before the Turks took over in 1453. Don't miss Cretan rusks, taramasalata, horta, and fried cod with skordalia. *AndyK* recommends ntakos (a Greek bread salad made with whole wheat bread, feta, tomatoes, olives, capers, greens, and olive oil), saganaki, meat bureks, and some of the best mussels in New York City. Also check out the grilled octopus (untried but looked amazing).

Brooklyn **TURKISH** Choices

Anadolu Halal Meat Market
  (Suffolk County)
1815 Deer Park Ave.
Deer Park, NY
631-274-4851
Turkish

Empire Kebab House (Brooklyn)
1103 Kings Hwy.
Midwood, Brooklyn, NY
718-627-3406
Turkish

Liman Trading (Brooklyn)
2710 Emmons Ave.
Sheepshead Bay, Brooklyn, NY
718-769-3322
Turkish

Taci's Beyti Restaurant (Brooklyn)
1955 Coney Island Ave.
Midwood, Brooklyn, NY
718-627-5750
Turkish

Tanoreen (Brooklyn)
7704 Third Ave.
Bay Ridge, Brooklyn, NY
718-748-5600
Lebanese

Veranda Turkish Cuisines
 (Brooklyn)
2424 Coney Island Ave.
Gravesend, Brooklyn, NY
718-376-0100
Turkish

Although Taci's Beyti looks like two separate adjoining restaurants, it's just one strangely spread between two unconnected buildings. Based on a first visit, *Micki* raves that every item is fresh, perfectly spiced, distinct in flavor and texture, and absolutely delicious. A combo meze platter included hummus, cacik (minty/dilly yogurt sauce), eggplant spread, eggplant with spicy tomato sauce, mushroom salad with cornichons, and fantastic grape leaves. To accompany the bounty of spreads: pillowy *pide*, along with three large and well-spiced lahmachun filled with tomatoes, slices of white radish, parsley, lemon wedges, and sumac-dusted raw onions.

It's easy to fill up on appetizers at Empire Kebab, and that may be the best way to approach this place. Baba ghanoush has much zing and intense smokiness. Cacik is fresh and goes well with hot bread. Shepherd salad (basically a Greek salad but don't call it that here!) is delicious, with a lemon flavor in the vinegary dressing, reports *JackS*. But he finds their lentil soup and a dish with lamb and spinach uninspired.

Liman is a Turkish seafood place with lots of Russian customers and really good simple grilled fish, reports *Erica Marcus*.

Turkish/Lebanese Tanoreen has a large display case full of mezes. Roasted eggplant slices (topped with chopped tomatoes, jalapeño, avocado, and parsley), baba ghanoush and slightly spicy stuffed rolls are delicious, according to *mark*, as is an entrée of baby eggplant stuffed with spiced lamb and pignoli (accompanied by a phenomenal rice dish). They have superlatively fresh and fragrant stuffed grape leaves, heavenly baba ghanoush and hummus, eggplant salad, amazing and unusual fried cauliflower, stuffed cabbage, and best of all, sautéed dandelion with caramelized onions, says *JKOS*, who also highly recommends the kibbe. BYOB with $5 corkage fee.

Out in increasingly Turkish-heavy Long Island, Anadolu is a prepared-foods market with a good selection of items. *Paul Trapani* recommends trying *simet,* a crescent roll topped with black sesame seeds and filled with cheese and oregano. Spinach boreks are amazing. There are lots more places along this part of Deer Park Avenue opening up all the time; it's an excellent chowhounding destination.

Newcomer **Veranda** is drawing attention for tasty Turkish foods. Don't miss lahmacun, a thin pizzalike disc topped with very finely ground meat, parsley, and spices and cooked in a brick oven, sporting a crisp, pliable crust. Shepherd's salad is made with fresh chopped tomatoes, cucumbers, red onion, and black olives flecked with mint and parsley. Meats (cooked well done unless you specify otherwise) like spicy lamb chops or shish kebab come with generous sides of rice, red cabbage, grilled tomato, and grilled green pepper, along with a yogurt-based sauce and a tame red sauce. Prices are moderate and the room is large, perfect for groups.

The Extremely Promising
TURKISH Strip in Paterson, NJ

King Shawarma (Passaic County)
899 Main St.
Paterson, NJ
973-977-8811
Turkish

King Shawarma is one store in a strip of Turkish and other Middle Eastern restaurants on Paterson's Main Street. A platter of baba ghanoush (creamy and smoky), hummus, stuffed grape leaves, chunky and delicious falafel, and tabbouleh covered with a pile of freshly roasted lamb costs under $10. *Jkos*, who pines to explore further in the nabe, notes that it's amazing that you can stumble on an ethnic pocket and have a meal like this when your alternative is fast food.

Brooklyn **UKRAINIAN**

Cafe Glechik (Brooklyn)
3159 Coney Island Ave.
Brighton Beach, Brooklyn, NY
718-616-0766
Russian

Ukraina (Brooklyn)
1214 Avenue J
Midwood, Brooklyn, NY
718-252-8887
Ukranian

Ukraina is a tiny Russian deli with a huge selection of goods, and *cooljerk* raves about most everything, including garlicky roast pork; chicken and rice stuffed peppers; and blintzes (cheese, apple, cherry). An amazing sausage selection from local sources includes several types of liverwurst (the fat kind is best). Also check out their wonderful candies, chocolates, and pastries. No English signs, but staff is very friendly.

Glechik is a small café that often has lines of people outside waiting to enjoy good Ukrainian home cooking. Very casual and pretty cheap.

Miscellaneous **UPSTATE** Tips

Bavarian Manor (Greene County)
866 Mountain Ave.
Purling, NY
518-622-3261
German

Green Duck LTD
    (Schoharie County)
584 Main St., #1
Cobleskill, NY
518-234-1605
American

Homer's Coffee Shop
    (Orange County)
2 E. Main St.
Port Jervis, NY
845-856-1712
Diner or Coffee Shop

Langdonhurst Market
    (Columbia County)
1450 Rte. 7A (Center Hill Rd.)
Copake, NY
518-329-7171
Farm or Farm Stand

Le Bouchon Brasserie
  (Putnam County)
76 Main St.
Cold Spring, NY
845-265-7676
French Bistro

Ripe Tomato (Saratoga County)
2721 Rte. 9
Ballston Spa, NY
518-581-1530
Italian/New American

Pueblo Viejo (Putnam County)
180 Rte. 52, in Shoprite
  Shopping Center
Carmel, NY
845-228-2504
Mexican

Bavarian Manor, in Purling, has been around for more than a century, and has been run by the same family since the 1930s. It's a big old Victorian inn with lots of fun and funky touches (paintings, mounted animals, old German folk art) on beautiful grounds with a large wraparound porch featuring lots of rocking chairs (for hanging out before or after dinner). That said, it really is about the food here, says *elvislives*. The menu's very German, as are wine and beer offerings. Sauerbraten is tender enough to cut with a fork and comes in an intricate but delicate sauce. Rouladen (thin pounded beef wrapped around bacon, a pickle, and carrot spear) comes in a rich brown gravy. Schnitzels and side dishes shine, as do dessert strudels, particularly apple. Their wild game dinners are very popular with area hunters, but we've had no firsthand reports as of yet.

Le Bouchon is a French bistro in Cold Spring where food's good and portions very generous. The house specialty is moules frites, and mussels come in a sweet curry broth flavored with apples. *Mekon1* says both shellfish and fries are great. Frisée salad with bacon comes with toast covered in whipped blue cheese. Mashed potatoes accompanying tiger shrimp with artichoke hearts had capers mixed in.

Carmel's **Pueblo Viejo** serves very fresh-tasting and wonderfully balanced Mexican food replete with really tasty sauces and specials. The host is gracious, the table salsa tastes freshly prepared, and the made-to-order, stone-ground-at-your-table guacamole is a real treat, reports *Gary Gladstone*. A strolling guitarist on weekends may or may not add to your dining pleasure.

The parking lot is always full at **Ripe Tomato**, a casual, family-type place in Ballston Spa with reportedly very good food. Recommended dishes: anything with pork (with homemade applesauce!), seafood fra diavolo, eggplant parmigiana. Nice service touches, e.g., offers to add sherry to lobster bisque. Wine specials a particular value.

Langdonhurst, in Copake, bakes outstanding blueberry pie, says *lucia* (not sweet, great real crust, fresh). Here's some info we dug up on the place: "Langdonhurst Market: A farm market located on a dairy farm where we grow our own vegetables without pesticides. We make homemade ice-cream right on the premises. You must try our Peanut Butter Brown cow flavor! We also have 15 other flavors. Our home baked pies, muffins and breads are baked fresh daily. Open seasonally from Mother's Day until the middle of September. Sonja Langdon. Phone: 518-329-7171."

Green Duck is a gem of a bakery in Cobleskill, says *Tim Kane*. "WOW! I've eaten breakfast in four- and five-star hotels and restaurants that weren't as good as this! Bacon and Swiss omelet, strawberry/banana pancakes (strawberries and bananas pureed right into the batter), real butter on the toast (bread baked right there), scrambled and over easy done to perfection and with great presentation, and the best home fries I've EVER had. Bar none. End of story. As if this isn't enough, the baked goods are INCREDIBLE! We took some apple turnovers and butterscotch chip cookies for the road that were out of this world."

Homer's Coffee Shop, in Port Jervis, is an all-around winner. It's the quintessential small-town blue-collar diner. Great waitresses, funky nostalgic-look atmosphere inside and out (the real deal, not retro done), and wide menu with amazing home-cooked food (everything is fabulous, especially their slow-cooked pork roast with gravy). Great for breakfast, lunch, or dinner. Portions are made for lumberjack appetites, reports *elvislives*.

See also Upstate *Barbecue, Adirondack* Chowhounding, and Chow off the *Taconic Parkway.*

Plus see nabe index for upstate counties.

URUGUAYAN in Jackson Heights

El Chivito d'Oro (Queens)
84-02 37th Ave.
Jackson Heights, Queens, NY
718-424-0600
Uruguayan or Paraguayan

El Chevito d'Oro is a Uruguayan meat and pasta house where grilled meats are fantastic and the pasta's not bad either, says *JH Jill*. There's chimichurri (garlicky green sauce) on every table, and lots of Argentine-style dishes . . . but Uruguayans do it better. Service is leisurely, so don't go if you're in a hurry.

VEG-FRIENDLY Brooklyn

Black Iris (Brooklyn)
228 De Kalb Ave.
Fort Greene, Brooklyn, NY
718-852-9800
Middle Eastern/North African

Bliss Cafe (Brooklyn)
191 Bedford Ave.
Williamsburg, Brooklyn, NY
718-599-2547
Vegetarian

Cambodian Cuisine (Brooklyn)
87 S. Elliott Pl.
Fort Greene, Brooklyn, NY
718-858-3262
Cambodian

D'Ital Shack (Brooklyn)
989 Nostrand Ave.
Flatbush, Brooklyn, NY
718-756-6557
Vegetarian Jamaican

D'Ital Shack (Brooklyn)
305 Halsey St.
Bedford-Stuyvestant,
   Brooklyn, NY
718-573-3752
Vegetarian Jamaican

Goga Vegetarian Cafe (Brooklyn)
521 Court St.
Carroll Gardens, Brooklyn, NY
718-260-8618
Vegetarian

Imhotep (Brooklyn)
734 Nostrand Ave.
Crown Heights, Brooklyn, NY
718-493-2395
Vegetarian

Sweets Village (Brooklyn)
702 Washington Ave.
Prospect Heights, Brooklyn, NY
718-857-7757
American

Mo-Bay (Brooklyn)
112 De Kalb Ave.
Fort Greene, Brooklyn, NY
718-246-2800
Vegetarian Caribbean/Southern

Vegetarian Palate (Brooklyn)
258 Flatbush Ave.
Park Slope, Brooklyn, NY
718-623-8808
Chinese (Buddhist/Veg)

Oznot's Dish (Brooklyn)
79 Berry St.
Williamsburg, Brooklyn, NY
718-599-6596
Middle Eastern/North African

Veggie Castle (Brooklyn)
2242 Church Ave.
Flatbush, Brooklyn, NY
718-703-1275
Vegetarian Jamaican

Vegetarian Palate is one of those faux-meat places, using combinations of soy protein, wheat gluten, and vegetable products to create meatless versions of, say, lamb chops that are way short of the mark. But if you just appreciate things for what they are, *Robin Snead* says Vegetarian Palate delivers some tasty items. Sugar cane drumsticks (breaded soy protein and fresh herbs wrapped around raw sugarcane, served with Thai sauce) are amazing, like chicken salad, pressed and shake-and-baked dark brown, balled up half-fist-sized around sugar cane. Order carefully, as quality is uneven (e.g. soups are disappointing, and cornstarch is a major player in sauces). Extensive selection of juices and smoothies.

Quick tips: **Mo'-Bay** is a Caribbean place with many veggie options (great mac and cheese and candied yams). At **Cambodian cuisine**, "BC10" is the menu's code name of a favorite vegetarian dish. **D'Ital Shack** might not have much going for it decorwise (there's only one table at the Nostrand Avenue location), but the food's good and it's all vegetarian. **Imhotep** makes great vegetarian food in the back of a natural foods store. **Goga Cafe** has tasty food and an energetic vibe; music lovers might enjoy the DJ. **Bliss Cafe** is hip and laid back . . . so laid back there can be a wait for a table. **Veggie Castle**, a former White Castle gone vegan-friendly, is a consistent chowhound favorite. **Oznot's dish** is an intimate spot with clever modernized takes on traditional Middle Eastern cuisine, including some good veggie options. For delicious veg-friendly fare, check out **Sweets Village's** good sandwiches, desserts, and juices or the eclectic Middle Easternish cooking at **Black Iris**.

- ○ **Imhotep:** *see also* p. 178.
- ○ **Veggie Castle:** *see also* p. 178.

VEGETARIAN MOCK MEAT

Red Bamboo (Greenwich Village)
140 W. 4th St.
Manhattan, NY
212-260-1212
Eclectic Vegetarian

Tchefa (Brooklyn)
510 Flatbush Ave.
Lefferts Gardens, Brooklyn, NY
718-284-8742
Vegetarian Caribbean/Southern

Vegetarian's Paradise (Chinatown)
33 Mott St.
Manhattan, NY
212-406-6988
Chinese (Buddhist/Veg)

Vegetarian's Paradise 2
    (Greenwich Village)
144 W. 4th St.
Manhattan, NY
212-260-7130
Chinese (Buddhist/Veg)

The menu at Red Bamboo runs all over the world (Japanese, Korean, Italian, Indian, Mexican, soul, et cetera) and almost everything's faux-meat vegan, though a few clearly marked dishes include dairy. Meat eaters will be happy here, too, as long as they take the food as it is and don't expect the fake meat to taste or feel like the real stuff. Soul renditions (which strike some as Asian-tasting) get the best marks, especially the soul chicken. Collard green rolls with "ham" are excellent, says *cj*, and collard greens are better than at most soul food joints. The texture of the soy ham might not fool anyone into thinking it's real ham, but this dish is all about the great greens and the crunch in the wrapping. Note: When they say spicy here, they mean it. Panko-breaded "chicken" nuggets served with both sweet Cajun and soy-based sauces, along with some lightly cooked vegetables, pleased *dzoey*. The mock chicken had an authentically firm texture, though the flavor's a bit mild. Chowhound *c212* liked mock-chicken roti canai and the tasty but mild Buffalo wings. Also good: an Indian stew appetizer and fried faux chicken with flavorful mashed potatoes (be sure to ask for them heated fully). A welcoming staff and affordable prices (most items around $10) round out the picture.

Vegetarian Paradise 2 next door serves a similar menu of mock meats, though *Mark M* prefers Vegetarian Paradise on Mott Street.

Out in Brooklyn, **Tchefa** serves veggie versions of many West Indian and South American comfort foods, as well as some Southern standards like mac and cheese. Lots of fake meat. Some vegan options. Lots of tofutti and fruit juice flavors. Cornmeal-crusted BBQ "shrimp" is a favorite, and jerk "chicken" has also garnered praise. Order a combo platter to sample the numerous options. Clean and friendly. They're about half a block from the Flatbush exit of the Prospect Park Q station.

Of course, there's an extensive Chinese Buddhist tradition of mock meat cookery. We haven't had recent reports about Flushing venues like Happy Buddha (135-37 Thirty-seventh Avenue, Flushing, Queens, 718-358-0079), so we haven't listed any.

Brooklyn **VIETNAMESE** Picks

Pho Nam Bo (Brooklyn)
7524 18th Ave.
Bensonhurst, Brooklyn, NY
718-331-9259
Vietnamese

Truc Mai Vietnamese Restaurant
(Brooklyn)
6102 7th Ave.
Sunset Park, Brooklyn, NY
718-567-8680
Vietnamese

There's been a recent outcropping of Vietnamese food in Brooklyn. We've done a pretty good job of vetting the Vietnamese sandwich choices (see our Comprehensive *Banh Mi* Roundup), but for full-service sit-down places, we have just two scant but superlative tips:

- **Pho Nam Bo** for great Vietnamese food and service to match.
- **Truc Mai** for excellent food, especially their delicate dumplinglike appetizers, grilled beef, and pho, all recommended by *Iron Frank*.

Chowhound Nametag: Jennifer Ehmann

○◯○

Location:
Brooklyn.

Occupation:
Book editor and knitting enthusiast.

Farthest Out of the Way Traveled Just for Chow: Every summer my family drives hours for hoagies from Voltaco's in Ocean City, New Jersey. They're hoagie alchemists who achieve just the right proportion of cold cuts to condiments to seasoning to bread.

Nabe Most Full of Explorable Unknown Chow: Church Avenue in Brooklyn (lots of West Indian restaurants).

Top Chinatown Pick: Dim Sum at Golden Unicorn. The endless variety is marvelous, and I love the chaos on a busy weekend afternoon!

Underrated by Chowhounds: Chestnut on Smith Street in Brooklyn. I think the food is quite good and the natural, earthy colors of the decor are artful and soothing, not bland (as some feel).

Favorite Comfort Chow: Coffee and a sandwich at Grey Dog Cafe on Carmine Street. The bread is always fresh, the music is always good, you're surrounded by happy dog pictures, and the friendly staff lets you sit for as long as you like. It was practically my living room for years.

Guilty Pleasure: A green "bubble" tea with milk and tapioca balls from Saint's Alp Teahouse and a large bag of Japanese fruit-flavored gummy candies from one of the Aji Ichiban "Munchies Paradise" shops in Chinatown.

Favorite Mail Order Chow: See's Candy makes me feel like I'm on vacation: www.sees.com.

Favorite Chinese Buns Bakery: Dragon land Bakery on Walker Street. I always get the tuna, but they have a whole wall of both sweet and savory buns.

WEST AFRICAN Options

Africa Restaurant (Clinton)
346 W. 53rd St., #8–9
Manhattan, NY
212-399-6100
African

Keur-Sokhna (Upper West Side)
225 W. 116th St.
Manhattan, NY
212-864-0081
Senegalese

Africa Restaurant
  (Upper West Side)
247 W. 116th St.
Manhattan, NY
212-666-9400
African

There are many businesses run by French-speaking emigrés
from West Africa on 116th Street, including some restaurants
and an outdoor market. An Ivoirian waiter tipped *JH Jill* off to
Africa Restaurant, which might be the best West African restaurant
on the block. UN delegates from Africa have been spotted at the
Hell's Kitchen branch of **Africa Restaurant** by *Wisco*, who recommends their fried fish dishes.

Whether it's the locals sitting at the few tables, French language news on the TV, or portraits of African figures on the
walls, **Keur Sokhna** feels so Senegalese you almost forget you're
in Manhattan. *Mafe yapp*, a mildly spicy lamb and peanut
butter stew, is "fork-droppingly, heavenwards-gazingly good.
Bones are cut for access to marrow. It is relentlessly heavy and
rich, even though it is served with rice," raves *Keith K*. Poisson
braise (grilled fish) comes with a slightly spicy mustard and
onion sauce. There are no side dishes on the menu other than
salad. The menu lists "special breakfast" of *thiaky*, *chawarma*,
nems (plat), sandwich, and pastel, available from 8:00 a.m. to
11:30 a.m.

WESTCHESTER Faves and Raves

Aberdeen Seafood
(Westchester County)
3 Barker Ave.
White Plains, NY
914-288-0188
Chinese (Dim Sum)/Chinese
(Cantonese)

Azteca (Westchester County)
125 W. Main St.
Mount Kisco, NY
914-242-9313
Mexican

Bengal Tiger
(Westchester County)
144 E. Post Rd.
White Plains, NY
914-948-5191
Indian

Cafe Brazil
(Westchester County)
37 N. Main St.
Port Chester, NY
914-934-1600
Brazilian

Cafe Tandoor
(Westchester County)
19 N. Broadway (Rte. 9)
Tarrytown, NY
914-332-5544
South Asian

Central Seafood
(Westchester County)
285 N. Central Ave.
Hartsdale, NY
914-683-1611
Chinese (Fujian)/Chinese
(Cantonese)/Chinese
(Dim Sum)

C-Town Supermarket
(Westchester County)
88-100 Croton Ave. (Rte. 133)
Ossining, NY
914-923-2395
Latin American/Middle
Eastern/North
African/Irish/Polish

El Taco Loco
(Westchester County)
5 N. Division St.
Peekskill, NY
914-736-0500
Mexican

Emilio's (Westchester County)
1 Colonial Pl.
Harrison, NY
914-835-3100
Italian

F.I.S.H. (Westchester County)
102 Fox Island Rd.
Port Chester, NY
914-939-4227
Seafood

Flames Steakhouse
(Westchester County)
533 N. State Rd.
Briarcliff Manor, NY
914-923-3100
Steak House

Francesco's Restaurant
(Westchester County)
600 Mamaroneck Ave.
White Plains, NY
914-946-3359
Spanish

Golden Village
(Westchester County)
365 Central Park Ave.
Scarsdale, NY
914-723-8888
East Asian Store

Jackie's Bistro
(Westchester County)
434 White Plains Rd.
Eastchester, NY
914-337-8447
French Bistro

Kalbi House Restaurant
(Westchester County)
291 Central Ave.
White Plains, NY
914-328-0251
Korean

La Manda's
(Westchester County)
251 Tarrytown Rd.
White Plains, NY
914-684-9228
Italian

La Panetiere (Westchester County)
530 Milton Rd.
Rye, NY
914-967-8140
French

La Puebla Restaurant
(Westchester County)
8 S. Kensico Ave.
White Plains, NY
914-684-5958
Mexican

Mei Di Ya (Westchester County)
18 N. Central Park Ave.
Hartsdale, NY
914-949-3669
East Asian Store

Pantanal (Westchester County)
29 N. Main St.
Port Chester, NY
914-939-6894
Brazilian

Piero's (Westchester County)
44 S. Regent St.
Port Chester, NY
914-937-2904
Italian

Ripe (Westchester County)
151 W. Sandford Blvd.
Mount Vernon, NY
Jamaican

Sal's Pizzeria
(Westchester County)
316 Mamaroneck Ave.
Mamaroneck, NY
914-381-2022
Pizza/Italian

Tamale woman
  (Westchester County)
C-Town parking lot at 88-100
  Croton Ave. (Rte. 133)
Ossining, NY
Mexican Street Cart/Truck

Thai House (Rockland County)
12 Park St.
Nyack, NY
845-358-9100
Thai

Thai House (Westchester County)
466 Ashford Ave.
Ardsley, NY
914-674-6633
Thai

Turquoise Gourmet
  (Westchester County)
1895 Palmer Ave.
Larchmont, NY
914-834-9888
Turkish

Unnamed Asian supermarket
  (Westchester County)
In the small mall at 200
  Hamilton Ave.
White Plains, NY
East Asian

Ye Olde Tollgate
  (Westchester County)
974 E. Boston Post Rd.
Mamaroneck, NY
914-381-7233
Steak House

Hounds reveal some favorite Westchester spots. (Note: for more
Westchester choices, check the nabe index.)

Latin/Caribbean:

Ripe (Mount Vernon) might be hard to find. There's no sign out
front and from the outside it looks like there's nothing going on
(if driving, take Hutchison Parkway to Sandford Boulevard).
Don't be fooled by appearances. Go inside to discover an old
takeout restaurant turned into a Caribbean lounge with tasty
food. *Lainey* says Ripe is an amazing restaurant amid nothing-
ness, serving real good peppery head-on shrimp and spicy,
smoky jerk chicken done on a huge grill in the backyard—
where, incidentally, you can also dine with tikki torches and all.
Also good: codfish roti and fried Jamaican butterfish (grouper).

  The C-Town (aka Four Seasons Market) in Ossining boasts a
large selection of goods catering to Ossining's diverse South
American population: aisles of specialty goods from Brazil,
Mexico, Peru, Ecuador, etc., as well as exotic fruits and vegeta-
bles. There are also sizable sections catering to North African,
Polish, and Irish shoppers. And after you stock up on Moroccan

sardines, Portuguese pasta, Brazilian gardenia salads, Mexican hot chocolate, and Polish jams, be sure to check out the woman selling fresh homemade tamales out of the back of a station wagon in the parking lot. She's always there Monday evenings, and *Fred Goodman* says her **tamales** are fantastic.

There are a few small tables at **La Puebla** (White Plains), but it's mostly a takeout operation. Tamales are especially good, reports *The Rogue*, but they usually run out before 1:00 p.m. (a new batch comes out around 6:00 p.m.). A half-dozen various daily hot specials cost around $5.50 each. Ask for more of their freshly made hot sauces. Good fruit shakes.

Azteca is noted for high-quality Mexican food in the increasingly Mexican town of Mt. Kisco.

English is definitely a distant second language at **El Taco Loco** in Peekskill, but that didn't prevent *Kingdog* from ordering outstanding-tasting enchiladas and burritos. There might be more interesting stuff buried in the Spanish-only menus.

Pantanal (Port Chester) is a Brazilian churrascaria that usually has five or six cuts of beef, pork loin, or chops; lamb and chicken are available at any time, though *cteats* has never spotted heart or any of the other funkier Brazilian cuts. The salad bar stocks almost two dozen selections, plus a large menu offers alternate entrée options. **Cafe Brazil**, also in Port Chester, is a cafeteria-style place with what *Uncle Dave* says is the best coffee to go in town. More substantial options include roast chicken, fish, various pork dishes, greens, cabbage, rice and beans, and crispy empanadas.

Indian:

Naan stuffed with sesame or spinach are winners at **Cafe Tandoor**, a Tarrytown BYOB where *LisaM* also recommends pureed eggplant. And **Bengal Tiger** (White Plains) is a model of consistent quality, says *Jkos*.

Italian and Pizza:

Piero's (Port Chester) can be loud and close, but they make up for it with very good southern Italian food. **Emilio's** (Harrison) is more refined Italian, with bountiful antipasti choices.

For old-fashioned nongourmet pizza, **Sal's** of Mamaroneck is much loved by many hounds (great chicken parm wedges, too, with perfectly browned cutlets with crispy edges, great crusty bread, well-seasoned sauce, and not too much cheese, according to *Pat Hammond*), but La Manda, in White Plains, also earns kudos for their Neapolitan pies. **Francesco's** in White Plains is an old-style Italian American restaurant making excellent thin-crusted pizza. *Jkos* raves about the extra gooey cheese and great pasta dishes (e.g. penne with sausage and broccoli di rabe, and top-notch baked ziti with meat sauce). The overall experience is very satisfying.

French:

Jackie's Bistro (Eastchester) serves tasty food in a nice setting that's particularly cozy in winter. For formal French, hounds suggest **La Panetière** in Rye.

Asian:

Kalbi House (White Plains) is a small, authentically Korean BBQ place with friendly service that outclasses its local competition. The array of panchan—kimchi, radishes, spinach, small minnows in tamarind, etc.,—impressed *spector 49*. As a bonus, grilled imported fish, (ong chi? in Korean) something like a delicate mackerel. The BBQ main courses of bulgogi and sliced pork are both very good, and meals close with an ethereal drink of cold, sweet cinnamon ginger tea containing two pinenuts.

Central Seafood (Hartsdale) has taken over the location of Hartsdale Garden. *Josh Mittleman* reports delicious congee with roast pork and egg, nicely flavored roast duck, and an outstanding dish of lightly breaded—and slightly spicy—head-on crispy shrimp. Standard dim sum items like soup dumplings, shumai, shrimp dumplings, etc., are all done properly as well. Coconut cake and egg custards provide a sweet finish.

Skip the standard menu and grab the one with the "must try" dishes at **Aberdeen**, a seafood/dim sum place in Harrison. You'll find lots of items you don't usually see in suburbia. Crispy chicken with minced garlic (half a deep-fried chicken with crispy, but not greasy skin, topped with a light sauce of minced garlic, scallions and soy) is excellent, reports *Shawn*. Black pepper sauce served with oysters is tasty, but the oysters can be too large. Dim sum is tasty.

Ardsley's **Thai House** has a bigger menu than the Thai House in Nyack. Both have interesting decor and lots of vegetarian options.

An **Asian supermarket** in downtown White Plains serves cooked food in front of the store, including stellar roast pig, according to *bruce*. Also a good selection of Asian groceries and baked goods. **Golden Village** (Scarsdale) and **Mei Di Ya** (Hartsdale) are also commendable Asian markets. *The Rogue* says that among the three stores you can find almost any Asian food/ingredient.

Other:

Turquoise (Mamaroneck) is the popular choice for Turkish food, and meat eaters will find good, if not great, steaks at either **Ye Olde Tollgate** (Mamaroneck) or **Flames** (Briarcliff Manor). As the name implies, **F.I.S.H.** (Port Chester) is a seafood restaurant, and has some innovative preparations and good desserts.

See also *Japanese* in Northern Suburbs and *New Rochelle* Tour.

'WICHCRAFT

'Wichcraft (Gramercy)
49 E. 19th St.
Manhattan, NY
212-780-0577
New American

Grilled pork loin with *coppa*—pickled pepper relish—is fantastic at 'Wichcraft. There's a "great unexpected melding of flavors. One minute great pork taste, the next a flash of hot pepper, then the acidity of the pickling spices and vinegar, all surrounded by the delightfully crunchy bread," describes *Jonathan Saw*. Italian tuna sandwich with lemon and fennel is really fresh and light and the bread is perfectly crunchy, adds *Iron Frank*. Peanut butter cookies sandwiched around peanut butter are fantastic. Not everything's equally good; e.g. bacon, cheddar and apple on grilled pumpernickel is too fruity, and the braised beef grilled sandwich can be stringy and tough.

○ 'Wichcraft: *see also* p. 267.

Coffee, Snacks, and **WIFI**

Alt.coffee
  (East Village)
139 Avenue A
Manhattan, NY
212-529-2233
Café

Chelsea Market
  (Chelsea)
75 9th Ave., in the Chelsea
  Market
Manhattan, NY
212-242-7360
Store

Dean & DeLuca Cafe
  (Lower Manhattan)
100 Broadway, at Pine St., in
  Borders Books Music & Cafe
Manhattan, NY
212-577-2153
American

Doma Cafe & Gallery
  (Greenwich Village)
17 Perry St.
Manhattan, NY
212-929-4339
Czech Café

DT-UT (Upper East Side)
1626 2nd Ave., #1
Manhattan, NY
212-327-1327
Bread/Pizza Bakery and Sitdown
  Café

Full City Coffee (Lower East Side)
409 Grand St.
Manhattan, NY
212-260-2363
Café

Soy Luck Club (Greenwich Village)
115 Greenwich Ave.
Manhattan, NY
212-229-9191
Eclectic American Vegetarian

Cafés set up for wireless Internet access are all the rage. Perk up, log in, and chow down . . . all at once!

- **DT-UT** offers wireless Internet access (WIFI) for a voluntary one-dollar donation. Nice selection of baked goods.
- The **Dean & DeLuca Cafe** inside Borders Books offers free WIFI.
- **Chelsea Market** offers free WIFI throughout the building (which includes a variety of food offerings from chowhound faves like Amy's Bread, Sarabeth's, Eleni's, and Fat Witch Brownies, and more—see the alphabetical index for more info on each).

- **Alt.coffee** has free wireless access along with a good mug of café au lait.
- **Soy Luck Club** has good soy-based drinks, healthy food, and wireless access in a funky atmosphere.
- **Full City Coffee** has great coffee and pastries . . . though we're not sure whether their WIFI is free.
- **Doma** is a cute spot for hanging out and using the Internet, and while some praise the Czech-style crepes (*palacinka*), *Peter Cuce* warns that their coffee is like toxic waste, and the food's nothing special.
- Bryant Park, Union Square Park, and Tompkins Square Park offer free wireless access anywhere in the park. (See the neighborhood index for local to-go possibilities.)

WINE BAR Paradise . . . Early Weeknights Only

Mae Mae Enoteca Di Vino (Tribeca)
68 Vandam St.
Manhattan, NY
212-924-5109
Italian

Mae Mae Enoteca Di Vino isn't open weekends, and it closes at 8:00 p.m. the rest of the week, but if you catch them open, you'll find a beautiful place serving great wines, panini, and cheese platters, reports *CiaoNewYork*. Live jazz Thursdays until 7:30.

A WINE BAR in Brooklyn??

Half Bottle Wine Bar (Brooklyn)
626 Vanderbilt Ave.
Prospect Heights, Brooklyn, NY
718-783-4100
Wine Bar

The **Half Bottle Wine Bar** has a limited menu (cheese and meat plates with some nice olives, plus a planned list of grilled sandwiches) to complement the large selection of wines. The friendly and knowledgeable owners put together an intriguing list of about thirty half bottles and twenty or so full bottles, with about ten to fifteen wines available by the glass. Recommended by *lambretta76*: Hirsch Gruner Veltliner, Hugel Riesling, and a $14 bottle of Shiraz from India(!). There's an excellent beer list, too, including Victory Storm King on tap. Check out the cozy, candle-lit back room right off the main room and the Lifestyle Shop, carrying a nice selection of wine accessories and assorted tchotchkes.

The Skinny on **WINE SHOPS**

Ambassador Wines
   (Upper East Side)
1020 2nd Ave.
Manhattan, NY
212-421-5078
Wine Store

Chambers Street Wines (Tribeca)
160 Chambers St.
Manhattan, NY
212-227-1434
Wine Store

Crossroads Wine
   (Greenwich Village)
55 W. 14th St.
Manhattan, NY
212-924-3060
Wine Store

Is-Wine (East Village)
225 E. 5th St.
Manhattan, NY
212-254-7800
Wine Store

Morrell Wine (Midtown West)
1 Rockefeller Plaza
Manhattan, NY
212-688-9370
Wine Store

Morrell's Restaurant (Gramercy)
900 Broadway
Manhattan, NY
212-253-0900
New American

Nancy's Wines (Upper West Side)
313 Columbus Ave.
Manhattan, NY
212-877-4040
Wine Store

Rosenthal Wine Merchants
   (Upper East Side)
318 E. 84th St.
Manhattan, NY
212-249-6730
Wine Store

Sherry-Lehmann (Upper East Side)
679 Madison Ave.
Manhattan, NY
212-838-7500
Wine Store

Union Square Wines
   (Union Square)
33 Union Sq. W.
Manhattan, NY
212-675-8100
Wine Store

67 Wine & Spirits
   (Upper West Side)
179 Columbus Ave.
Manhattan, NY
212-724-6767
Wine Store

- **Rosenthal Wine Merchants** is recommended by *NinaW*. Be aware it is closed Sundays and Mondays.
- **Chambers Street Wines** has an informative staff and, says *djk*, stocks smaller producers—wines made from hand-harvested grapes, with low yeast content, etc. Limited stock; European wines predominate.
- The knowledgeable staff at **Nancy's Wine** have tasted all wines carried and love to recommend (*love to eat* suggests asking for Evan). Main strength: German wines and French Sameurs.
- **Union Square Wines** has a friendly staff and a great selection of wines (especially dessert wines).
- **67 Wines** has the best selection of half bottles in the city, says *adam*.
- **Ambassador Wines** has the best sake selection.
- Knowledgeable wine shoppers who don't need hand-holding will appreciate **Sherry-Lehmann** for one of the deepest selections around (inexperienced clerks, though), says *Chicago Mike*.
- **Is-Wine** has a good mix of affordably priced foreign and domestic wines. You can trust the personable owner to recommend something interesting, says *plum*.
- **Crossroads Wine** has an enormous selection for its size, and for the most part, a very knowledgeable staff.
- **Morrell's** is an upscale wine shop, but prices are better than you'd expect. Their restaurant offers a large selection of wines by the glass.

○ **Morrell Wine:** *see also* **p. 267.**

Delicious Chicken **WING** Sampler

Utopia Bar & Grill (Brooklyn)
446 Park Pl.
Prospect Heights, Brooklyn, NY
718-638-4600
American Pub

Utopia serves a sampler plate with two each of a variety of wings (buffalo, BBQ, honey BBQ, and jerk), all made from scratch, for $8. According to *at203* the wings are large, meaty, and delicious.

e**X**tremely Important

It's extremely important that we never settle for anything undelicious when there are so many geniuses, holdouts, and proud craftsmen investing hearts and souls in cooking edible treasure that can sate our deepest hankerings. Just venture a bit farther and care a bit more, and all occasions can be special . . . and the good guys will win.

Good Places for **YAKISOBA** Noodles

ONY (Greenwich Village)
357 6th Ave.
Manhattan, NY
212-414-8429
Japanese

Otafuku (East Village)
236 E. 9th St.
Manhattan, NY
212-353-8503
Japanese

Rai Rai Ken (East Village)   Sapporo (Midtown West)
214 E. 10th St.   152 W. 49th St.
Manhattan, NY   Manhattan, NY
212-477-7030   212-869-8972
Japanese   Japanese

Yakisoba, or pan-fried buckwheat noodles, are a quick and relatively inexpensive meal. You can find them at Japanese noodle shops **Rai Rai Ken, Ony,** and also at **Otafuku,** the tiny octopus ball shop. **Sapporo** serves yakisoba as well as many other noodle dishes.

- **ONY:** *see also* p. 234.
- **Rai Rai Ken:** *see also* p. 234.
- **Sapporo:** *see also* pp. 179, 234.

YALE'S South Asian Food Trucks Evolve into Real Restaurant

Noor Mahal (New Haven County)
157 Boston Post Rd.
Orange, CT
203-799-8162
North Indian/Pakistani

The family behind the Moghuli Foods trucks, which ply the Yale campus in New Haven (near Ingall's ice hockey rink), have opened a sit-down restaurant in nearby Orange. It's good news for anyone who's sampled the feather-light samosas served up by the trucks, says *Kelly Monaghan*, who praises a couple of unusual menu items. Chicken haleem is chicken and five kinds of lentils, cooked separately and then mashed into a puree. Shami kebab appetizer is pureed beef mixed with chana dal and spices, formed into patties and lightly fried, and served with lemon and minted yogurt. Naan is heartier than the common soft variety. There is a $5.95 lunch buffet ($7.95 on weekends). BYOB.

YANKEE STADIUM–Area Food

Court Deli (Bronx)
96 E. 161st St.
Bronx, NY
718-993-1380
Store

El Molino Rojo II (Bronx)
101 E. 161 St., just down the
    block from the Yankee
    Stadium subway stop
Bronx, NY
718-538-9642
Puerto Rican/Dominican

Feeding Tree (Bronx)
892 Gerard Ave., Suite 161
Bronx, NY
718-293-5025
Jamaican

La Orquidia (Bronx)
149th St. and Brook Ave.
Bronx, NY
Honduran

Press Cafe (Bronx)
114 E. 157th St.
Bronx, NY
718-401-0545
Italian Sandwich Shop

Venice Restaurant & Pizzeria
    (Bronx)
772 E. 149th St., west of
    Southern Blvd. and the
    Bruckner
Bronx, NY
718-585-5164
Italian/Pizza

Don't want to pay ballpark prices for lukewarm, soggy hot dogs? Check out these nearby alternatives. All offer food to go, but heightened stadium security may bar your carry-in. (We opt for the classic "mule" approach of swallowing the stuff first.)

Hounds love the **Feeding Tree**, even if it's dipped a bit from previous levels. (Jerk chicken can be dry, which *Helen F.* fixes by ordering all dark meat). Lunch specials run about $5.00. Generous portions.

Intrepid chowhound *Eric Eto* advises picking up a Cubano or some roast pork with rice and beans from **Molino Rojo**, the twenty-four hour cuchifritos place on 161st Street before the game.

The deli in the stadium can't match the quality or the prices at **Court Deli**, which makes great sandwiches and hot dogs, says *Phil DePaolo*, plus knishes, fries, etc. Lots of seating, but it fills quickly before and after games.

Panini don't come immediately to mind as baseball fare, but **Press**, a block or so from the stadium, provides a tasty alternative to overpriced, undercooked hot dogs and insipid knishes.

There are salads, bruschetta, and beer and wine besides the pressed sandwiches, and a large plasma-screen TV to catch the game should you decide to linger.

Venice is an antiquated Italian restaurant that's unthrilling yet a great resource if you're near Yankee stadium. Solid renditions of old favorites like large, decently moist meatballs over linguini, warm and tasty veal parmigiana sandwiches, and a spicy scungili salad filled with an abundant amount of fresh scungili, says *mrnyc*.

While in the nabe, check out **La Orquidia**, a lunch counter serving ultrarare Honduran food.

The shish kebabs, gyros, and knishes from The Gyro Twins are really cheap, and *fedex guy* says he's been able to sneak them into the games. We can't locate the place, but he says it's under the train, across from bleacher entrance.

○ **El Molino Rojo II:** *see also* p. 101.

ZONA ROSA:
Spicy Midtown Eclectic

Zona Rosa (Midtown West)
40 W. 56th St.
Manhattan, NY
212-247-2800
Eclectic Caribbean/Latin American

Zona Rosa (a sibling of Babalu) is a large and comfortable space with dining room downstairs and bar/lounge upstairs where you can sample a variety of tequila-based beverages like the eponymous Zona Rosa (José Cuervo Especial with Cointreau infused with hibiscus and rose petals). Spicing is bold, says *JoanN*, who reports that spicy and thick guacamole is served with homemade chips, and terrific empanadas are filled with wild mushrooms, corn, and huitlacoche and are served with jalapeño and tomatillo salsa. Also worthy: steamed mussels with chipotle in *hoja santa* broth with epazote dumplings; mixed ceviche of scallops, octopus, clams, mussels, and calamari with chile piquin; mahimahi with toasted pumpkin seed crust; and lobster-mango pico de gallo with visible chunks of flavorful lobster. Zona Rosa does well with meat dishes like tampiquena (a flavorful and tender piece of grilled hangar steak served with rajas poblanas and mole). Don't miss the dessert crêpes.

○○○ Manhattan ○○○

CHELSEA

CHINATOWN

MIDTOWN EAST

Nabe Index: Manhattan

SOHO

SPANISH HARLEM

THEATER DISTRICT

TRIBECA

UNION SQUARE

UPPER EAST SIDE

○○○ Queens ○○○

ASTORIA

JAMAICA

KEW GARDENS

LITTLE NECK

LONG ISLAND CITY

REGO PARK

○○○ Middlesex County ○○○

Restaurant/Store	Cuisine	Page

WANTAGH

Cafe Le Monique	French	225
Salpino's	Italian	170

WESTBURY

Roman & Ann Soul Food	Southern	278

WOODBURY

Poppa Rick's Fine Food/Real Texas BBQ	Barbecue, Street Cart/Truck	226

○○○ New Haven County ○○○

BRANFORD

Indian Neck Market	American	41
Lenny's Indian Head Inn	Seafood	41, 88
Scotty's Breakfast Connections	Diner/Coffee Shop	41
Waiting Station	American	41

MADISON

Lenny & Joe's Fish Tale	Seafood	88

ORANGE

Noor Mahal	North Indian, Pakistani	339

○○○ New London County ○○○

STONINGTON

Sea Swirl Restaurant	Seafood	88

○○○ Orange County ○○○

FLORIDA

Chumley's BBQ Hut	Barbecue	29

Restaurant/Store	Cuisine	Page

○○○ Ulster County ○○○

○O○ Warren County ○O○

○O○ Westchester County ○O○

Nabe Index: Westchester County

Restaurant/Store	Location	Page

○○○ Bagel Shop ○○○

○○○ Bakery ○○○

Cuisine Index: Bakery

○○○ Café ○○○

Alt.coffee	East Village	334
Ambrosia Cafe	Grand Central	135
American Pie	Sherman	90
Brown	Lower East Side	116
Cafe Mozart	Upper West Side	68
Ceci-Cela	Soho	67, 96, 201
Chikalicious Dessert Bar	East Village	103
City Bakery	Gramercy	96, 161, 207
Cupcake Cafe	Clinton	110, 240
Doma Cafe & Gallery	Greenwich Village	334
DT-UT	Upper East Side	334
Fauchon	Upper East Side	97, 136, 161
Fortunato Bros.	Williamsburg	68
Full City Coffee	Lower East Side	334
La Bergamote Pastries	Chelsea	97
La Nueva Bakery	Jackson Heights	38, 175
Marie Belle	Soho	161
Pasticceria Bruno	Greenwich Village	22
Petrossian Boutique & Cafe	Midtown West	239
Tea & Tea	Chinatown	75
Tea & Tea	East Village	75
The Donut Pub	Chelsea	110
Wild Lily Tea Room	Chelsea	302

○○○ Cheese Shop ○○○

Artisanal Cheese Center	Clinton	66
King Umberto	Elmont	246
Murray's Cheese Shop	Greenwich Village	53
Murray's Cheese Shop	Grand Central	53
Rocco Pastry Shop	Greenwich Village	22

○○○ Chocolate or Candy Shop ○○○

Got Chocolates	Islip	62
Jacques Torres Chocolates	DUMBO	97
La Maison du Chocolat	Upper East Side	161
Martine's Chocolates	Midtown East	84
Marine's Chocolates too	Upper East Side	84
Ortrud Munch Carstens Haute Chocolature	Midtown East	84
Philips Candy	Staten Island	286
Vosges Haut-Chocolat	Soho	84

○○○ Store (Grocer, Supermarket, Meat, Fish, Produce, Et Cetera) ○○○

○◯○ African ○◯○

AFRICAN

ETHIOPIAN OR ERITREAN

GHANAIAN

SENEGALESE

○◯○ American ○◯○

AMERICAN

BARBECUE

CAJUN OR CREOLE

DINER OR COFFEE SHOP

NEW AMERICAN

PIZZA

SEAFOOD

SOUTHERN

STEAK HOUSE

○○○ Caribbean ○○○

CARIBBEAN

CUBAN

DOMINICAN

○○○ East Asian ○○○

CHINESE

CHINESE (BEIJING)

CHINESE (BUDDHIST/VEG)

CHINESE (CANTONESE)

CHINESE (DIM SUM)

PAN-ASIAN FUSION

TIBETAN

○○○ Eclectic ○○○

○○○ European ○○○

AUSTRIAN

BELGIAN

BOSNIAN OR SERBIAN

BRITISH

CENTRAL ASIAN

CENTRAL OR EASTERN EUROPEAN

CROATIAN

CZECH

EASTERN EUROPEAN JEWISH

FRENCH

FRENCH BISTRO

FRENCH BRASSERIE

GERMAN

GREEK

POLISH

PORTUGUESE

ROMANIAN

RUSSIAN

SPANISH

PERUVIAN

SALVADORAN

○○○ Middle Eastern/North African ○○○

YEMENI

○○○ Pacific ○○○

AUSTRALIAN

○○○ Scandinavian ○○○

DANISH

SCANDINAVIAN

SWEDISH

○○○ South Asian ○○○

BANGLADESHI

○○○ Southeast Asian ○○○

CAMBODIAN

INDONESIAN

LAOTIAN

MALAYSIAN

PHILIPPINE

THAI

VIETNAMESE

○◯○ Vegetarian ○◯○

VEGETARIAN

Cuisine Index: Vegetarian